THEORY AND PRACTICE OF DISTANCE EDUCATION

Distance education is practised in all parts of the world and in recent years its scope has developed enormously and rapidly. It has become an intrinsic part of many national educational systems and an academic discipline in its own right. Research into the area has produced a body of theory which is now being used to improve its practice.

This new edition of *Theory and Practice of Distance Education* has been thoroughly updated both by describing how practice has changed, and by examining recent research in the field. Like the first edition, this book provides a comprehensive survey of distance education, looking at it globally and discussing the different lines of thought and models used. It describes the place of distance education in educational thinking, its various theories, principles, and techniques of presentation, its organization and its administration.

Börje Holmberg has worked in distance education since 1955. He was for many years head of one of the largest distance-teaching organisations in the world, Hermods in Sweden. He was then appointed as Professor and Director of the Institute for Distance Education Research at the FernUniversität in Germany. He is a pioneer in research on distance education and is the author of many books, project reports and articles on the subject.

ROUTLEDGE STUDIES IN DISTANCE EDUCATION
Series editor: Desmond Keegan

THEORETICAL PRINCIPLES OF DISTANCE EDUCATION
Edited by Desmond Keegan

DISTANCE EDUCATION: NEW PERSPECTIVES
Edited by Keith Harry, Magnus John and Desmond Keegan

COLLABORATION IN DISTANCE EDUCATION
Edited by Louise Moran and Ian Mugridge

OTTO PETERS ON DISTANCE EDUCATION
Edited by Desmond Keegan

THEORY AND PRACTICE OF DISTANCE EDUCATION

SECOND EDITION

Börje Holmberg

London and New York

First published 1989
by Routledge
11 New Fetter Lane, London EC4P 4EE

Reprinted 1990, 1992

Second edition published 1995
by Routledge

Simultaneously published in the USA and Canada
by Routledge
29 West 35th Street, New York, NY 10001

© 1995 Börje Holmberg

Phototypeset in Baskerville by Intype, London

Printed and bound in Great Britain by
T. J. Press (Padstow) Ltd, Padstow, Cornwall

British Library Cataloguing in Publication Data
A catalogue record for this book is available from the
British Library

Library of Congress Cataloging in Publication Data
A catalogue record for this book has been requested

ISBN 0–415–11292–3

CONTENTS

CONTENTS

FIGURES

PREFACE

The study of distance education as a discipline of its own, or as an academic field of study composed of parts of other disciplines, has developed considerably during the last couple of decades. In 1960, when I published my first monograph on what is today called distance education, that term had hardly been thought of. Very little had been written about the subject, apart from some studies of the relative effectiveness of correspondence education (home study, independent study) and of the practices of some schools and universities.

The picture looks very different in the 1990s. There is now a wealth of literature on distance education, in the form of monographs, articles and case studies of various kinds. This literature reflects the development of practice, of research on education and other disciplines relevant to distance education and of theoretical approaches. The development has been rapid and is of wide scope, on the one hand covering applications, recognition and social impact, on the other, methods and media. Information and communication technology has made considerable improvements possible, for instance by eliminating or minimizing the procrastination previously inherent in student–tutor interaction. However, the intrinsic nature of distance education has remained unaltered. Distance education did and does offer mediated teaching and learning with a one-to-one relationship between learner and tutor, it did and does serve individual learners independently of time and place. It is evolution rather than revolution that characterizes its development.

This is the second edition of this book, which was first published in 1989. The content has been thoroughly updated on the basis both of changing practice and of new scholarly contributions to the field. The presentation is organized in a way meant to make the logical structure clearer than in the first edition.

It remains my ambition with this book to provide a thorough study of facts and thinking in the field, a vade-mecum with a reasonable degree of inclusiveness. I hope it will prove useful to both colleagues in distance education and scholars chiefly interested academically in the subject.

Börje Holmberg

1

TODAY'S OVERALL PICTURE OF DISTANCE EDUCATION

Distance education is practised in all parts of the world to provide study opportunities for those who cannot – or do not want to – take part in classroom teaching. This does not mean that there is universal agreement about its characteristics. To some, distance education is identical to private study of prescribed texts with or without special study guides, to others, it is a teaching–learning system including specially prepared study materials and regular, mediated contacts between students and tutors, individually or in groups. There are distance-teaching universities that offer their students printed and recorded courses but no mediated communication, although they sometimes provide supplementary face-to-face teaching. This applies, for example, to the Dutch Open Universiteit and the Colombian Unisur. Others like the British Open University, make provision not only for course materials but also for correspondence, telephone and computer communication between students and tutors and others in the distance-teaching school or university, which – following Delling (1987b) and earlier – I call the supporting organization. This use of pre-produced course materials and non-contiguous communication, sometimes supplemented by face-to-face contacts, no doubt represents the praxis of most distance-teaching institutions in the world. In some cases arrangements are also made for peer-group interaction, i.e. for individual students communicating with other students.

Usually students learn entirely individually and at their own pace. They then neither belong to a group or class, nor feel that they do so. A great number of exceptions to this rule occur, however. Universities sometimes teach some groups of students by distance-education methods and other groups face-to-face –

1

they are so-called dual-mode organizations. Even single-mode organizations – like distance-teaching universities – in many cases endeavour to some extent to keep students together in groups and do so by imposing regulations of various kinds. Nevertheless, individual study basically characterizes distance education.

THE DISTANCE-EDUCATION CONCEPT

The concept of distance education that this book is based on implies consistent non-contiguous communication between the supporting organization and its students. This communication is of two kinds:

1 One-way traffic in the form of pre-produced course materials sent from the supporting organization and involving students in interaction with texts; this can be described as simulated communication
2 Two-way traffic, i.e. real communication between students and the supporting organization.

As far as it is non-contiguous, this communication must be mediated. The media used for the one-way traffic are in most cases the printed and recorded word and for the two-way traffic correspondence and telephone interaction. More sophisticated media are now widely used (telefax and electronic mail, for example). They are discussed in Chapter 6.

Distance education thus has two constituent elements, the teaching exposition referred to as one-way traffic and the real communication by means of which students have access to personal tutoring and counselling. With this understanding of its two constituent elements I would define distance education as covering the various forms of study at all levels which are not under the continuous, immediate supervision of tutors present with their students in lecture rooms or on the same premises but which, nevertheless, benefit from the planning, guidance and teaching of a supporting organization.

The term distance study is sometimes used in the sense of distance education (no doubt a translation of German Fernstudium, which means university-stage distance education), but should be limited to denoting the activity of the distance students while distance teaching denotes that of the supporting organization, particularly its writers, editors and tutors. Others have gone further in their descriptive definitions of distance education, thus including the role of possible supplementary face-to-face sessions and organizational-administrative aspects. See Keegan (1980a, b and 1990) as well as Bååth (1981).

The addressees of distance education are usually individual students although it sometimes also serves group learning, by tele-conferencing, for example.

THE EVOLUTION OF DISTANCE EDUCATION

Teaching and learning by correspondence is the origin of what is today called distance education. Correspondence education has been known for several generations, mainly as part of adult education. References to what was probably correspondence education occur as early as the 1720s and to what was indisputably correspondence education in the 1830s (Battenberg 1971: 44; Bratt 1977: 161; Holmberg 1986: 6–7). Correspondence education is taken to denote teaching in writing, by means of so-called self-instructional texts, combined with communication in writing, i.e. correspondence between students and tutors.

As, for both of these elements, media other than the written word became common and grew in importance, the term correspondence education was felt by many to be too narrow. In North America, independent study (cf. Wedemeyer 1981) and home study (Lambert 1983) have been used as competing terms. The same applies to external study in Australia and New Zealand; hence the name, the Australian and South Pacific External Studies Association. Since the early 1970s, distance education is the designation that has gradually been adopted in the United Kingdom and Ireland (though resisted by the Association of British Correspondence Colleges), in North America, Australia, New Zealand, and other parts of the English-speaking world, as well as internationally. Usage in this context can be studied in the periodicals concerned with this type of education. 'Distance' occurs in the very first issue of the British Open University journal, *Teaching at a Distance* (1974: 1, 35 and 55), and in the names of the Australian journal, *Distance Education,* the Canadian *Journal of Distance Education,* and the US *American Journal of Distance Education.* A degree of formal recognition of the term distance education occurred in 1982 when the International Council for

Correspondence Education (ICCE) changed its name to the International Council for Distance Education (ICDE).

Whereas from the end of the nineteenth century up to the 1960s the distance-teaching organizations had – with few exceptions, among them the University of Chicago under William Harper and the University of Wisconsin inspired by William Lighty – been private correspondence schools (one of which, Hermods in Sweden, had in 1958 become an official examining body for its own students), a new era saw publicly supported and established universities and schools becoming more and more numerous and important while the private organizations continued their development with gradually more sophisticated use of methods and media (see Holmberg 1986 Chapter 3). An outstanding pioneer heralding the influence of public distance-teaching organizations was the University of South Africa, which emerged as a development of the University of Good Hope, founded in 1873 as an examining body based on the model of the University of London. It started teaching at a distance in 1946. The University of South Africa was definitely established as a distance-teaching university through a governmental decree of 1962 (Boucher 1973). However, it was the founding of the Open University in the United Kingdom in 1970 that above all marks the beginning of the new era. It gradually created general public recognition of distance education. With few exceptions, as in Scandinavia, educational authorities had until then been sceptical in their appraisal of this kind of education. The image of distance education in many countries changed from one of possibly estimable but little respected endeavour to one of a publicly acknowledged type of education, far from seldom acclaimed as an innovative promise for the future.

DISTANCE EDUCATION AND OPEN LEARNING

The adjective 'open' occurs frequently in connection with distance education, no doubt because of the strong influence of the British Open University and other distance-teaching organizations that have adopted practices corresponding to and names containing this adjective (see pp. 9–10). In these names, 'open' originally referred to access and to the avoidance of certain restrictions; in itself it has nothing to do with distance education, as Dewal makes clear:

As distance education refers mainly to mode of delivery, open education refers to structural changes. A distance education institution can also be an open institution but not necessarily so. Open education refers to structural changes so as to make an institution open: open with respect to place; time; content of learning; mode of learning; etc . . . A distance teaching institution could also be a 'closed' one.

(Dewal 1986: 8)

This contradicts a statement by Lewis and Spencer (1986: 17) to the effect that 'distance learning is a sub-category of open learning', which was derived from the frequent use of 'some features of distance learning' in open learning (ibid.). To judge from the use made of the term open learning in the UK, this seems to be a fairly common interpretation. However, see Foks (1987):

Open learning is not synonymous with distance education; nor is distance education a sub-set of open learning. Distance education is a mode of learning with certain characteristics which distinguish it from the campus-based mode of learning. (p. 74)

Open learning is a state of mind. It is an approach taken to the planning, design, preparation and presentation of courses by educators, and an approach taken to the selection and use of learning strategies and associated resources by students. This approach seeks to provide students with as much choice and control as possible over content and learning strategies. (p. 76)

See also Cirigliano 1983; Keegan 1986: 23–24; Lewis 1986; Northcott 1986; Boot and Hodgson 1987; Cunningham 1987; Holmberg 1989a. Cunningham equates open learning with self-managed learning (p. 41).

In today's usage the distinction between open and distance learning is blurred. Mary Thorpe testifies to this development: 'Undoubtedly "correspondence education" as a term has been overtaken by "distance education", which, in the United Kingdom at least, has in turn been overtaken by "open learning" ' (Thorpe 1987: 56).

Frequent references to what are called open-learning methods seem to indicate that a change of meaning in this direction is a distinct possibility, however undesirable it may be from the point of view of conceptual clarity. Thorpe and Grugeon (1987: 2) describe open learning as 'an umbrella term which refers to a whole series of varied educational initiatives and provision'.

Against this background it seems doubtful if open learning is really a helpful term. It would be if the distinctions made by Dewal and Foks were observed. But perhaps its very vagueness makes it acceptable to common usage. Educators who find distance education a forbidding term may feel like replacing it by open learning.

MODES OF TEACHING AND LEARNING IN DISTANCE EDUCATION

Teaching and learning in distance education are based on the two constituent elements described: a pre-produced course and non-contiguous communication between students and the supporting organization with its tutors and counsellors. Modern technology has made a number of useful developments of both elements possible.

The pre-produced courses used are, or are meant to be, of a self-instructional type. They are usually in print and often supplemented by recorded audio presentations. Sometimes broadcast programmes (radio and/or television), video recordings, viewdata/videotex and other supplementary media are used (see p. 79ff.). Pre-produced courses may be self-contained or may function as guides to the study of set or suggested texts, recordings, etc. (see pp. 71–2). They are usually divided into units, at the end of which students are invited to answer questions, compute, translate, solve problems, write essays, etc. and to submit this work for correction and comment. Tasks for submission to the supporting organization are usually referred to as assignments.

The role of the second constituent element, non-contiguous communication (by which, of course, is meant two-way traffic, primarily student–tutor interaction), whether in writing, on the telephone, on audio tape, by computer, or in any other way, varies in distance-education systems. In some it is the basic element, in others it is partly or even largely replaced by self-checking exercises and/or face-to-face sessions. Between these extremes there are various intermediary positions, acknowledging face-to-face interaction as a subsidiary procedure. For instance, on the one hand, the British Open University, though catering for complete non-contiguous two-way communication, systematically organizes face-to-face contacts in study centres and during summer courses; on the other hand, many private distance-teaching organizations in Europe, the USA and elsewhere, offer two-way communication mainly by non-contiguous means but make occasional use of face-to-face sessions.

The role of distance education within the organizations that offer it and the ways in which it is provided and supported also vary. Two opposite, general approaches should be mentioned as typical of well-known distance-teaching organizations. There are what I have elsewhere (Holmberg 1985a: 9–10) called large-scale and small-scale systems of distance education. Whereas the former develop courses for hundreds and thousands of students, often as a result of team work, and then engage groups of tutors to comment on students' work and teach in other ways, the small-scale approach implies causing teachers to develop courses exclusively for their own students, so that the course author is identical with the tutor. The large-scale organizations, as typically represented by the British Open University, the German FernUniversität and the large correspondence schools, can be regarded as innovations outside the traditional educational systems in that they apply what Otto Peters (1973 and 1983) calls industrial working methods (division of labour, rationalization, economies of scale, etc.; see p. 16). The small-scale organizations, on the other hand, find it important to keep within the main stream of education. The University of New England in Australia can be seen as the prototype of small-scale distance-education organizations, which commonly occur among Australian 'dual-mode' universities, i.e. universities with both traditional, on-campus activities for resident students and external study for distance students. Far-reaching parallels between these two forms of study are considered desirable and are effected. Periods of residential teaching are usually required also of the external, 'distant' students.

The two approaches outlined, large-scale and small-scale, represent different views of distance education: the latter often functions merely as a form of distribution, replacing, when necessary, traditional types of teaching and learning. This aspect will be discussed later on pp. 137 and 161. Important financial implications are further concerned in the differences between the two approaches, as investigated on p. 201.

Distance education is often regarded as an innovation which gives students a high degree of independence. This has been expressed by, among others, Charles A. Wedemeyer (1981: 36), a leading representative of American independent study, in a list of *desiderata*:

1 Instruction should be available any place where there are students – or even only one student – whether or not there are teachers at the same place at the same time.
2 Instruction should place greater responsibility for learning on the student.
3 The instructional plan or system should free faculty members from custodial duties so that more of the teacher's and learner's time can be given to truly educational tasks.
4 The instructional system should offer learners wider choices (more opportunities) in subjects, formats, methodologies.
5 The instructional system should use, as appropriate, all the teaching media and methods that have been proven to be effective.
6 The instructional system should mix and combine media and methods so that each subject or unit within a subject is taught in the most effective way.
7 The media and technology employed should be 'articulated' in design and use; that is, the different media or technologies should reinforce each other and the structure of the subject matter and teaching plan.
8 The instructional system should preserve and enhance opportunities for adaptation to differences among individual learners as well as among teachers.
9 The instructional system should evaluate student achievement not by raising barriers concerning the place where the student studies, the rate at which he studies, the method by which he studies, or even the sequence in which he studies, but instead by evaluating as directly as possible the achievement of learning goals.
10 The system should permit students to start, stop, and learn at their own paces, consistent with learner short- and long-range goals, situations, and characteristics.

This quotation can be regarded as a summarizing declaration of intent with which many distance educators can identify.

8

FACTS AND NUMBERS

Distance teaching primarily serves professional/occupational training, secondary and tertiary education. There can be little doubt that the former two applications are much more widely spread and also exert stronger social influence than the last-mentioned field of action. However, university education at a distance seems almost everywhere to enjoy a higher degree of prestige than applications in the other two areas. As shown above, this particularly applies to the official distance-teaching universities offering duly authorized degrees. In comparison with the many highly professional correspondence schools and other, often private, distance-teaching organizations, this may seem unjustified; nevertheless this impact of the distance-teaching universities is a historical fact.

Organizations offering distance education

It would be almost as difficult to say how many distance-teaching institutions exist in the world as to state the number of conventional schools or universities. A comparative study of international distance education carried out at the FernUniversität in West Germany in 1986 listed some 1,500 distance-teaching institutions.

Well-known distance-teaching universities are:

Allama Iqbal Open University, Pakistan
Andhra Pradesh Open University, Hyderabad, India
Athabasca University, Alberta, Canada
Central Broadcasting and Television University, Beijing, China
FernUniversität, Hagen, Germany
Indira Gandhi National Open University, New Delhi, India
Korea Air and Correspondence University, South Korea
Kota Open University, Rajasthan, India
Kyongi Open University, South Korea
Nalanda Open University, Bihar, India
Tha National Open University of Taiwan
Open Universiteit, The Netherlands
The Open University, United Kingdom
The Open University of Israel
Ramkhamhaeng University, Thailand
Sri Lanka Institute of Distance Education
Sri Lanka Open University

Sukhothai Thammathirat Open University, Thailand
Télé-Université (part of the network of the University of Québec, Canada)
Unisur (Unidad Universitaria del Sur), Colombia
Universidad Estatal a Distancia, Costa Rica
Universidad Nacional Abierta, Venezuela
Universidad Nacional de Educación a Distancia, Spain
Universidade Aberta, Portugal
Universitas Terbuka, Indonesia
University of Distance Education, Union of Myanmar, Burma
University of the Air, Japan
University of South Africa
Yashwantrao Chavan Maharashtra Open University, Nashik, India

There are a number of distance-teaching organizations which do work similar to that of these universities and which might have been included in the list, among them the following:

The International University Consortium, Maryland, USA
The National Distance Education Centre, Ireland
North Island College, British Columbia, Canada
The Open Education Faculty of Anadolu University, Turkey
The Open Learning Agency, British Columbia, Canada
The Open Learning Institute of Hong Kong

For university distance education within a dual-mode framework Australia has had, since 1989, eight distance-education centres, as follows:

Deakin University and Monash University, Victoria
The University of New England and Charles Stuart University, New South Wales
The University College of Central Queensland and The University College of Southern Queensland
The University of South Australia
The Western Australia Distance Education Centre (Murdoch University)

A central brokering company was founded in 1993 at Monash University. It is called the Open Learning Agency of Australia (King 1993).

In the USA many universities offer distance courses as well as their regular teaching on campus. The Open College in the UK, a creation of the late 1980s, has produced a range of 'training packs' serving open learning.

A great number of other private, state-owned, church or foundation-financed distance-teaching organizations, university departments, colleges of advanced education, and schools offering distance education are active in various parts of the world. Some of them are members of national and/or multinational professional bodies, such as the International Council for Distance Education (ICDE), the Association of European Correspondence Schools (AECS), the European Association of Distance Teaching Universities (EADTU), the Distance Education and Training Council, until 1994 called the National Home Study Council (NHSC) (based in the USA), the Open and Distance Learning Association of Australia (ODLAA), which until 1993 was called the Australian and South Pacific External Studies Association (ASPESA).

Whereas the distance-teaching universities are creations of the 1970s and 1980s (with the exception of the University of South Africa) many distance-teaching organizations which teach mainly at the secondary level or offer professional training are much older. Among traditional, still leading distance-teaching organizations of this kind can be mentioned the Australian TAFE colleges (TAFE = technical and further education) and the following, with dates of foundation:

International Correspondence Schools, USA (1891)
Wolsey Hall, England (1894)
American School, USA (1897)
Hermods, Sweden (1898)
NKS, Norway (1914)

Both the size and the working methods of the distance-teaching organizations vary to an extreme extent, as already shown in the presentation of the two opposing approaches (mentioned on p. 7). There are small, highly specialized institutions (teaching management, for example) with a total student body of one or two hundred people. At the other end of the scale are both officially established universities and private distance-teaching organizations which simultaneously teach hundreds of thousands of students. While in the 1990s the British Open University and the German FernUniversität have student bodies of between 120,000 and 40,000 participants, the French Centre National d'Enseignement à Distance has more than 250,000 students enrolled (Dieuzeide 1985: 32), the big home-study schools in the USA each register 200,000–300,000 students (about four million students 'are enrolled at any given time' in schools accredited by the American National Home Study Council according to Verduin and Clark 1991: 19) and their European counterparts in the private sector have about a million students together. The distance-teaching universities in Thailand and the Central Broadcasting and Television University in China work with even larger numbers of students (Walter Perry 1984 and Doerfert, Schuemer and Tomaschewski 1989).

The methods and media used also vary greatly. In some developing countries, the written word is the only medium available and communication is frequently hampered by faulty postal services. Radio is often either used or considered desirable. Television and satellite communications are available in many areas, not only in the developed parts of the world, and serve mass audiences, whereas the use of both mainframe and personal computers is on the whole limited to the more affluent countries.

Descriptions of the situation in individual countries can be found principally in detailed case studies. A number of descriptive and partly explanatory surveys of the international state of distance education are available, among them Walter Perry (1984); Keegan (1990); Kaye and Rumble (1981); Jenkins and Perraton (1980); Doerfert, Schuemer and Tomaschewski 1989; Minnis 1990; Peters 1990; Khoul and Jenkins 1990; Rumble (1985); Rumble and Harry (1982); Sewart, Keegan, and Holmberg (1983); Graff and Holmberg (1988); Henri and Kaye (1985); Holmberg (1985b).

Facts about distance students

There is no evidence to indicate that distance students should be regarded as a homogeneous group. The only common factor is that, with few exceptions, these students are adults and consequently are gainfully employed and/or look after their families. The 25–35 age group seems to be the largest in most organizations. Distance study evidently contributes to upward social mobility. Gradually older students too, not only those around 40 and 50 but also old-age pensioners, seem to show a preference for distance education.

These general statements are borne out by a great number of studies, among them Glatter (1968); Glatter and Wedell (1971); McIntosh, Calder, and Swift (1976); Ansere (1978); Flinck (1980); McIntosh, Woodley, and Morrison (1980); Bartels (1982, 1983); Woodley (1986b). Of interest also are the studies by Fritsch (1980) and Woodley (1983) of the reasons why applicants have withdrawn their applications to university study at a distance.

The reasons why adults choose distance education, as shown in both the sources mentioned and others, are primarily the convenience, flexibility and adaptability of this mode of education to individual students' needs. A predilection for entirely individual work is frequently referred to. In Flinck's study, 63 per cent of the population investigated (about 4,000) stated that they liked working on their own at the same time as they largely referred to the support given by the distance-teaching organization as an important reason to choose distance education; 73 per cent of the students mentioned this second reason. Free pacing, although a privilege not given to all distant students, was found to be an even more important argument in favour of distance education (Flinck 1980: 6–9).

Many distance students mention poor previous educational opportunities as a background for distance study. Physical handicaps, hospitalization, and even imprisonment occur as background factors, but apparently a majority of students in developed countries, which do offer real choices, choose distance education because they genuinely prefer it to other modes. This is, of course, to be expected from adults whose family, professional and social commitments make face-to-face teaching, bound by a fixed timetable, less attractive or unrealistic.

There are indications that distance students consider themselves independent and capable. An investigation by Göttert (1983), in which he reports on an interview study of more than 500 FernUniversität prospective and real students, is interesting in this context. These people 'saw themselves as more competitive, achievement oriented and assertive' than the average general population and student groups investigated. 'Only small differences were found between dropouts and persisters (after one year in distant study): the persisters (before enrolment) had portrayed themselves as more competent and successful in coping with academic and social demands' (Göttert 1983: summary before list of contents). Nevertheless, quite a few university dis-

13

tance students seem to doubt their ability to cope. This has produced counselling activities and various attempts to understand the distance learner as a 'whole person' (Kelly and Shapcott 1987: 7).

THE ASSUMED POTENTIAL OF DISTANCE EDUCATION

It is often assumed that distance education is suitable exclusively or mainly for subjects wholly relying on printed study material, i.e. cognitive learning, mainly in arts subjects. Through the use of audio and video recordings, laboratory kits, computer programs, telephone contacts, and other media, a great number of other subject areas have shown themselves teachable and learnable at a distance. In fact, the results of language learning by means of distance-education courses have in some cases proved extraordinarily good, even as far as pronunciation (for which phonetic transcription has proved vital) is concerned.

Evidently work requiring equipment that individual distance students do not have available or experiments that could be dangerous if not performed under the supervision of a subject specialist have to be arranged face to face; also, in other cases supplementary face-to-face sessions can be useful (see pp. 113–16).

Experience shows, however that there is no need to exclude certain subjects from the possible application of distance education; even some aspects of medicine and surgery have proved to be subjects suitable for this form of education. The distance-education work done by the Centre for Medical Education of the University of Dundee in Scotland testifies to this.

The training of skills in the so-called psychomotor domain is often seen as more of a problem in distance education than it actually need be, above all at fairly elementary stages, in developing countries and elsewhere (see *About Distance Education* 23 1986: 6).

Distance education claims to serve students who are not situated or willing to benefit from comprehensive face-to-face instruction. Unless special measures are taken, it is thus an individual activity and mainly a means of study for adults mature enough to decide on their own ways of learning and to study on their own. Teleconferencing makes it possible to 'assemble a class of students who may interact not only with the teacher but with each other' (Garrison 1990: 15). Educators tend to regard this as a considerable advantage, whereas many students claim that they prefer individual study. Distance education above all attracts mature people with professional, social and family commitments and facilitates recurrent and permanent education. It is true that distance-education procedures are also used in schools for young people but, as this is a special application, it is disregarded here (see, however, pp. 146–9).

In a paper reflecting the position of distance education in the early 1990s Ljoså describes 'several roles which distance education should fill', i.e. balancing 'inequalities between age-groups', offering 'second-chance upgrading', providing 'information and education campaigns for large audiences', training 'key target groups', speedily and efficiently, catering for 'otherwise neglected target groups', offering education 'in new areas', extending 'geographical access to education', facilitating the combination of study 'with work and family life', developing 'multiple competencies' and offering 'trans-national programmes' (Ljoså 1992a: 28–29).

The repeated reference above to the maturity of distance students is indicative of the relevance of student independence in our context. At the very least, students are independent in carrying through a programme of study, i.e. in deciding where and when to learn, how much of a course to undertake at a time, when and how much to rest, when and how often to revise texts and exercises, etc. The independence can go much further, via entirely free pacing, free choice of examination periods, if any, to independent selection of learning objectives and course elements. How far student independence can and should go is a bone of contention which will be discussed further on pp. 165–72. Suffice it to say here that distance education undoubtedly has special potentials for student independence.

This brings to the fore the possibility of catering by distance education for academic socialization, which belongs to so-called affective learning (see p. 42). In the affective domain, which is concerned with values, emotions and attitudes, it is usually taken for granted that non-contiguous communication has less power to influence students than face-to-face meetings. However, experience shows that distance education can be effective in bringing about attitude change. This is borne out by studies of distance-education programmes in health and welfare work in, for example, Sweden and the United Kingdom (Rogers 1986). Sparkes rightly points to unforgettable television programmes as one of 'the most effective external influences in the affective domain' (Sparkes 1982: 7).

While it is thus in the nature of distance education that it can serve individual learners in the study they do on their own, in the cognitive, affective and psychomotor domains, courses developed can easily, and to great financial advantage, be used by great numbers of students. Distance education can be, and often is, a form of mass communication. This union of individualization and mass communication may appear as something of a paradox. Personal approaches and a conversational style are compatible with individualization (see pp. 125–7). In preparing a mass communication programme, on the other hand, it is practical to apply industrial methods including planning, rationalizing procedures, division of labour, mechanizing, automation, and controlling and checking. Peters, as already referred to, has made a systematic study of these methods. He describes distance education as an industrial form of teaching and learning (Peters 1973, 1983). The implied technological approaches do not prevent personal communication of a conversational character from being a basic characteristic of effective distance study. This applies even when computerized communication occurs.

Distance study is self-study but the student is not alone; he or she benefits from a course and from interaction with tutors and the supporting organization constituted by the distance-teaching institution. A kind of conversation in the form of two-way traffic occurs through the written or otherwise mediated interaction between the students and their tutors and others belonging to the supporting organization. Indirectly, conversation is brought about by the presentation of study matter if this one-way traffic is characterized by a personal approach (as it were, conversing with the students) and causes the students to discuss the contents with themselves. The conversation is thus both real and simulated. The simulated conversation is not only what Lewis calls internalized conversation caused by the study of a text (Lewis 1975: 69) but a relationship between the course developers and the students, created by an easily readable and reasonably colloquial style of presentation and the personal atmosphere of the course. This style of presentation stimulates activity and implies reasoning, discussing for and against, referring to the student's previous experience and thus avoiding omissions in chains of thought.

As will be evident from the following remarks, the present author finds the personal character of both real and simulated communication a most important characteristic of distance education, and indeed regards organized distance education as a mediated form of guided didactic conversation.

The picture that emerges shows distance educaton to have vast application potentials not only for independent study attractive to adults but also for mass education, through what has been described as industrial methods, and for highly individualized study and personal approaches with a great deal of rapport between the teaching and learning parties.

2

THE BACKGROUND OF
DISTANCE EDUCATION

Distance education is neither an isolated concept, nor in its practice an isolated creation. It is education of a special type, like all types of education dependent on and influenced by values, opinions, experience and external conditions. While it is different from conventional schooling and has so many characteristics of its own that as an academic area of study it may be regarded as a discipline in its own right (see Chapter 11), its basis is general educational thinking and experience.

BASIC QUESTIONS CONCERNING EDUCATION, TEACHING AND LEARNING

Every educational endeavour has a purpose. Distance teaching and learning, like any kind of teaching and learning, can serve different ends. It makes little sense on the basis of purposes to distinguish between education proper and training of certain skills (Wedemeyer 1981). Any learning can be an educational experience. Distance learning primarily serves those who cannot or do not want to make use of classroom teaching, i.e. above all, adults with social, professional and family commitments.

Learning implies more than acquisition of knowledge, for example, abstracting meaning from complicated presentations and interpreting phenomena and contexts; '[it] is the process of transforming experience into knowledge, skills, attitudes, values, senses and emotions' (Jarvis 1993: 180).

Regarding learning as acquiring the capacity to provide a number of replies that are correct (stage 1) is a primitive view that, at least according to William Perry (1970), ordinary university students give up fairly early. The reason why they do so is

18

that they realize, through varied reading, that in many cases there is no such thing as an answer or solution that is absolutely right. This relativism (stage 2) represents an important experience, on the basis of which students may reach conclusions and positions of their own (stage 3). Perry's study of the three stages of the understanding and application of learning should be an eye-opener to distance educators. There is definitely a risk that distance-study courses may degenerate into spoon-feeding or presentation of given truths in larger doses. Developing awareness of problems and of the plausibility of different approaches and solutions, as well as inspiring (or provoking) students to take up positions of their own, is an important educational task for academic distance education.

Teaching is frequently regarded as knowledge transfer 'from one vessel to another' (Fox 1983: 151), a view which must be rejected as too narrow from the points of view mentioned. The author last quoted, Dennis Fox, identifies three further views of teaching:

> There is the shaping theory which treats teaching as a process of shaping or moulding students to a pre-determined pattern ... There is the travelling theory which treats a subject as a terrain to be explored with hills to be climbed for better viewpoints with the teacher as the travelling companion or expert guide.
>
> Finally, there is the growing theory which focuses more attention on the intellectual and emotional development of the learner.

Only the last view meets the demands of complete education. However, there can be no doubt that the shaping and travelling theories to which Fox refers represent not only widespread but also, in many contexts, well-founded views of teaching, for example in occupational training.

The aims of education, including distance education, cover a wide spectrum: from the development of personality and cognitive structure, via guided learning and problem-solving, to the training of knowledgeable and well-adapted professionals or examinees. Each of these aims means more than merely conveying information or imparting knowledge.

To the present author, teaching means facilitation of learning (see Rogers 1969), which is seen as a basically individual activity intended to lead to a goal of some kind (self-realization, an examination, professional competence, or some other goal). This definition is important for ridding us of an otherwise well-grounded objection to treating teaching and learning as one package. The objection would be that teaching and learning are sometimes little related to each other. It has rightly been said that, when something has been learned in a teaching–learning situation, learning may have been caused by influences other than those of the teaching. When something has been taught, we do not know whether something has been learned; and if something has been learned, we do not automatically know what it is – it is possibly something different from what was intended by the teaching (Loser and Terhart 1977: 29). Teaching is an attempt, sometimes successful, to facilitate learning towards some goal. It is in this light that distance education should be viewed. Like other educational activities, it encompasses learning and teaching in the senses indicated.

The purpose of distance education is thus to offer teaching and learning facilities, with a view to promoting the aims of education as referred to above. They concern the promotion of productive and critical thinking. Distance education must promote these goals by means that are useful and acceptable to students, usually adults, who either cannot or do not want to benefit from face-to-face teaching.

What makes this complicated is that

> many distance-education courses are characterized by a high level of structuring and by the fact that the knowledge to be learned is presented as a ready-made system; for such a teaching method Weingartz (1981) coined the term 'system-oriented' teaching method, which she contrasted with the term 'problem-oriented' teaching method.
>
> (Schuemer 1993: 3–4)

Schuemer warns of the danger that highly structured learning packages may lead to dependence on the teaching system rather than promote independence. This is a concern that engages quite a few social scientists wary of the possible alienation effects of the individual approaches that are typical of much distance education.

PAVING THE WAY FOR TEACHING AND LEARNING

Anyone concerned with teaching and learning methodology has unavoidably to face the question whether there can be a useful general structure, or methodology, or if each subject has characteristics so special that the principles applying to, say, language courses can have little or nothing to do with those for courses in, say, mathematics, chemistry, or social science. It is evident that this question is acutely relevant to any attempts to discuss specific approaches, such as distance education, to teaching and learning.

This is a classical issue to which Amos Comenius, the great seventeenth-century educationist, gave much thought. He based his recommendations on his view of nature and in his *Didactica magna* included a number of observations that are relevant in this context. They imply that there are structures inherent in certain learning matter, generated from the characteristic and unchangeable nature of reality. Compare the following quotations from Comenius 1657 cols. 72 and 78: Natura sibi parat Materiam, antequam introducere incipiat Formam (Nature prepares matter before it begins to introduce form) and Natura Materiam praedisponit, ut Formae fiat appetens (Nature predisposes matter so that it may find its proper form). This kind of thinking has greatly influenced the educational debate, not least in Germany, where the word didactics (Didaktik) is often used to refer to teaching principles specially related to content as opposed to methodology. In the German debate there has been much insistence on the 'Primat der Didaktik' (Klafki 1970: 70), i.e. the leading role of content-related principles in teaching. It is doubtful, however, whether Comenius' nature equals subject content or the way humans grasp matter to be learnt, which would include learning conditions and allow subject-bridging principles for teaching and learning.

At least one attempt has been made in the distance-education debate to demarcate the areas of general teaching theory and discipline-based teaching theory in relation to each other. Müller, Schneider and Schulz argue that 'general teaching theory is not directly interested in the orientation of pedagogic activity in formal teaching–learning situations but confines itself to analyses of pedagogic processes from which generalizations can be made', whereas the objective of discipline-based teaching theory is 'to give the particular discipline a concrete teaching format' and 'to judge the practical value of the theoretically determined teaching concepts in concrete teaching situations. So it attempts to define practical forms of pedagogic behaviour' (Müller, Schneider and Schulz 1985: 95).

No doubt the content of many learning areas or subjects has its intrinsic logic causing an order of presentation to be followed. The question is whether this required order represents the disciplinary order of the subject concerned. It can well be argued that a subject area to be taught and learned acquires its logical order from the requirements of teaching and learning. Look at the following example of hierarchical presentations concerned with the teaching and learning of mathematics:

> At the bottom of the diagram are basic aptitudes which students bring to the learning task, such as symbol recognition. Next to these are the simple, general components of knowledge or competency, such as recognizing that $1x = x$. Higher up in the pyramid are skills like performing multiplication of numbers in sequence. Continuing progressively upward in the hierarchy are combining fractions with the denominators simplifying an equation by adding and subtracting numbers to both sides, etc.
>
> (Briggs 1968: 6)

We may ask ourselves if this hierarchical approach primarily depends on the discipline of mathematics or on what is called for from the points of view of teaching and learning methodology.

This is not to deny that there are cases of subject logic that are decisive for the structure of teaching and learning. It must, on the other hand, be recognized that attempts to teach a subject can impose a teaching-learning logic on the subject. This problem was dealt with by Dewey as early as 1916 and has later been analysed by Hirst. The latter distinguishes between what he calls the logical grammar, i.e. 'the rules for the meaningful use of the terms' that a domain of knowledge employs, and the logical sequence of a subject. Whereas the logical grammar is something that is given and cannot be dispensed with, there can never, in Hirst's view, be only one logical sequence in any domain of knowledge:

> In so far as the logical grammar reveals elements of logical order, then the teaching must equally respect these too.

What they are in any given subject is a matter for the detailed analysis of the concepts of that subject.

There is . . . no one logical sequence in which the truths of a subject must be communicated, even in those subjects which seem most strictly sequential.

(Hirst, in Hirst and Peters 1970: 53, 54)

The relative characters of subject logic and teaching–learning logic are apparently inevitable facts. Everyone realizes today that science and scholarship are not ontological in character, i.e. generated from nature, but represent results or findings based on research methods. See Loser and Terhart, who stress that subject content does not become teaching content until it has been subjected to special processing ('Aufbereitung') (Loser and Terhart 1977: 14).

There is a case for discussing forms and methods of education across disciplinary boundaries. This applies to distance education and the structuring of courses on the basis of subject logic and psychological considerations. Among the approaches relevant in this context are those concerned with learning starting out from attempts to solve specific problems rather than from the systems of knowledge available, which has been called genetic learning (Wagenschein 1975), for instance, when studying gravitation, asking the questions of Aristotle and Galileo in the way that Einstein and Infeld do instead of starting by learning the solutions found (Lehner 1978: 76–7). Attempts to apply this kind of problem learning as well as various structuring principles to distance education will be looked into on pp. 35 and 64f.

THE IMPACT OF THEORY ON PRACTICE

In the above discussion of teaching and learning as elements of (distance) education, the relation of these two elements to each other was briefly described as of a not necessarily causal nature. Learning can occur without teaching, and teaching can occur without learning. As the purpose of teaching is learning, and the basic assumption (theory) behind teaching is that it causes or facilitates learning, what has been said is tantamount to querying the impact of theory, or at least its dominating influence, on practice in this context.

As a rule, teaching intent is not regarded as theory, however.

23

On the contrary, there are theories prescribing what teaching should be like, under what circumstance and how it should be provided. The question is to what extent logico-deductive theories are immediately applicable to teaching practice. In the spirit of Popper, it would seem to be possible to draw practical conclusions from theoretical considerations, although these are primarily concerned with true statements and explanations and only secondarily with practice. This applies if we accept Popper's statement that the task of scholarship is on the one hand theoretical, to bring about understanding and explanation, and on the other hand practical, to provide for application or technology (Popper 1972: 49). Popper makes it clear that he is mainly concerned with the explanatory power of theories and that he rejects a merely instrumental view, although their predictive power is recognized and seen as a control instrument (Popper 1980: 61). See also the section Epistemological Concerns below.

An example of a theory in our field that has had immediate and direct consequences for practice is behaviourism, in the form of Skinner's operant conditioning applied in programmed learning (Skinner 1968; Mager and Beach 1967). Both the theory and its applications have been widely rejected, however, largely with reference to the facts that humans and human learning are complicated and that learning is influenced by the individual personality and will of the learner. From the points of view of education (teaching and learning) developed above, consistent behaviourism must be rejected as irrelevant, as it is concerned with conditioning rather than with education.

If a free will is postulated, there are nevertheless possibilities to base practice closely on theory. Following and simplifying Herrmann (who has chosen another example than the one used below), we seem to be entitled to relate theory and practice in the following way. If we believe in and find logical and empirical support for a hypothesis of the type 'If A, then B', this can guide practice. Let us suppose that we operationalize the concept of readability, so that it is quite clear what is meant, and then hypothesize: 'If the style of a distance-teaching course is characterized by a high degree of readability, then students will learn easily.' This will evidently lead to a practical rule to be followed: 'Develop courses in such a way that they are highly readable if you want students to learn easily' (see Herrmann 1979: 141f). A number of hypotheses or theories, i.e. logically connected series of hypotheses of this kind, have been developed, also for distance education. See Chapter 9.

However, there is little hope (or fear) that any scholarly theory or agglomeration of theories would ever be able to give enough and sufficiently detailed prescriptions to allow us to state, as a reasonably acceptable rule, that all practice in education (distance education) can be consistently guided by theories of the kind described. One reason for this is the impossible expectation of an unfailing cause-effect relationship in human behaviour (pp. 180–1).

As will be shown in the following chapters, this view of theory as only to a limited extent guiding practice will not mean neglect of theoretical considerations. On the contrary, they will be given much attention as indicators of possible solutions. While the testing of theories is a purely rational procedure, their emergence is almost always due to personal observations, intuition and creative thinking.

This influences our view of instructional design. It has been claimed to be a science and 'a discipline separate unto itself' (Richey 1986: 8). This claim has been rejected and even ridiculed. Barrow argues that the claim is that 'one may learn how to design curricula as one may learn how to skate, how to weld or how to fill in tax returns' (Brown 1986: 73), but that instructional (curriculum) design

> is more like some branch of the arts, landscaping or interior decorating than it is like engineering or cake-making, inasmuch as it is an open flexible domain due to uncertainty and disagreement over ends, crucial concepts being contested or unclear, our relative ignorance about cause and effect, and the likelihood that in this case there are many good ways to kill a fox.
>
> (Barrow 1986: 75)

However, instructional design is undoubtedly, and often successfully, concerned with scholarly inquiry, the verification of observations and the practical application to teaching of findings made. For further viewpoints, see Snellbacker (1983); on its potentials in distance education see Benkoe de Rotaeche (1987).

In the development of course materials for distance education, instructional design is inevitably an important concern, whether it is interpreted as a 'science' based on scholarly analysis of empirical findings or simply as a system for bringing reasonable expectations, experiences and insights into useful order. Its purpose is to develop validated recommendations for the structuring of effective teaching. It is often combined with the so-called systems approach which here implies considering teaching as a system with interrelating sub-systems (Andrews and Goodson 1980; Hannum and Briggs 1982; Romiszowski 1981a).

3

PLANNING DISTANCE EDUCATION

The introductory comments made so far make it clear that distance education in theory and practice encompasses a number of diverse considerations and actions. The interaction between these, their relations to and influence on one another are important to our picture of distance education as a manageable whole.

What this means to distance-teaching organizations and their overall planning is far from universally clear. Needs and conditions in the societies concerned are decisive, but real knowledge about relevant circumstances is seldom easily available. What can be called market research and a kind of corporate planning are required. In the early 1970s the present writer made what proved to be an abortive attempt to develop a generalizable approach to such planning and published a booklet in Swedish about this (Holmberg 1972). A more fecund approach of immediate relevance in the 1990s has been introduced by the Canadian Open Learning Agency in a 'scan of the British Columbian Environment' (Bates 1990b and 1993; Segal 1990).

While strategic planning must remain a concern of each national, regional and local organizing body there are more easily generalizable principles that apply to the planning of the processes of distance education. Here we have to consider the system itself, its students and their learning, course planning based on the needs of the target groups concerned, the goals and objectives of the teaching and learning. This type of planning concentrates on what has been called the endogenous concerns of distance education, i.e. what it is like and how it can be optimized. There is, however, particularly among social scientists, a strong consciousness that exogenous factors such as the reciprocal influences of society and distance education are of considerable interest and should be investigated. This will be briefly discussed in the last chapter of this book.

A SYSTEMS APPROACH

The so-called systems approach embodies a somewhat vague but nevertheless helpful principle related to what has been called holism (from Greek *holos* = whole). See von Wright, who characterizes systems theory as a rather immature mixture of loose philosophical ideas and 'mathematical quasi-exactitude' (von Wright 1987: 112). Holism stresses the whole (the system) and studies its parts not as separate entities but as components of the whole. Knowledge of the purpose that a system serves, for instance, makes for understanding of the functions of the parts. The components of the distance-education system are, for example, students with their needs and wishes, tutors and others representing the supporting organization, subject and curriculum requirements, goals, the presentation of subject matter, students' interaction with tutors, counsellors and fellow-students, the assessment of learning, course and systems evaluation, and organizational–administrative arrangements. In our examination of distance-education practice it is the processes we are above all concerned with, thus, e.g., the development of learning materials rather than courses, tutoring rather than tutors, students' learning rather than students.

The system of distance education has been aptly described by Renée Erdos. She illustrates the system as shown in Figure 1. Another systems view of distance education occurs in an Alberta publication (Figure 2).

From less organizational–administrative starting points, a further interesting systems approach to distance education has been developed by Tony Wright. In his case, the system is 'a model of teaching and learning, showing how various factors influence the personal development of a student' (Figure 3).

Systems and sub-systems of distance education are both listed and discussed analytically in Casas Armengol's 1987 survey in Spanish.

From these and other attempts to identify the system of distance education, we seem to be entitled to describe the following eight processes from an educator's point of view, as the most essential components:

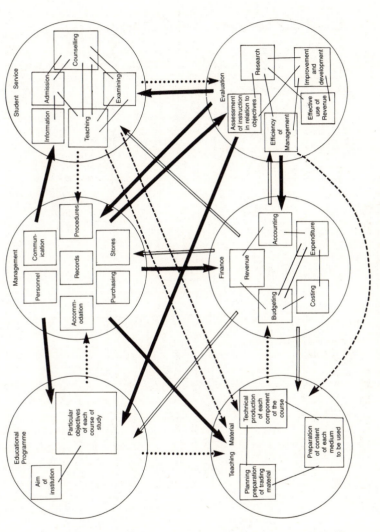

Figure 1 System of distance education
Source: Erdos 1975b: 11

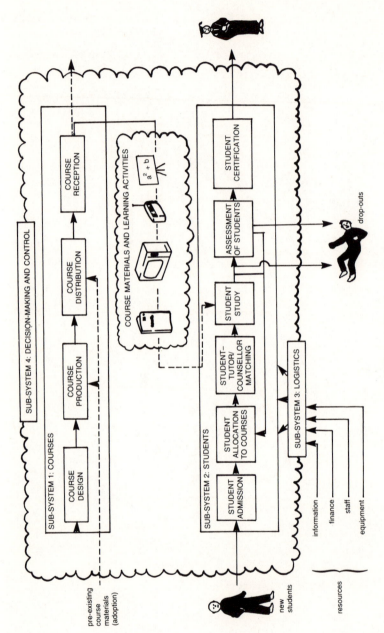

Figure 2 System of distance education
Source: Perspectives on distance education 1987: 28

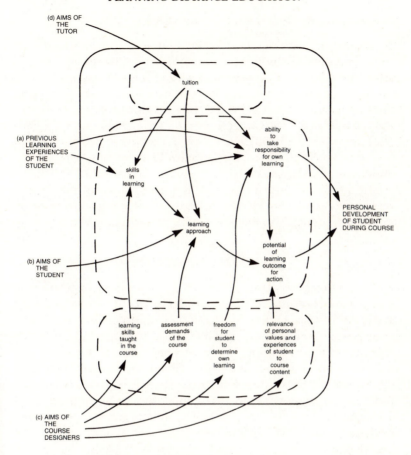

Figure 3 System of distance education
Source: Wright 1987: 5

1 Student learning
2 Course planning
3 Developing course materials.
4 Catering for instructive communication.
5 Counselling students.
6 Administering course development, course-material distribution, instructive communication, counselling, etc
7 Creating a suitable organizational structure for distance education.

31

8 Evaluating the functioning of the system.

In agreement with systems thinking, it is to be expected that these components influence one another (a change in one will affect the others). 'The systems approach is not necessarily a step-by-step process. Analysis, synthesis and evaluation are recurring stages repeated throughout the process and not necessarily in the traditional format of beginning, middle and end' (Romiszowski 1986: 58). Seven of the above components will be investigated in some detail below. The eighth component, evaluation, will be discussed at length in Chapter 10.

The systems approach is sometimes, irrespective of media use, referred to as educational technology. On educational technology in distance education, see Sauvé, Gagné and Lamy (1989).

STUDENT LEARNING

Helping students to learn is any educator's most important task and is a concern that must be considered already at the planning stage. All of what follows in this book is more or less relevant to endeavours that aim at facilitating and supporting distance students in their learning. While later sections will approach this from an educator's viewpoint, this chapter will briefly look into descriptive studies of how students actually learn. This is done in order as far as possible to make sure that optimizing attempts are realistic and to the point. The heterogeneity of distance students makes it difficult to attain generally applicable knowledge.

The starting point of our considerations must be our view of what learning is, as discussed in Chapter 2. Learning should not be understood as a passive process with the learner as the object of teaching, someone who merely receives information, but rather as an active process 'in which the learner interprets information and tries to connect it with already existing knowledge and to fit it into existing cognitive structures' (Schuemer 1993: 3). A consequence of this thinking may be that rote learning (i.e. merely committing facts, names, and figures to memory without looking into purposes, logical relations, reasons, and consequences) is considered relatively uninteresting. On the importance of fact learning see below, however. What Ausubel has called meaningful learning (Ausubel 1968: 55ff) is our main concern. Meaningful learning implies anchoring new learning matter in cognitive structures already acquired.

By non-arbitrarily relating potentially meaningful material to relevant established ideas in his cognitive structure, the learner is able effectively to exploit his existing knowledge as an ideational and organizational matrix for the incorporation, understanding, and fixation of large bodies of new ideas. It is the very non-arbitrariness of this process that enables him to use his previously acquired knowledge as a veritable touchstone, for internalizing and making understandable vast quantities of new word meanings, concepts, and propositions with relatively little effort and few repetitions. Because of this factor of non-arbitrariness, the potential meaning of new ideas *as wholes* can be related to established meanings (concepts, facts, and principles) *as wholes* to yield new meanings. In other words, the only way it is possible to make use of previously learned ideas in the processing (internalization) of new ideas is to relate the latter non-arbitrarily to the former. The new ideas, which become meaningful, in turn, also expand the base of the learning matrix.

(Ausubel 1968: 58)

As will be shown on pp. 59f. and 75, Ausubel's thinking can be of decisive importance for the structuring of learning matter in distance-education courses.

The awareness that people learn different things from the same teaching endeavours and from the same texts has caused some interesting attempts to identify types of learners and of learning. Gordon Pask's identification (Pask 1976b) of holist and serialist learners has been well summarized like this:

Serialists (partists) followed a step-by-step learning procedure concentrating on narrow simple hypotheses relating to one characteristic at a time. Holists (wholists) tended to form more complex hypotheses relating to several characteristics . . . Irredundant holists made use of analogies in their explanations which were appropriate and correct. Redundant holists made, if anything, wider use of analogies but many of these were not strictly accurate and some were entirely fictitious, invented to help the student remember certain characteristics . . . These personal 'props' seem to be the mark of the extreme holist.

(Entwistle 1978: 255)

From reading this, it could be asked if there are methods to help students to become 'irredundant holists'. Pask and Scott fear that it would be deleterious to teach serialists in a holist manner and holists in a serialist manner. Instead, they endeavour to find different strategies adapted to the two types of learners (Pask and Scott 1972; however, see Laurillard below).

A study of learning styles by Marton and Säljö has proved highly relevant to distance education. Their identification of deep-learning and surface-learning habits is particularly important for distance educators for two reasons: first, it is a study of reading, which dominates most distance learning; second, learning habits have great operational importance and bearing on the learning outcomes.

Surface learning basically endangers the educational outcomes of distance study, as it leads to priority being given to the external characteristics of the text concerned rather than to its contents, to examples rather than to principles of general relevance. Apparently many students are 'capable of using "deep" or "surface" strategies'. What is expected of them in an examination may influence the choice of strategy. Focusing the attention on 'the underlying meaning', i.e. promoting deep learning, can probably be brought about 'by ensuring that the assessment procedures demand deep-level processing' (Marton and Säljö 1976: 125).

While neither Pask nor Marton and Säljö pay particular attention to distance students, examinations of the study habits of students of the British Open University have led to the identification of the same deep- and surface-learning approaches as those described by Marton and Säljö (Morgan, Taylor and Gibbs 1982, Morgan 1984). Overcoming the dangers of surface learning must be seen as an important concern in distance education. See below pp. 35–6 as well as p. 129.

An alternative approach 'based on a system for classifying the mental activities reported by students' has been developed by Marland, *et al.* (1984). Data from an interview study offer 'specific leads about textual design' which are listed 'together with propositions for research' (op. cit. p. 233). These include considerations about metacognitive skills, access structure (see below Chapter 4) and deep-level textual processing.

To some extent related to this discussion is the dichotomy between problem-solving approaches and presentations of intellectual knowledge as ready-made (already discovered and described) systems. Weingartz, on the basis of a consistent view of learning as understanding and problem-solving, has provided an in-depth analysis of some distance-study courses from different parts of the world that illustrate these differences (Weingartz 1980, 1981), and Lehner has developed a learning theory bearing on this. He describes all learning as problem-solving in the sense that it is composed of making assumptions (i.e. developing hypotheses) and modifying these as the learning progresses: an application of Popper's epistemological principles of 'conjectures and refutations'. This leads him to the so-called 'genetic learning approach' mentioned above (Lehner 1978, 1979; see p. 23).

Weingartz' theoretical approach is linked with Lehner's and has resulted in her study of current practice in distance education. Apparently much remains to be done to improve problem-solving learning in distance education; on the whole the 'ready-made systems' presentation dominates, although guidance in far-reaching problem-solving occurs in some courses.

The evident conclusions of the studies referred to are that deep-learning and problem-solving approaches can and should be developed further in distance education. On the other hand, it must be realized that the 'genetic' method of retracing the paths of scholars and scientists in the search for the solutions to problems – including drawing the wrong conclusions (making the wrong hypotheses or conjectures) and later rejecting these in favour of new hypotheses – is much too time-consuming a procedure to be applied throughout, although without doubt an extremely educational experience.

The procedures to be applied to support deep learning, in the sense of Marton and Säljö, would seem to have to direct students' attention towards the subject matter of the texts studied and away from the textual presentation as such. How this is to be done is far from self-evident, however, unless making students conscious of their own learning, by advance organizers (see p. 59f.), 'learning conversations' (p. 47ff.) and other means as well as influencing the learning strategies by means of assessment procedures

35

are regarded as the answer. The problem is worth investigating further.

There seems to be little cause for resignation or belief that students' learning habits are rigid or necessarily difficult to influence. A study by Laurillard shows that 'students' styles and strategies of learning are context-dependent' (Laurillard 1978: 1). She rejects 'the assumption that learning is a process that is independent of other external factors, or that students possess inherent, invariant styles of learning' (op. cit. p. 10).

Stressing deep learning and problem-solving may lead to neglect of the learning of facts. In some cases it may be argued that, when students' retention of facts turns out to be poor, the sacrifice made is small, as long as they understand and can apply principles. This is not always a sound conclusion. A student of a foreign language must learn the accidence of that language in toto, and in languages such as German or Finnish must automatically be able to use the correct case after individual verbs, adjectives, or prepositions. Such learning can hardly be achieved without a number of repetitions and rather mechanical exercises and so, in certain instances, repetition and over-learning are still to be recommended. Interest in rote learning has now faded, and a sceptical attitude to both repetitions and over-learning has become quite fashionable. However, learning by heart, which is sometimes unavoidable, need not be rote learning only, as will be evident from the discussion of the structuring of a language course on p. 60ff.

In agreement with a view of teaching as facilitation of learning the following chapters will discuss the teaching–learning processes relevant to distance education.

COURSE PLANNING

Bringing about distance-education processes, whether meant to serve personality development, problem-solving as a purely academic exercise, or training leading to an examination or professional competence, requires planning to be useful. The most important considerations for planning are the characteristics of the target groups, the general conditions (social, financial, etc.) under which the study is to be performed, and the needs and intentions behind the educational endeavour, i.e. the study goals and objectives to be catered for.

The target groups

It is evidently important to know what types of students are to be taught. Their general education and previous study experiences, if any, as well as their specific prior knowledge of the subject to be learnt must necessarily exert decisive influences on the teaching. Under the influence of behaviourism, the following principle, among others, has been expressed.

> The course must be designed for the target population (students) that actually exists. It is foolish and wasteful to design a course without defining the target population. The major characteristics of the target population constitute the starting-point of the course, the performance called for in the course objectives constitutes the finishing-point, and the process of turning the incoming student into the skilled graduate constitutes the course itself. In other words, the substance of the course is derived by subtracting what the student already is able to do from what you want him to be able to do.
>
> (Mager and Beach 1967: 25)

Those who think in different terms have to accept the point that students' prior knowledge and proficiency must be the basis of any educational endeavour. However, it is only rarely that a student body is both homogeneous and well known when a course is planned. The only characteristic common to most distance students is that they are adults and active citizens (cf. pp. 14 and 205–6).

As a rule, course planners select their students by prescribing a certain standard of competence for enrolment. If, as in popular education, a broad student body is expected or desired, assumptions have to be made on the basis of existing knowledge of the population concerned. The same applies to selected target groups with certain common characteristics as far as intellectual interests, inclinations, prior knowledge, experience, and attitudes are concerned. For instance, these groups might be teachers, or nurses, or accountants; or they may be wider groups, such as those who have acquired university entrance qualifications, or have passed some other educational milestone, or have taken part in a preparatory course of study.

General background factors

The general circumstances under which the study is to be performed can be influenced to a limited extent only. Family situations, social and economic conditions, work requirements, and other background factors must be considered when a study programme is planned. In some cases these factors can be influenced in a way that improves the study situation of individuals or groups, for example, by the offer of paid work-free periods, baby-sitting facilities, scholarships, etc. Distance students in Germany, the United Kingdom, Scandinavia, and elsewhere have experience of such measures to improve their situation. Whether or not this type of intervention occurs, the study situation of distance students usually has some special characteristics to which attention must consistently be paid: students' maturity, their jobs and social commitments, their family responsibilities. One aspect of this is that adult distance students can only rarely give first priority to their study. This, of course, requires adaptability and flexibility of the study arrangements.

Data about factors of the kind discussed occur in, for example, Bååth (1984b); Balay (1978); Bartels (1983); McIntosh, Woodley and Morrison (1980); Wångdahl (1980).

Goals and objectives of study

It is a truism to say that the goals of an undertaking are of paramount importance for how this is to be performed. In education, goal orientation has caused much discussion, however. While it is commonplace that education is an intentional activity, the extent to which pre-determined goals are to direct study is a contentious issue.

What has caused most of the modern discussion in this respect is the insistence of the behaviourist school of thought that all teaching should be oriented towards detailed, behavioural goals, i.e. objectives specifying not what the students should learn or know but what they should be able to do after the study. A list of objectives described in this way is thus a presentation of what has been called the terminal behaviour.

As distance education in most cases relies on pre-produced courses, which have to be planned in detail, this approach seems attractive to many distance educators. They realize that saying that students should learn to know French grammar or the principles of combustion, for example, really means nothing. More detailed goals are required if they are to guide course development.

In the case of an elementary course on combustion, the following goals might be agreed upon:

1 To develop problem-solving skills.
2 To understand scientific method.
3 To develop skills in using scientific apparatus and in measurement.
4 To develop understanding of the theory of combustion.
5 To learn how to interpret and evaluate data.

Not only behaviourists would object that these goals are too vague to function as guidelines to course content; they can be interpreted in different ways. A more useful definition of the objectives might be expressed as follows:

When the student has completed the programme he/she should be able:

1 To tell one way in which a scientist might attempt to answer the question, 'What is necessary for combustion?'.
2 To demonstrate how water can be made to boil in a dish made of paper, without burning the paper.
3 To state several hypotheses as to why the paper will not burn in the demonstration.
4 To conduct experiments to determine which hypothesis is correct.
5 To tell how a scientist might explain the results of the experiments which have been conducted.
6 To tell how the findings of the experiments might be put to practical use.

See De Cecco (1964: 308–9), the source of this example.

In fact, distance educators usually think that the aims and objectives of a course should be clarified as far as possible in order to ensure that the needs and interests of students are catered for rather than the whims of course developers. This leads to the requirement that objectives should be communicable and as lucid as possible. It has been found to be good practice when defining study objectives to avoid verbs of state, such as 'know', 'understand', 'realize', 'grasp', 'master', since these are particularly ambiguous. Verbal expressions of action, such as 'recognize the symptom of', 'conduct experiment', 'demonstrate', 'do', 'enumerate', 'calculate', 'quote arguments for and against', 'prove', 'write an account of', 'report orally on', are found to be more acceptable in definitions of objectives.

As a rule, it has also been found necessary to determine the extent to which each objective is to be achieved, i.e. how well the student should perform after the training. This has been done by grading the required performance, for instance as follows:

Grade 1: Merely recognizing the knowledge matter.
Grade 2: Performing without answering why-questions.
Grade 3: Explaining and discussing.

This borders on what has been called a taxonomy of educational objectives (Bloom 1956), which is discussed below under Content and structure in Chapter 4).

Other methods of grading performance are to state that students are expected to solve a certain percentage of selected types of problems, to give a certain number of examples, theories or reasons, or to demonstrate something by a certain number of different experiments.

The insistence on objectives in behavioural terms stems from thinkers such as Skinner and Mager, who have developed and apply behaviourist theory to education (Mager 1962). When non-behaviourists use definitions of objectives to guide course development, they take over a technique, not a psychological theory. They stress communicable rather than behavioural objectives, realizing that some objectives simply cannot be expressed in behavioural terms.

Thus, there is fairly general agreement that there are educational goals in distance education that transcend measurable cognitive or manipulative skills. Sometimes training aims at influencing attitudes: for instance, making students critical readers, seeing through propaganda and prejudices, or encouraging a feeling of co-operation, understanding, positive relations towards (and treatment of) customers, patients, etc.

There are also other good reasons generally to regard and apply the objective-defining technique with critical judgement. Thus, we must realize that it is almost impossible to avoid ambiguity completely in the formulation of objectives, even if we exclusively use verbs of action ('do', etc.) and avoid verbs of state ('know', etc.). Even action verbs, such as 'deduce', 'recognize' and 'solve', have been shown to be ambiguous. 'There is a limit to the extent to which any human can understand the intention of another, no matter what, though in practice and in certain circumstances the risk of serious error can be minimized' (Macdonald-Ross 1973: 35–6).

A further counter-argument is that defining learning objectives in operational terms with tests, against which their attainment is checked, need not necessarily lead to any kind of proof that the objectives have or have not been attained. It is perfectly possible to make the right operation for the wrong reason, as shown by the following example borrowed from Lewis. Anyone who believes that 0.3×0.3 makes 0.9 (instead of 0.09) and that 0.2×0.2 makes 0.4 (instead of 0.04) will no doubt, on the basis of a false understanding, come to the conclusion that $0.3 \times 0.5 = 0.15$, which happens to be correct (Lewis 1974: 16). It is evident that the operation is not enough; we must pay attention to the knowledge and understanding on which it is based.

On the other hand, there can hardly be valid complaints about the use of behavioural objectives in cases where accurate performance can be measured against them and where there is an indisputably correct answer (as, for example, in certain points of grammar in a foreign language, such as saying and writing 'he takes/speaks', etc. but 'I take', 'you take', etc.).

A basic question is who decides what the learning objectives are to be. If they are determined in an authoritarian way, students are most likely (and in some cases no doubt well advised) to protest. Study objectives thus determined can be powerful instruments of indoctrination. However, it should be clear that it is not the possible effectiveness as such that is the danger but the very content of the objectives and the way in which they are defined.

In the so-called affective domain, special caution is advisable. First we must ask ourselves to what extent and in what areas distance students should be subjected to emotional influence. Naturally, educational policy cannot neglect the requirements of society to provide some sort of moral upbringing. On the other hand, the indoctrinating character of any endeavour of this kind cannot be disregarded. In order to ensure that people are not brainwashed, it is necessary that a reasonable plurality should characterize their upbringing and their general socialization.

It is doubtful, however, to what extent this is really an issue in distance education for adults with a number of social responsibilities and commitments. I would submit that adult distance students automatically acquire the kind of community socialization expected of mature citizens. Following their upbringing as children, they do this in their day-to-day social life through their families, jobs and the company that they keep. In planning distance study, particularly at the university level, we would thus seem to be entitled to limit our socialization efforts to the requirements of academic life, study, research, and professional socialization.

However, it seems important that study objectives in the affective domain should be specified in all cases when there are such objectives, for instance, those concerned with professional socialization or similar goals. The reason for this is that, to my mind, the students should always be made aware of any attempts made to influence them. As soon as any persuading or convincing is intended, this should be made explicit so that individual students may be in a reasonably fair position to protect themselves. This is particularly important in relation to subjects where there are competing schools of thought, relying on or supporting political ideas or religious beliefs. Transparency in this respect seems to be a matter of intellectual honesty. For objectives of this kind, behavioural descriptions are of little avail. This, however, does not mean that communicable objectives should be dispensed with. Contrary to expectations among most educationists, distance education has proved to be a powerful means to bring about attitude change (see p. 15f.).

In cases where affective objectives could possibly be interpreted as indoctrination plans, it is evident that the declaration of objectives should be made available to students before they choose the course or enrol. In other cases it is doubtful if study objectives need necessarily precede the actual course. If they do, however, they can, if suitably and comprehensively worded, act as 'advance organizers' that 'bridge the gap between what the learner already knows and what he needs to know before he can successfully learn the task at hand' (Ausubel 1968: 148) or act at least as directors of attention.

The extent to which students use statements of objectives as guides to what they should give particular attention is uncertain, however. According to Macdonald-Ross, evidence collected in the Open University 'by questionnaire surveys suggests that objectives are not used in this way by the students' (Macdonald-Ross 1979: 19). Using statements of objectives as check lists at the end of course units, to make sure that students have learned what is expected of them, for instance in a forthcoming examination, is another application. Specified objectives can also facilitate selective reading, as part of what Waller calls the 'access structure of texts' (Waller 1977b). Whether the objectives should be placed at the beginning or the end of a course unit would seem to depend on how students wish or are expected to use them.

Although it is thus uncertain how and to what extent students benefit from reading a list of specified learning objectives, there can be little doubt that they serve a useful function as planning devices, as control instruments to be used by course developers, and as eye-openers to the developers when they confront their pet subject areas with the needs of students.

The above discussion will have shown that the application of detailed objectives 'needs to be tempered with an understanding of its inherent deficiencies' (Macdonald-Ross 1973: 47). Once this is recognized, I think that there is a strong case for detailed objectives in distance education (see Popham 1987).

One reason for this is that distance-study courses are prepared in advance and give little scope for improvization and references to day-to-day occurrences. They can thus be consistently planned to cover what is considered important. Such planning usually entails a detailed analysis of what is desired, makes exactitude necessary, and provides a basis for judgements of the results of the course, i.e. for evaluating procedures. It would be an illusion, however, to believe that the definition of objectives is normally an initial activity only, completed when the media are selected and the real course creation starts. It is often desirable and necessary to modify the original objectives in the light of information, considerations, and experiences made available through the actual development work: a consequence of the systems approach (see Romiszowski, as quoted on p. 32). It could also be regarded as adherence to Popper's attractive 'piecemeal' approach (a suggestion made by Davies 1978: 140–1). It is, of course, possible (and desirable) to include independent work under the objectives, which will lead to open-ended tasks of a project type in the course to be developed.

The basic problems connected with definitions of study objectives do not concern their efficiency as control instruments but their appropriateness from the points of view of both the individual and society. The relevance and necessity of the objectives for the main educational goals, their appropriateness as seen from a wider perspective than that of the course that is being planned, their influence on the self-actualization of individual students whose integrity must be safeguarded, and their compatibility with pluralistic approaches which encourage unprejudiced study are matters of vital importance to be considered in the course of the planning process.

A question that should be looked into further in this context is how students themselves, by selecting their own learning objectives, can influence or even independently decide not only how but also what they are to study. This is the key question related to student autonomy in distance study. Individualized learning is not brought about by freedom of pace or even freedom of method and medium if others than students decide the content of study. To what extent is it possible to provide a wide range of study opportunities, with clearly defined and declared study objectives for each small unit, and to make possible a completely free choice of such units for students in individual combinations? Constructive approaches which engage the students in the selection of study objectives have been developed by both Potvin (1976) and Ljoså and Sandvold (1983). Potvin 'denies the institution and the tutor the right to prescribe what the learner should learn and how he is to learn it' (Potvin 1976: 30). How this philosophy is to be practised is worth considering. It is evidently possible only to a very limited extent in studies which have to follow fixed curricula.

4

COURSE DEVELOPMENT – FUNDAMENTAL CONSIDERATIONS

The presentation of learning matter has been described above as one of two constituent elements of distance education, the other being interaction between students and their supporting organization with its tutors, counsellors and its administrative infrastructure. Any discussion about how this presentation occurs, how its goals can be attained and what methods and media are used, should be preceded by a consideration of its basic character. In distance education it is brought about by other means than face-to-face sessions.

OVERARCHING PRINCIPLES

Evidently (see pp. 23 and 35), the presentation of learning matter cannot be confined to dissemination of information. As an educational endeavour it must engage students in an intellectual activity that makes them try out ideas, reflect, compare and apply critical judgement to what is studied. This necessarily includes making use of insights acquired in various connections and cannot be limited to purely intellectual experiences; there is an affective aspect to be considered, as there is in anything that engages the mind and develops the personality.

It is the task of course developers to assist students' learning by examining the learning matter by argument, reflection in writing or recording, and causing students to reflect. Reflection in this context has been understood as 'a generic term for those intellectual and affective activities in which individuals engage to explore their experiences in order to lead to new understandings and appreciations. It may take place in isolation' (Boud, Keogh and Walker 1985: 19). These activities are compatible with

45

personal approaches, bring out communicative aspects, and can lead to conversation-like principles of presentation.

Learning-matter presentation simulating personal communication

This means more than rejecting information dissemination as the sole function of learning-matter presentation. It necessarily entails consequences for the general approach, the way in which students are addressed and treated. Under no circumstances can students be seen as passive recipients of wisdom conveyed by the medium of the distance-teaching course. Instead, they are partners whose knowledge, experience, and capacity are relied on to contribute to a real and/or simulated communication that promotes learning and the development of new insights.

While it is true that the presentation of learning matter in a pre-produced course, written, recorded, broadcast, or made available in any other way, is technically a case of one-way traffic (to be supplemented by interaction, i.e. two-way traffic), the approach described can simulate informal communication which causes and – in the author's opinion – requires personal rapport between course developers and students. Empathy would thus seem to be an important quality for a course developer. See Swanepoel (1987), according to whom dialogue and personal relationships are necessary prerequisites for education; she states that 'education is primarily a personal relationship which becomes concrete through affective and cognitive means' (Swanepoel 1987: 185).

The author of an Australian (Gippsland Institute of Advanced Education) sociology course states, in an audio tape introducing the study, that in the printed course materials a style has been adopted which 'is rather more personal or chatty than is conventional in social science writing. This should make these books easier to read' (Nation and Elliott 1985: 12). An accompanying research project (based on 'participant observation' and detailed records of telephone conversations with students)

> confirmed the effectiveness of the 'personal style' which had been used in our printed course materials. It pointed out, particularly, that for some students anyway, the 'personal style' broke down feelings of isolation and assisted

46

students to take up our offer to use the telephone and other forms of informal contact.

(Nation and Elliott 1985: 19)

Guided didactic conversation

The present author has long been concerned with the characteristics of distance-teaching courses meeting the requirements indicated and has introduced and operationalized the concept of guided didactic conversation in this context (Holmberg 1960: 15; 1983a; and elsewhere; Holmberg, Schuemer and Obermeier 1982).

My approach to guided didactic conversation as a pervasive characteristic of distance education is based on seven postulates:

1 That feelings of personal relation between the teaching and learning parties promote study pleasure and motivation.
2 That such feelings can be fostered by well-developed self-instructional material and two-way communication at a distance.
3 That intellectual pleasure and study motivation are favourable to the attainment of study goals and the use of proper study processes and methods.
4 That the atmosphere, language and conventions of friendly conversation favour feelings of personal relation according to postulate 1.
5 That messages given and received in conversational forms are comparatively easily understood and remembered.
6 That the conversation concept can be successfully translated, for use by the media available, to distance education.
7 That planning and guiding the work, whether provided by the teaching organization or the student, are necessary for organized study, which is characterized by explicit or implicit goal conceptions.

A basic general assumption is that real learning is primarily an individual activity and is attained only through an internalizing process.

The conversation that can be simulated in a pre-produced, usually printed course is primarily felt to be one between the course developers and the individual students. The former build up an image of the students who are expected to study their

47

courses and endeavour to address them as individuals. This leads to a simulated 'conversation', which tends to encourage individual text elaboration.

Thinking aloud is a frequently occurring form of text elaboration which has been studied in different contexts (cf. Ericsson and Simon 1980; Chafe 1979, 1980; Graff 1980: 149). Elaborative processing of text, i.e. the interaction of the text content with the prior knowledge of the reader, has actually proved conducive to retention (Weinstein *et al.* 1979; Ballstaedt and Mandl 1982). Whereas a student who does very little elaborating does not secure the new learning matter sufficiently, those who do a lot of elaborating seem to risk having difficulties in retracing the text information in the multitude of connections that they have established. Thus moderate use of text elaboration seems profitable (Mandl and Ballstaedt 1982; see Ballstaedt and Mandl 1982: 5; and Pask 1976b on 'redundant holists' as discussed on pp. 33–4).

Text elaboration has something of a conversational character also when it does not literally mean thinking aloud. See Lewis, who rejects any contrasting of 'conversational activity with more solitary activities such as private reasoning and silent reading', which he characterizes as 'internalized conversation'. 'As we mull things over quietly and in solitude, we are actually holding a conversation with ourselves' (Lewis 1975: 69). This is tantamount to interaction with a text and indirectly, with its author, by means of which the reader influences the outcome and implies affinity to what is called discourse theory (Juler 1990).

If we accept that discourse in the sense of elaborative text processing and 'internalized conversation' represent a useful learning strategy, it is logical to draw conclusions from this to a teaching strategy. In its simplest form this would imply causing students to apply an appropriate extent of text elaboration to their learning.

These are considerations behind my concept of guided didactic conversation, the qualities of which I have described as follows:

1 Easily accessible presentations of study matter; clear, somewhat colloquial language, in easily readable writing; moderate density of information.

2 Explicit advice and suggestions to the student as to what to do and what to avoid, what to pay particular attention to and

consider, with reasons provided; for example, along the following lines: 'Here you may draw the conclusion that . . . This is tricky, however. Compare . . . and consider if what we discussed in Course Unit X causes you to . . .

3 Invitations to an exchange of views, to questions, to opinions and comments.
4 Attempts to involve the student emotionally so that he or she takes a personal interest in the subject and its problems.
5 Personal style including the use of personal and possessive pronouns: I, my, you, your, etc.
6 Demarcation of changes of themes through explicit statements, typographical means, or, in recorded, spoken communication, through a change of speakers (e.g. male followed by female) or through pauses. (This is a characteristic of the guidance rather than of the conversation.)

Using this operationalization of the concept of guided didactic conversation, I have developed a theory implying that course presentations which follow the principles described are attractive to students, support study motivation, and facilitate learning. This is expected to apply to most learners at all levels, but particularly to those with little or modest experience of study and limited independence. This reservation is rejected by Mitchell who insists that 'the principles of guided didactic conversation are relevant in all aspects of education' (Mitchell 1992: 130). As exceptions are foreseen (a minority of students are expected to be indifferent or, in extreme cases, even negative to the style of guided conversation), this is not what the critical–rationalist school of epistemology would call a nomological theory.

I assume that if a distance–study course consistently represents a communication process that is felt to have the character of a conversation, then the students will be more motivated and more successful than if the course studied has an impersonal textbook character.

My main formal hypotheses, based on the general postulates and the assumptions about what constitutes guided didactic conversation, can therefore be summarized as follows:

1 The stronger the characteristics of guided didactic conversation, the stronger the students' feelings of personal relationship between them and the supporting organization.
2 The stronger the students' feelings that the supporting

organization is interested in making the study matter personally relevant to them, the greater their personal involvement.

3 The stronger the students' feelings of personal relations to the supporting organization and of being personally involved with the study matter, the stronger the motivation and the more effective the learning.

4 The more independent and scholarly experienced the students, the less relevant the characteristics of guided didactic conversation.

By three empirical investigations (Holmberg, Schuemer and Obermeier 1982), these hypotheses, as one unified theory, have been subjected to rigorous falsification attempts in the spirit of Popper. These attempts, among other things, caused testing to be done under circumstances as unfavourable as possible to the theory. The tendency apparent in all of the three studies favoured the theory, although no consistent, statistically significant corroboration emerged. The students who took part in the investigation stated that they felt personally involved by the conversational presentations, their attitudes were favourable to them, and they did marginally better in their assignment attainments than the students who took the original course.

Apparently independently of this theoretical approach and its empirical testing, other distance educators have adopted similar principles.

Learning conversations

Learning conversation is a designation used by Harri-Augstein and her group of scholars to denote

a form of dialogue about a learning experience in which the learner reflects on some event or activity in the past. Ultimately, it is intended that people will internalize such conversations so that they are able to review learning experiences systematically for themselves, but at the beginning, the learning conversation is carried out with the assistance of a teacher or tutor ...

It must first of all be said that a learning conversation is not idle chatter, nor is it an exchange of prescriptions, instructions or injunctions. Instead, it is a dialogue on the process of learning: the learner reflects on his or her learning with the assistance of a teacher or tutor.

(Candy, Harri-Augstein and Thomas 1985: 102)

There can be little doubt that this approach is less directive and has more of a metacharacter in its relation to learning than my guided didactic conversation. It is concerned with bringing 'to a level of conscious awareness the [learning] strategies and values which were previously implicit' with a view to putting students 'in a position to modify them' (ibid. p. 115). This, to quote from another paper,

> requires three parallel dialogues. Together these reflect the learner's cognitive process back to him, support him through painful periods of change and encourage him to develop stable referents which anchor his judgement of the quality of his assessment. The three dialogues can be described as:
>
> (a) commentary on the learning process;
> (b) personal support of the learner's reflection; and
> (c) referents for evaluating learning competence.
>
> Each of these three dialogues can become internalized, but people differ in the ease with which they can sustain each of them. Effective internalization of the complete learning conversation produces the self-organized learner and the fully functioning man or woman. Such people learn from experience and continue to learn through life. Frozen internal conversations disable us as learners, and it is only when the external conversation is re-established that the frozen process can be revived. Living then becomes an ongoing opportunity for learning.
>
> (Thomas and Harri-Augstein 1977: 101–2)

The tutorial-in-print

A more directive approach strongly characterizes what Derek Rowntree has called a tutorial-in-print. Like any tutorial it has a conversational character but it seems to be concerned more with knowledge acquisition than with discussing problems, more with down-to-earth suggestions and exhortations than with reflection on the learning.

Rowntree advises course developers to imagine that they are tutoring one individual learner, thus providing a substitute for individual face-to-face teaching:

> Everything you might want to say to this individual will need to be written down, forming what I have called a tutorial-in-print.
>
> This is what you will need to do in your tutorial-in-print if you are to teach your individual learners:
>
> • Help the learners find their way into and around your subject, by-passing or repeating sections where appropriate.
> • Tell them what they need to be able to do before tackling the material.
> • Make clear what they should be able to do on completion of the material (e.g. in terms of objectives).
> • Advise them on how to tackle the work (e.g. how much time to allow for different sections, how to plan for an assignment, etc.).
> • Explain the subject matter in such a way that learners can relate it to what they know already.
> • Encourage them sufficiently to make whatever effort is needed in coming to grips with the subject.
> • Engage them in exercises and activities that cause them to work with the subject-matter, rather than merely reading about it.
> • Give the learners feedback on these exercises and activities, enabling them to judge for themselves whether they are learning successfully.
> • Help them to sum up their learning at the end of the lesson.
>
> (Rowntree 1986: 82–3)

The conversational character of the 'tutorial-in-print' is stressed more clearly in other contexts, for example by Donnachie in a discussion of history teaching at a distance, in which it is said not only to involve 'the teacher in a one-to-one relationship with the student' but also to challenge 'the student in a dialogue with the tutor' (Donnachie 1986: 55). This implies stressing the importance of simulated communication in a way closely resembling my guided didactic conversation.

The same applies to a presentation by Cooper and Lockwood:

> The simulation of a 'tutorial in print' (Rowntree 1975) is the procedure whereby an author regards the student time spent working on his material as time spent by the student in the author's company. In such a situation it is unlikely that an author would expect a student to simply read an exposition from start to finish without reacting to it in some way or producing anything themselves. They may, for example, be asked to recall items of information, define concepts, draw together arguments, justify particular statements, consult other sources, interpret data, compare different interpretations of the same data, work out examples, and so on. In short to exercise certain study skills by which they can construct their own picture of a subject and integrate what they have just been taught with what they had learnt before.
>
> (Cooper and Lockwood 1979: 253)

Conversation theory

A sophisticated conversation theory has been developed by Gordon Pask, who applies a cybernetic approach to networks of concepts and interaction with a computer; he describes his theory as 'an attempt to investigate the learning of realistically complex subject matter under controlled conditions' (Pask 1976a: 12).

Pask's theory is complicated, indeed. Entwistle, who recognizes its difficulties, provides the following presentation:

> Essentially this theory describes learning in terms of a conversation between two representations of knowledge. In the most familiar situation these representations reflect the cognitive structures of two people, the teacher (or subject-matter expert) and the student. Learning takes place through a dialogue between the two and, in conversation theory, understanding has to be demonstrated by applying that knowledge to an unfamiliar situation in a concrete non-verbal way (often using specially designed apparatus). Reproductive responses based on memory are not accepted as evidence of understanding.
>
> Learning need not, however, involve an interaction between the cognitive structures of two people. The student

may converse silently with himself in trying to understand a topic, or he may interact with a formal representation of the knowledge structure and supplementary learning materials which have been specially designed to facilitate understanding of the chosen subject-matter area. Such a 'surrogate tutor' is described as a conversational domain in a standard experimental condition.

(Entwistle 1978: 255)

Pask's thinking has been very fruitfully applied and further developed by Kathleen Forsythe, a distance educator with experience of the Canadian Knowledge-Network. Her approach to conversation theory is based on

second order cybernetics, a relatively new theoretical construct for not only assessing systems and interactions but also how we see ourselves as we interact. . . . The intriguing insight of Conversation Theory is that the inquiry may be between perspectives within the mind of one person and that Conversation Theory enables the mind to deal with a variety of truth valuations. Unlike the functionalist school, where the ontology of dual states of truths is exemplified in true and false, Conversation Theory is a science of process, encompassed by an ontology of many truth valuations which exist as distinct entities and which form their own necessarily dynamic phenomenology.

(Forsythe 1986: 4 and 5)

Forsythe considers instructional design primarily as design for learning interactions and has developed a 'learning system as a new paradigm for the information age' (Forsythe 1985), in which the learner, the learning partner (the teacher) and 'the knowledge that may be the substance of their conversation' (Forsythe 1986: 10) are the basic components. She elaborates this system to facilitate the understanding of the effectiveness of media, on which see p. 85 (Forsythe 1986).

Forsythe's identification of the evocative, provocative, and convocative functions characteristic of 'interactions for learning' can be seen as something of a guideline for a conversational approach to distance education:

Evocative. The conversation with another, or the conversational agent, evokes or calls forth a reaction within the

54

participant that is often based on a feeling of awakening or of experiencing. This often comes from experiencing one thing in terms of another – the isophor. In designing systems that evoke interactions for learning, use of isophor is particularly helpful.

Provocative. The conversation with another, or the conversational agent, rouses forth a reaction from the participant that is often unsettling or disturbing, often because it represents a perspective or state significantly different from our own. The feeling of provocation is experienced as we feel we must reassess our own point of view in light of the new perspective.

Convocative. The conversation or the conversational agent gathers participants together for a shared experience mediated by the conversational agent.

(Forsythe 1986: 22–3)

Further comments on personal, conversational approaches as guidelines

The personal, conversational approaches are not exclusively applied to distance education but also to the development of study materials for other purposes. Nevertheless it seems to have originated in distance education (see Holmberg 1960). My studies of guided didactic conversation, Nation's of the personal style in course development, and Forsythe's learning system are primarily intended to serve distance education. Further, Sparkes emphasizes educational conversation as a teaching mode in distance education (Neil 1981: 112; Sparkes 1982: 4). An interesting near parallel is what Chang, Crombag, van der Drift, and Moonen, in their plan for the Dutch distance-teaching university, call paradigmatic presentation (Chang *et al.* 1983: 21). See further Morgan's insistence on dialogue (Morgan 1985: 44).

Empathy and personal approaches are thus considered guidelines for presentation of learning matter in distance education. They can do the same for tutor-student interaction in distance education, as will be shown on pp. 125–7.

CONTENT AND STRUCTURE

In a great number of cases, the analysis of learning objectives and their final definition automatically lead to a description of the course content. In other cases, the objectives will have to be translated into categories of content defined qualitatively and quantitatively. We have to consider internal criteria, i.e. those that intrinsically characterize the subject, and external criteria, which are those derived from students' needs and interests, from society and the labour market. This applies whether the learning objectives have been expressed behaviourally or in a more general way. It is important to specify what students must know, what they should know, and what they might find useful to know; to define this, as far as possible, in terms of what they will be expected to be able to do and under what circumstances they will be expected to perform. It is also useful to specify the manner (orally, in writing, by laboratory demonstration, creation of something, etc.) in which students are to prove their acquired competence. It is no less important, as implied on pp. 41–2, to state aims bearing on such intellectual skills as cannot easily be checked by performance (behaviour), and the affective objectives, if any, so that they may duly influence both the contents and the course structure.

Learning levels

In the so-called cognitive (intellectual) domain Benjamin Bloom has identified a classical hierarchy of objectives of immediate relevance to course development. He lists six cognitive levels as shown in the pyramid opposite.

When a distance-education course is planned, considerations of the importance of each of these levels for the course under preparation can provide directing influences. See Ray Taylor on the 'Blooming of education' (Taylor 1991). Other hierarchies of interest have been developed. A project-team at Leeds Metropolitan University has in its work on a degree model focusing on the application of 'work-based' learning defined the following stages also presented here in a pyramid on p. 58.

The same team has identified five problem-solving stages:

1 Formulating the problem (involving detection, identification and definition).
2 Interpreting the problem.

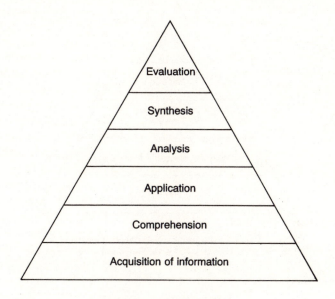

Figure 4 Cognitive levels
Source: Bloom, in Bloom *et al.* 1956

3 Constructing courses of action.
4 Decision-making.
5 Implementation.
(*Mentoring* 1: 7–8)

These hierarchies would seem to offer useful guidelines comparable to Bloom's.

Structuring learning matter

Structuring the presentation of content selected on the basis of such taxonomies of objectives or other principles is sometimes fairly unproblematic and occasionally a tricky matter. In most subjects there is, as shown on pp. 21–3, a logical order or a conventional pattern which is usually felt to be natural by subject specialists. This order is sometimes such that it must be followed, at least partly, because one part is based on another, knowledge

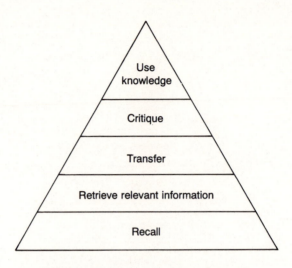

Figure 5 Stages of work-based learning
Source: *Mentoring* 1: 7–8, Leeds Metropolitan University

and understanding of the latter being necessary prerequisites for tackling the former. It is important for course developers to specify what prior knowledge of neighbouring disciplines is necessary (for instance, what mathematics is necessary for a physics or statistics course), to make provision, if possible, for the acquisition of this pre-knowledge, and in any case to make would-be students and administrators aware of the necessary sequence. Concepts and methods within a discipline usually serve as organizers which must decisively influence the structure of most courses. at university level at least. See Hirst's 'logical grammar' (p. 22).

The structuring of any presentation of learning matter is always based on the implicit or explicit goals at which the learning aims, the character of the learning content, and the types of learning concerned. Attempts have been made to develop firm rules for structuring and sequencing content on this basis. These attempts include a search for algorithmic solutions, information mapping and concept mapping, for which sophisticated methods have been created, such as network analysis, mathematics (T.F. Gilbert's system for developing special skills), and the so-called critical path method (Landa 1976; Horn and Green 1974; Wyant 1974; Rowntree 1974: e.g. Ch. 4). Learning hierarchies and relational networks further exemplify attempts made in this area. Reigeluth, Merrill, and Bunderson (1978) have endeavoured to clarify the discussion about content mapping and content relations in a paper that introduces their own approach to structuring. They provide illuminating examples of learning structures, procedural structures, taxonomic structures, and theoretical structures as 'pervasive content relations'.

Inductive and deductive approaches

A basic question is whether in a course to start out from the parts of a subject area or from the whole, to proceed inductively or deductively. There is, in fact, a philosophical controversy related to structuring principles. The atomistic, associative and inductive approaches, based on David Hume's thinking, have inspired modern behaviourism. Logically, the result of this should be – and among behaviourists often is – an insistence on starting out from the smallest items of knowledge, from the particular, in order to come to grips with the general. This is entirely contrary to the philosophy of Karl Popper and his school of rationalists. Popper rejects inductive methods and in his epistemology starts with the general, i.e. basic abstract assumptions, from which he deduces the particular. Strike and Posner (1976) relate these two contradictory views to education and argue convincingly that whereas the ' "bottom up" approaches to curriculum of the sort represented by the work of Robert Gagné' are based on inductivist thinking, the ' "top down" varieties of the sort often associated with Jerome Bruner' are influenced by the deductive philosophy of Popper and others (Strike and Posner 1976: 115).

A most influential representative of the deductive approach in education is David Ausubel. He suggests the use of 'advance organizers' which

> are introduced in advance of the learning material itself and are also presented at a higher level of abstraction, generality, and inclusiveness; and since the substantive

content of a given organizer or series of organizers is selected on the basis of their appropriateness for explaining, integrating, and interrelating the material they precede, this strategy simultaneously satisfies the ... criteria ... for enhancing the organizational strength of cognitive structure.

(Ausubel 1968: 148)

Ausubel, who distinguishes advance organizers from summaries or overviews which 'are ordinarily presented at the same level of abstraction ... as the learning material itself' (ibid.), argues in favour of a hierarchical theory of cognitive structure. New learning materials are seen as items which are subsumed under already existing cognitive structures. Early research on the whole gave proof of the effectiveness of advance organizers, but later studies have produced conflicting evidence as to their effectiveness (Macdonald-Ross 1979: 20).

The advance organizers describe the basic concepts of the immediately following part of the course and 'bridge the gap between what the learner already knows and what he needs to know before he can successfully learn the task at hand'. They have proved helpful to students because 'not only is the new material rendered more familiar and potentially meaningful, but the most relevant ideational antecedents in cognitive structures are also selected and utilized in integrated fashion' (Ausubel 1968: 148 and 137). They can thus promote deep learning and make students aware of how they learn. They do this by relating what they already know to the learning task. The research on advance organizers has been summarized in a useful way, and practical guidelines on the when and how of their use have been presented by Marland and Store (1982: 77–81).

Ausubel's thinking thus agrees with the top-down approach as opposed to the bottom-up approach of the behaviourists. In practice both approaches are often applied by one and the same course author and are not always easy to identify as applications of one or the other of the two.

In this context, let us consider language learning concerned with forms of grammar. If, in a course of German, one purpose of teaching and learning is that the student should learn how to use dative and accusative forms respectively in objects of the verb and learn it so well that the application of the principles involved becomes almost automatic (an inevitable requirement if the learner is to use the language learnt), the following sequence is possible.

1 Typical sentences selected from a text read, from which the student sees which principles govern the usage (as, 'Ich gab ihnen die Bücher. Gab er euch die Bücher? Er gab ihr den Ring. Ich sah sie auf der Strasse. Sie gab ihm den Ring. Sie bat ihn um Hilfe. Schickte er Ihnen keine Blumen?').

2 A discussion of the findings made, specifying the principles illustrated, and explaining, say, why the dative form is used after the verb in five of the sentences and the accusative form in the other two; this can be done in a Socratic way, referring to the students' observations.

3 Exercises of a self-checking character.

4 A discussion of the exercises, relating the individual examples to the general principle discovered according to 1 and 2.

5 New, more complicated examples.

6 A discussion of findings.

7 New self-checking exercises.

8 A discussion of the new exercises relating them to the principle as explained under 2 and 6.

Is the presentation of this item of language learning an example of an inductive or a deductive approach? The procedure suggested is open to alternative interpretations. Superficially it would seem to represent a typical application of the inductive method: particulars (case forms) are looked for and identified, and from these findings conclusions are drawn about general principles. Nevertheless, it would be possible to interpret the initial analysis of sentences as an introduction to the general insight that in German there are case forms of articles and pronouns related to logical syntax. On the basis of this general approach, particular forms are identified and learned. No doubt parallel alternative interpretations occur when the structuring of other presentations of knowledge are studied.

The type of learning discussed would seem to some extent to exemplify what has been called reproductive learning and reception learning. However, it also involves the understanding and application of a principle and thus an element of problem-solving: tracing a direct and an indirect object, its person, gender and number, the correspondence between 'ihr' and 'euch',

'Sie' and 'Ihnen', etc. Thus, it is a case of not only reproductive but also productive learning.

The problem-solving concerned here is limited to the application of principles discovered, explained, and laid down as a codex, which is pertinent because there are, in fact, correct replies that cannot be doubted. The same would apply to some forms of mathematics.

Although in pure rote learning (with which we need not concern ourselves here), it may not matter at all in what order the various items are introduced, i.e. the learning can be done in an unstructured form, much productive learning is of hierarchical nature. Thus, for example, it would make little sense to introduce the object forms of pronouns (the accusative and dative) as above before the subject forms have been learned.

Psychological sequencing

It is the logical structure of the learning content that is decisive for these considerations. Apart from this logical structure, didactic and psychological considerations must be taken into account. A perfect logical presentation is of no avail in a course of study if it is not comprehensible to the students who constitute the target group. A teacher in class does not try to cover all aspects of a subject but limits himself to what the students concerned can benefit from; nor does he try to teach at one time more of a given section of the subject than he expects the students to grasp and remember. Those who develop courses for distance study must observe the same principle to make it possible for the students to digest and benefit from the course. This seems self-evident but is not always observed. When writing or recording, many scholars more or less consciously have their colleagues (and critics) in mind, as a kind of secondary target group, and are thus tempted to prove their scholarly standard by means to which the students are, at best, indifferent and which may even be harmful by creating confusion and uncertainty.

In some subjects, particularly those where the teaching aims at providing the students with certain attainments that need repetitive practice, the requirement that the teaching should be student-centred leads course developers to adopt a kind of concentric method. They give their students a small part of the difficult matter at a time, make them consolidate their newly acquired knowledge in various ways, support it by bringing in secondary material of both motivating and elucidating types, and also help them to check their knowledge and proficiency prior to bringing in new learning matter in the same subject area. Before this process is completed, another part of the subject is also brought in and treated in a similar way. Then attention is again given to the first topic, with a view to consolidating and widening the students' knowledge, understanding and skill in this particular field. Thus, one body of problems may be dealt with in several study units, along with various other parts of the subject. This means that the authors and other members of course teams identify with teachers and tutors who have to consider the receptivity of their students.

The method described is applied above all in the planning of language courses, in which problems of text analysis, phraseology, idiomatic expressions, grammar, style, phonetics, etc. are often dealt with concentrically. However, fundamentally the same method is found in courses of mathematics (where, for example, algebra and geometry may be taught side by side) and physics and chemistry (where theory, discussion of experiments, and the solution of problems may be brought together). In some cases, the various aspects of a subject are considered in different courses, the units of which alternate in the students' programme of study. From the point of view of teaching method, this application of concentric instruction is only superficially different from the one described earlier.

However, a presentation is seldom really concentric, which would imply nothing but continuous review, discussion, and training in the same parts of a subject, but rather spiral. Ausubel uses the expression 'the spiral curriculum' (Ausubel 1968: 209).

The so-called elaboration theory developed by Charles Reigeluth and his co-workers is a contribution in the spirit of Ausubel. Reigeluth compares his approach with the use of a zoom lens, offering first a wide-angle view and then zooming in on a part of the picture at a time, i.e. operating 'in steps or discrete levels'.

In a similar way the elaboration model of instruction starts the student with an overview of the major parts of the subject matter, it elaborates on one of those parts to a certain level of detail (called the first level of elaboration), it reviews the overview and shows the context of that part within the overview (an expanded overview), it continues this pattern of elaboration/expanded overview for each part of the overview until all parts have been elaborated one level, and it follows the same pattern for further levels of elaboration.... To summarize, the elaboration model of instruction starts by presenting knowledge at a very general or simplified level... Then it proceeds to add details or complexity in 'layers' across the entire breadth of the content of the course (or curriculum), one layer at a time, until the desired level of detail or complexity is reached.

(Reigeluth 1979: 9)

While Reigeluth agrees with Ausubel in starting by presenting knowledge at a general level, the overview referred to is not identical with Ausubel's advance organizer, but is described as an epitome, apparently implying a small-scale presentation with a single orientation, 'which means that it emphasizes a single type of content' (ibid., p. 10). It should contain a 'generality', some instances of the generality and an exercise giving students an opportunity to apply 'the generality to new instances' (ibid., p. 11).

Reigeluth's approach (along with Merrill's component display theory linking in with it, on which see Merrill, Reigeluth and Faust (1979)) has been applied by Koeymen as a guideline for a Turkish distance-teaching university (Koeymen 1983).

In the cases where problem-solving is the core of the learning matter, the order of presentation will evidently not be hierarchical, as no ready-made edifice of knowledge is to be presented. Here, the beginning is made by the problem and the search will be made along the lines of scholars who have looked for and finally found solutions. Their search can then also be followed when they make errors and correct them, which implies learning by Popperian 'conjectures and refutations' in the spirit of Lehner and Weingartz, as discussed on p. 35.

Further approaches

Attempts have been made to analyse the consequences of organizing a text strictly from the points of view of general subject content, and from special aspects applying to individual content items. Empirical research causes Schnotz to state:

With a text organized by aspect essentially all learners do integrative as well as comparative processing. With a text organized by object only the integrative processing is done by all learners. In the latter case, comparative processing is optional. Therefore, only some of the learners will engage in it, needing relatively much time. Rate of processing depends on prior knowledge more strongly in the case of organization by aspect than in the case of organization by object, presumably because of the frequent mental switches. Learners with higher prior knowledge seem to have less difficulty with these switches, whereas with low prior knowledge this type of processing tends to be a handicap. Hence, with organization by aspect learning results are affected more strongly by differences in prior knowledge, whereas organization by object seems to be less sensitive in this respect.

(Schnotz 1982: 95)

Schnotz's studies of 'object-oriented' and 'aspect-oriented' texts have been summarized by Picard (1992), who recommends initial object-oriented sequencing followed by aspect orientation since object orientation seems to suit learners with lower prior knowledge while aspect orientation appears to be useful for learners with good prior knowledge.

The use of questions in the text is another procedure applied to structure the learning. Rothkopf initiated a series of studies on the effectiveness of questions placed before the text passages concerned, inserted into them, or placed after them. Not unexpectedly it was found that, whereas introductory questions tend to lead the student towards what would answer them specifically, to the detriment of the study of other parts of the text, questions placed after the text passage have a more general effect, stimulate more careful learning, and lead to slower learning of later passages. The delaying effect seems to disappear gradually, maybe because better study skills have been acquired with the help of the questions.

Research at the Open University

supports, but so far does not add to, the practice of inserting into texts higher-level (not rote recall) questions after the relevant teaching material. This practice was adopted at the Open University in 1969 on grounds of common sense, teaching experience and the distilled experience of practical work on programmed instruction.

(Macdonald-Ross 1979: 24)

Reservations have been made by students about the use of inserted questions. See p. 77 below. To the extent that they make students aware of how they learn and direct their attention to reflection, inserted questions are likely to support learning.

While these various approaches are interesting and contribute to our understanding of the learning process, they exert only limited influence on practical educational activities. Whether they apply or not, course developers have to consider didactic as well as logical aspects when structuring a course. A mixture of information presentation, examples, quotations, discussions, suggestions for student activity, and exercises is usually found valuable in the interests of motivation, of variation to counteract tiredness and lagging attention, and of securing the acquisition of knowledge. Inspired by Gagné (1970: 304), distance educators tend to point to the following functions of course materials as being essential:

1 To arouse attention and motivate; the presentation of objectives that are within close reach appears to be of particularly great importance in this respect.
2 To make students aware of the expected outcomes of the study.
3 To link up with previous knowledge and interest.
4 To present the material to be learned.
5 To guide and structure, offering guidance for learning.
6 To activate.
7 To provide feedback.
8 To promote transfer.
9 To facilitate retention.

My list almost entirely follows Bååth's adaptation of Gagné's model (Bååth 1982: 68); see also Lampikoski and Mantere (1976: 13–14), and Ahlm (1972) (the first distance educator to use Gagné's model).

A useful general survey of implications of text structure on text design is provided in Jonassen (1984), in which various theories and approaches to structuring and sequencing are commented on, among them schema theory and elaboration theory (on which see pp. 63–4) While these attempts have not succeeded in producing generally applicable guidelines (see Shavelson and Stasz 1980), they contribute to the understanding of the problems of structuring learning matter and make rewarding reading.

The resignation expressed as to the possibility of identifying generalizable and always practicable principles for the structuring of course materials should not be interpreted as a rejection of the findings made. Any application of principles must be guided by common sense and intuition, however. In spite of all reservations it must finally be stressed that learning takes place more easily if it is connected with concepts already known and if the knowledge that is being acquired is applied to problems that the student is interested in or becomes aware of. To arrange this, by guiding students through the problem areas, and to help them to find themselves in the situation where they can successfully solve problems of increasing difficulty is an extremely important obligation for course developers. It actually means helping students to attain success step-by-step, thus developing a strong continuous motivating force. The conversational approaches discussed above as over-arching principles are highly relevant also in this context.

5

STRUCTURES AND MEDIA OF DISTANCE-EDUCATION COURSES

While the principles so far discussed may serve distance educators as guides to course structure, there are a number of further considerations of how to organize the presentation of course content that deserve our attention.

In most cases, distance teaching and learning are based on courses pre-produced for the purpose. As print is the dominating medium for the presentation of learning matter in distance education, the relation between distance-study courses and other presentations in print is of prime interest.

A printed study course is basically different from a textbook with questions. A textbook gives all relevant facts and, if it is a good textbook, does so in a clear and logical way, but it does not guide or teach. That is to say, it does not induce the student to learn, as we must expect a distance-study course to do. The presentation of facts in a textbook has normally to be supplemented by the exposition of a teacher, who kindles the interest of the students, tells them what to pay most attention to, what comparisons to make, directs their inquisitiveness towards profitable framings of questions, etc. A distance-study course guides and teaches by causing discovery learning and/or giving complete explanations with elucidating examples, by providing exercises of various kinds, by constantly referring to what the student has already learned to master, and by paving the way for successful problem solutions. This can be done by means of mediated guided conversations (see section *Overarching principles* in Chapter 4 above). The course is thus a substitute for both a conventional textbook and the exposition of a teacher (unless the course is attached to one or more books or other sources, in which case it replaces a teacher's comments and the discussion of the exposition inspired by a teacher only). Naturally, this does not mean that a pre-produced course can be a complete substitute for the teacher in class (who not only lectures but also listens, argues, illustrates by means of experiments, etc., and generally interacts with the students). It must be borne in mind that the communication between the student and the distance tutor has essential tasks, however 'conversational' the pre-produced course is and however successful it is in meeting the requirements made clear by the Gagnerian functions listed on p. 66.

The subject matter to be taught is divided into parts, suitable as course units, which are usually sent to students as their work progresses. After students have completed their study of one unit, they answer certain questions, solve set problems, report on experiments made according to instructions, do some other written (or, in some cases, orally recorded) work which is to be submitted for corrections, comments and suggestions. They also ask questions, request advice, and may initiate communication in other ways.

The idea behind the division of the material into course units is that students should be offered a suitable quantity of learning matter at a time so that they can regard the study of each unit as a separate task and can always survey the material to be learned. The theory is that in this way it is possible to prevent the bulk of possibly difficult study material from being intimidating. With each finished unit and with the tasks in it completed, the students see the result of their work.

The size, i.e. length, of course units varies considerably with the schools and universities that develop them. (In German and in the Scandinavian languages, course units are often referred to as 'letters' to emphasize the correspondence character of the communication they initiate.) Units from eight small pages to more than 100 large-size pages exist. Some attempts have been made to define criteria for what should be regarded as a suitable size (and the frequency of communication desirable), but so far nothing conclusive can be said. This is discussed on pp. 123–5.

The length of time that students spend at any one study session can be – and has in some cases been – a criterion for the size of course units. David Roberts concludes from an Australian study of his:

Students like to feel they have achieved something each

time they have a study session. It makes good educational sense, therefore, to divide learning materials into consumable morsels that can be intellectually devoured by the average student in a two-hour study session. Producing learning packages in two hour work-load modules may be to the benefit of students if only because the production team is forced to think very carefully about the integration of notes, readings, self-assessment questions and other activities that will comprise each session.

(Roberts 1986: 37)

There can be little doubt that effective structuring of contents determined by the supporting organization to some extent becomes autocratic. Distance teaching may then mean 'teacher centred education, where the media are used as substitutes for the teacher, "telling" students what they ought to know' (Ljoså 1977: 79).

Most distance-education courses with their various components aim at leading their students straight to specific goals and do so on condition that the students are capable of following the exposition, doing the exercises, and solving the problems set. The course developers then tend to regard each study unit as an integral part and thus as a compulsory course component which is only rarely regarded as replaceable. The most common exception to this principle is no doubt an adaptation of the starting point to suit the prior knowledge of individual students.

This all-embracing course structure is often considered too rigid. It is felt only proper that the students should be offered a choice of which units of a course are to be regarded as relevant in each case. Such an approach leads to each unit or each small set of units being separate and providing sufficient treatment of a limited, and strictly defined, part of the subject. When that is the case, students can build their own curricula from units or sets of units belonging to different courses. This is what in German is called the 'Baukasten-prinzip', the principle of the box of bricks.

The advantage of this principle, which is usually stressed, is that each study unit or set of units can be used in different contexts. This is economical and can contribute to widening the offer of educational opportunities. Further, it makes a provision for requirements to study only one little part of a subject (and possibly acquiring a certificate; through a credit-point system, this can be tantamount to securing what may be regarded as a mortgage on a degree or other formal competence) (Ljoså and Sandvold 1983).

The modular principle would seem to have another consequence of considerable importance in that it lends itself to supporting the general autonomy of the students. If each unit or set of units is provided with a kind of product declaration including statements of the objectives, the availability of sufficient numbers of units on related topics will allow individual students to select their own study objectives.

SELF-CONTAINED AND STUDY-GUIDE COURSES

A self-contained course in principle provides all the learning matter that is necessary. It has proved particularly valuable when the course content is fairly elementary and does not call for a study of different sources. Elementary courses in foreign languages can serve as typical examples. Such courses are complete in themselves and provide texts, grammar, vocabulary (with so-called synonyms), phraseology, phonetics, pronunciation exercises, exercises in composition, translation, etc. Other proficiency subjects, such as mathematics, are usually taught in the same way at a distance.

Sometimes, however, students must be made to see a complicated picture of a subject with conflicting theories and views, or they have to learn how to trace facts and arguments from different presentations and to study various sources critically. In such cases, self-contained courses may not offer the best solutions. Instead, a study guide steering or facilitating the study of set texts is usually more suitable in that it causes students to read and/or listen to presentations of various kinds, to compare and criticize them and to try to come to conclusions of their own. This study-guide approach is generally practical when the learning is to include part or the whole of the content of various books, papers, and other sources of knowledge. See also Holmberg (1977b, 1989c) Ljoså (1975); Weltner (1977).

Evidently study guides, like self-contained courses, can be and are used in different manners. Du Plessis underlines that

study guide design should afford individual students the opportunity of developing their own learning styles. Once they have identified the teaching objectives, they should find, and be able to use, multiple access points to the subject matter. The study guide should enable students to keep to the order of presentation if they wish, or to select areas they consider relevant, skip material they have already encountered and do not wish to repeat, or evaluate themselves on any section where they wish to ascertain their standing, even if they do this before studying the relevant part in any great detail. It follows that study guides can hardly be 'too easy' in this regard. They should, however, provide a measure of 'difficult' work as well by, for example, inserting appropriate self-evaluation questions that challenge even the best of students.

(du Plessis 1987: 13)

Study guides should, preferably, in the interest of plurality, encourage students to use a number of different sources. This usually necessitates the availability of library services. A second best is the use of specially prepared readers which contain contributions representing different approaches. This practice evidently tends not to diminish interest in library facilities. On the basis of research by Winter and Cameron, Jevons states:

Where books of readings are supplied as well as study guides, students make more use of almost every other source of library material or information than do students who do not get readers. Their appetite is whetted rather than satiated.

(Jevons 1984: 32)

Making regular use of scholarly papers in periodicals is one way both of making students aware of different approaches with possibly conflicting views and of keeping courses up to date. Reprinting, with due permission, suitable articles for distribution among students is a procedure apparently widely adopted, for example in Australia where copyright legislation seems less restrictive to distance education in this respect than in most other parts of the Western world (L. Moore 1987: 26).

CONTRACT AND PROJECT LEARNING

The learning can also be organized on the basis of individual students' and tutors' predilections, needs and interests. This means removing the choice of subject-matter from the preparation (in the terminology of Michael Moore 1975: 5, the preactive element) to the very teaching–learning process: tutor and student agree on which course literature is to be selected, what tutor support is required, etc. This is what happens in contract learning, which inevitably stresses tutor–student interaction more than many other applications of distance education.

Since 1836, London University has acted as a pioneer in this field by conferring degrees on students who have not attended any of its classes but have prepared themselves for examinations in other ways (Tight 1987: 51). Individual tutoring is based on the study of literature prescribed or agreed between the professor and the individual students. Recent developments along this line have occurred in the contract learning initiated in the USA by Empire State College, NY (Coughlan 1980; Worth 1982), in a diploma curriculum at the University of East London, formerly North East London Polytechnic (Bradbury *et al.* 1982; Hinds 1987), and at Murdoch University in Western Australia (Marshall 1984). The individual student exerts strong influence on the objectives of his/her study. In these cases, distance education is characterized by adaptability to students' needs and wishes, as far as content, time and methods are concerned. These are applications of far-reaching student independence at all levels. Contract learning unrelated to traditional distance education has proved very successful. See Lehmann on an early Empire State evaluation:

'Relatively few students stated they were frequently worried (10%), bored (4%), confused (7) or concerned about mentor evaluation of their work (13%). On the other hand, most students said they were frequently interested (87%), challenged to do their best thinking (79%), and found the connections of life and learning exciting (81%).

(Lehmann 1975: 7)

An analysis of the potential and applications of contract learning in distance education is presented by Weingartz (1991).

Similar activities occur as parts of otherwise more pre-structured courses of study. They are then usually referred to as projects. The higher the level of study, the more important is the project work. The requirements for advanced project work have been worded as follows by Bynner and Henry:

- The project should represent continued work over an extended period of time.
- The project should provide opportunities for the student to undertake original work based on the student's use of local resources.
- There should be an opportunity to display higher cognitive skills (analysis, synthesis, evaluation), organizational and problem-solving skills in the conduct of the project and writing up of the report.
- Supervision and guidance must be available at appropriate times to ensure the work is both feasible and that it stays on course.

(Bynner 1986: 28)

While this type of work demands excellent library services and availability of highly competent supervisors, there is much evidence to show its effectiveness in distance study at the university level (see Bynner 1986 and his sources on post-graduate distance study).

Study starting out from individual problems rather than from the systems of knowledge known (see Lehner and Weingartz, whose research is mentioned on pp. 35 and 64) would seem to go well with contract learning and project work at various levels.

INDIVIDUALIZED COURSES AND COMMON-SENSE APPROACHES

The possibility of individualizing more traditional distance education should also be looked into. To base the presentation of distance education courses of a mass-communication character on the individual student's cognitive structure is naturally an unattainable goal. Nevertheless, there are practicable (and practised) procedures for individualization. Referring to 'increasingly sophisticated technology' Kathryn Atman claims that it is 'possible to develop interactive, individualized orientation pro-

individualized study

grams, based on psychological type differences that focus on personal skills' (Atman 1990: 149).

No sophisticated technology is required to allow students in the interest of individualization to start their distance study at different levels, i.e. to take additional introductory course units or skip some of the regular units. Students may also be offered supplementary study material related to the weaknesses which they find that they have as they work through their course. Such adaptations may be based on special diagnostic tests, on students' and tutors' conclusions from work done. They may also be left to the students' own initiative. It is helpful to arrange the presentation in such a way that the students' selection of what is relevant to them is facilitated. On this, see what Waller calls access structure (see p. 98).

Within the framework of the aptitude–treatment–interaction research, Salomon has developed a remedial model, a compensatory model, and a preferential model. The first two correspond to the provision of additional study material, mentioned above, for the purpose of either correcting misunderstandings and generally putting things right or filling in gaps, thus compensating for prevailing deficiencies. The third tries 'to capitalize on what the student is already capable of doing' (Crombag 1979: 178; Salomon 1972). This implies a choice related to students' needs and predilections. It would seem to be implemented in distance education primarily through the choice of courses, although other applications are also possible and indeed practised (Moore 1983).

This is, of course, a reminder of Ausubel's basic principle, namely, 'If I had to reduce all of educational psychology to just one principle, I would say this: The most important single factor influencing learning is what the learner already knows. Ascertain this and teach him accordingly' (Ausubel 1968: motto before preface).

This declaration of Ausubel's reflects not only his research orientation but above all common sense, a commodity that is a sine qua non as much in education as in other human endeavours. The studies and principles referred to above are all undoubtedly of value to distance educators, but in practical work they must be coupled with both common sense and elements of educational feeling. In fact, original thinking and intuition are required for us to make good use of any scholarly finding. The point was recognized by William James as early as 1899 and has been further developed by Gage (1978), who points out that neither doctors nor engineers can limit themselves to relying on scientific information. Educators are no less dependent on their own thinking and intuition. See also Huber, Krapp and Mandl, who stress that the search for applicable scholarly results 'remains a creative act on the part of the practitioner' (1984: 33). This very much applies to the structuring of distance-education courses. It may be based on psychological rather than logical sequencing as suggested by John Bååth. The presentation may begin

> with a topic calculated to catch the students' interest and motivate them to read and to learn the other parts of the subject. You may compare this with the ways in which good fiction writers often begin a novel or a short story. They do not normally describe the whole background of the principal characters, their environment, their birth, childhood, adolescence, etc., before they proceed to the real story. Instead, they often throw the reader directly into the action, and introduce environment, background etc. afterwards. Something of this technique could very well be used in a correspondence course!
>
> (Bååth 1986: 14)

SELF-CHECKING EXERCISES

The simulated conversation which is seen as an important characteristic of the style of course presentations can be, and is, also brought about by exercises which students do not submit but check themselves.

Self-checking exercises can be of different kinds. Some are introduced to help students solely to learn facts and to memorize, whereas others aim at providing opportunities for practical applications, normally based on the understanding and solution of problems.

To help students to learn facts, it has been found useful to provide them with a series of detailed questions intended to make it possible for them to check that they retain all important items. In most cases no answers to these questions are given, the idea being that the student, when in doubt about a question, should carefully re-read the relevant section of the course unit or other work concerned and then tackle the question again. Some correspondence schools have a system of numbering small sections of their units and then referring to the numbers in the questions. Others reject this system, as they fear that it does not require sufficiently solid knowledge for the student to be able to answer the questions and that it may encourage him/her not to make an endeavour but merely to look up the answers while reading the questions. On the other hand, questions with full answers given on a following page occur in some courses. Sometimes answers to questions of this type on a topic already studied are included in a later course unit.

It is important not only to check knowledge but also to provide actual teaching by means of suitable questions and exercises, i.e. to make students think and thereby learn. Of course, this is nothing new but simply an attempt to apply an old method known as Socrates' 'maieutics', i.e. midwifery. Socrates put his questions in such a way that he made his listeners bring out into clear consciousness conceptions that were previously latent in their minds and made them draw the correct conclusions. He made his listeners see the solutions on their own. Something of the same kind can be brought about by suitable questions and exercises in a distance-study course. However, according to Thorpe, some Open University students tend to cut such inserted questions and exercises as expendable and one student comment runs like this: 'I don't know if they're helpful or not. Sometimes I feel they get in the way. They make me think. I don't want to think, I just want to get on' (Thorpe 1986: 39).

Lockwood, as quoted by Thorpe, adds: 'When students were asked what their reaction would be if activities were omitted from future teaching material, many said they would feel relieved. It would remove the feeling of guilt they experienced when skimming over or ignoring them' (ibid.). See also Clyde *et al.* (1983).

These findings would seem to indicate a need for course developers to consider carefully the level of difficulty of the tasks which they set, the lucidity and completeness of the subject-matter presentation that is offered and, above all, what kinds of questions can be helpful. They should help the students consciously to control their own learning.

Skill at solving problems and applying knowledge acquired is essential, even at an elementary stage, in mathematics, physics, chemistry, technical subjects, languages, accountancy, etc. and so it is of great value to the student to get an appropriate amount of practice. It is not enough for the student to follow a theoretical discussion leading to the correct conclusions; he/she must be able independently to produce solutions to problems similar to those discussed in the course. Much practice is needed in some subjects, such as foreign languages. To cater for this, it has proved practical to include in the various course units a series of problems for self-checking. Thus, a considerable amount of active work on the part of students can be brought about to stabilize their knowledge and practical skills. In some cases, printed or duplicated forms, where the students fill in gaps, solve problems, answer self-checking questions, etc., can contain the exercises, and specially prepared exercise books of this type are in use.

As already indicated, model answers and complete solutions to problems given in this way are often provided in the course, either in the unit containing the exercises or in the following unit. Marland and Store, who find that 'the practice of providing model answers makes good pedagogical sense', also point out that their 'usefulness to students will increase if the purposes of the model answers are explained to them and if they are told how to use them' (Marland and Store 1982: 95).

It has proved useful and even necessary to supplement some of these model answers or solutions with comments explaining, with reference to the course, why the solution given is the correct one, how it has been reached, and what possible alternatives there are. All educators should remind themselves from time to time that the average student cannot be expected to see, without assistance, all of the logical contexts that a tutor may wish or, judging from what has been taught, expect him or her to see; course developers must be on their guard against regarding as self-evident the reasoning behind correct answers or proper solutions once a correct reply has been provided.

Comments of the type mentioned in connection with exercises are more often required than they actually occur. A discussion based on the solution of even simple problems is very often valuable in considerably improving the students' capacity to benefit from the course. Discussions in writing or on audio-tape are naturally necessary in all cases when there is no self-evident correction solution.

Bååth (1980) reports on an empirical research project that in courses examined it seemed possible, 'without any noticeable effects – neither negative nor positive – to replace substantial numbers of assignment questions by self-checking exercises with model answers and pre-produced comments within the teaching material' (p. 152).

The computer is a valuable instrument for self-checking exercises bringing about simulated communication. See the following section on media.

MEDIA FOR SUBJECT-MATTER PRESENTATION

There can be no doubt whatsoever that print, in the form of printed texts, is the most important medium for subject-matter presentation in distance education. It is more or less regularly supplemented by illustrations, diagrams, blueprints and sketches, occasionally for three-dimensional viewing, and in some cases by elements programmed in short-step frames, linear or branched. Print allows individualization of information, functions in a wide range of study environments, and is easily accessible for revision. The potential and functions of printed course materials have been analysed by Peters (1973, 1979); Bååth (1986); and others. The use of the printed word in distance-education courses is an important theme in this work.

Recordings, mostly on cassettes, have become a second very common medium, functioning in most study environments (cassette players, earphones). Students often seem to feel that audio and video recordings provide a certain closeness to reality and have something of an enactive character. In some subjects, such as science and technology, concrete materials like models and kits with oral work instructions on tape occur as supplementary media for the enactive mode of presentation (Holmberg and Bakshi 1982; Kember 1982).

Radio and television belong to some systems of distance education, and recorded television programmes for use in video-recorders have gradually become important elements in several distance-education programmes. Ether media have long attracted distance educators as being likely to be both motivating and effective. Distance educators have amassed a considerable amount of experience of the use of radio and television programmes, mainly as supplements but also to some extent as the main teaching media, thus, for instance in the Chinese distance-education system (Peters 1990; Zhao 1988). A further example is the *Envision* programme of Laurentian University in Ontario (Gervais 1987). In some cases, use is made of satellite communication, a characteristic feature of the teaching of the University of the South Pacific, for instance, and of increasing interest to work elsewhere (Forsythe 1984).

Systematic use of radio and television as supplementary media occurs in the British Open University where the main medium of instruction is the written word, i.e. correspondence study. Most European countries, the USA, Canada, Australia, New Zealand, and several African, Asian and Latin American nations have experiences of using ether media for general educational purposes or as a back-up to organized distance study.

In spite of this, it is difficult to find a consensus of opinion about methodology. Probably, a majority of distance educators have come to the conclusion that television, apart from its potential for demonstrations, can have a strong motivating influence and that this to some extent also applies to radio. Television has also proved to be a powerful means for bringing about attitude change (see pp. 15–16). These characteristics are important not only in connection with the choice of media but also for the methods used when these media are applied.

The University of Mid-America tested television as a means to attract people who are assumed to find it difficult to learn from print. It was found that 'television was liked when its content was closely related to the course, and disliked when it tried to amuse and entertain'. Further, there were signs both that students considered television less important than the printed course material provided and, on the other hand, that 'where and when television is not available, course numbers are smaller and attrition rates higher' (Hawkridge 1978: 40–1). The pacing influence of the television programmes was evidently felt to support completion of the courses.

A case study of some relevance is the Swedish Delta project, an updating course on mathematics for teachers of that subject. It was offered as an integrated television–radio-correspondence course in 1969–71. A study of the attitudes of the students (i.e. the participating teachers) showed that, whereas more than 90 per cent of them found the correspondence and radio parts of the course satisfactory, more than 50 per cent of them reacted negatively to the television elements, which were found to be neither motivating nor providing good surveys (Holmberg 1973b: 47–52).

There have been similar experiences elsewhere. This probably reflects exaggerated expectations as far as the television element is concerned rather than a rejection of television as a medium of instruction. Critical students evidently do not want course items presented on television which can equally well be presented in print, nor do they normally want to hear formal lectures which, if provided in print, they can read in much less time than is required for listening and can then consult again and again. However, audio cassettes with recorded lectures are occasionally used in distance education (Leslie 1979, 1986).

It must be borne in mind that what suits one target group may not suit another. At an advanced level, television and radio should probably be reserved for such items as cannot be dealt with entirely in writing. Demonstrations in medicine, surgery and science, and study of such objects, circumstances, and processes as should be seen but cannot be made available to students individually would thus be suitable for television, whereas dramatic presentations, discussions, and talks on items of day-to-day current interest would be suitable for radio and/or television.

This, however, is more a general declaration of intent than a methodological guideline for the use of ether media in distance education. But see Laaser (1984) and (1986); Bates (1984: 29–41); Brown and Fortosky (1986).

It is tempting to regard broadcast radio and television programmes as educationally more or less identical with audio and video recordings respectively. This would be highly inaccurate, however, as succinctly explained by Bates:

> Broadcasts are ephemeral, cannot be reviewed, are uninterruptable, and are presented at the same pace for all students. A student cannot reflect upon an idea or pursue a line of thought during a programme, without losing the thread of the programme itself. A student cannot go over the same material several times until it is understood.
>
> (Bates 1984: 31)

Recordings can be used in a different and usually more profitable way. See Nicola Durbridge (on audio cassettes):

> For students, study material presented on cassettes offers

81

considerable freedom. Students can choose to listen at a time and place convenient to themselves and thus use the material as and when it appears most relevant to their individual needs. They can moreover exploit the hardware of cassette-players – the stop, pause and replay devices – to organise their study approach according to personal style and preference. Thus, it can be argued that cassettes provide students with a learning medium which shares many of the advantages inherent in a written text; it is adaptable to such study techniques as skimming and reviewing and listeners can, to a large extent, control the pace and methods with which they engage with particular content. This point alone goes some way towards compensating for the ephemeracy of a sound medium.

(Durbridge 1984: 101)

Technology contributes further possibilities, for instance in connection with television. This would seem to apply to video discs with their large storage capacity coupled with freeze-frame and fast-search equipment (interactive video). Graphics whose construction is shown by animation techniques belong here.

Presentation of text and graphics on a screen instead of on paper is becoming more and more common (viewdata/videotext, teletext), but may not be a wholly desirable development. It undoubtedly is useful when ephemeral, urgent, really new information is provided, i.e. information not available in books or articles (the parallel with information about rates of exchange, aeroplane bookings, etc. is illuminating). For teaching purposes, the presentation of verbal subject matter in print is decidedly superior to screen presentation: it is easier to read, it facilitates leafing and browsing and it is open to all printed sources. There can be little doubt that, for serious study, the reading of printed material will remain a prime medium. Using computer-stored information available for screen reading (or on printouts) is a fashion that makes sense only if it means making data accessible which would otherwise be hard to come by. This is a far from unusual situation, however. Search for relevant information in computerized data bases and problem-solving by computer processing are valuable methods and can be useful academic exercises. It is nevertheless harmful to wean students from using printed sources when they look for occasional data. To use handbooks, encyclopaedias, dictionaries, reports of various kinds and other reference books, and do so with ease, remains a necessity.

Reservations of this kind do not detract from the potentials of modern information technology. These are considerable, particularly for student-tutor and student-student interaction, on which see Chapter 6, but also in our present context, the one-way traffic by means of which subject matter is presented. Apart from relevant motion pictures, for instance such as illustrated processes and the development of graphics, the opportunities to make unprinted data available should be mentioned. Artificial intelligence, including so-called expert systems and knowledge representation, may lead to further developments of interest (Naughton 1986). 'Hypertext' systems are being looked into. They imply non-sequential presentation of learning matter, in which the student can browse and find his/her own way through the material available. Mandl *et al.* (1991) have studied hypertext empirically. Their conclusions are cautious; they recommend further studies before its value is judged. Schnotz warns that 'free navigation' may hinder rather than help learners with poor prior knowledge (Schnotz 1990: 15; cf. above Chapter 4, *Further approaches*). On hypertext see further Hall *et al.* (1989) and Schulz (1989).

As mentioned under the section *Self-checking exercises* computer media can – and to an increasing extent do – bring about programmed, i.e. simulated, interactivity as part of distance-education courses. Drill exercises, for example when learning language patterns, and problem-solving tasks when indisputably correct solutions exist, are examples of interactive computer use.

On-line communication also occurs in simulation exercises and in the study of branched programmes. Early experiments of interest were made at the Open University, e.g. in the CICERO project (Lockwood and Cooper 1980) and viewdata/teletext, 'in which a television screen is linked to a telephone, and hence to pages of data stored in a computer' (King, Sewart and Gough 1980: 14), as well as elsewhere (Kaufman 1986). Various kinds of progress have been made with the use of on-line systems (Bates 1984 and 1990a; Kaye 1985; Mason and Kaye 1989).

Programmed interaction of the kind that makes students interact not with a human being but with a computer program can in a truly educational situation supplement but hardly replace real interaction between students and tutors. On media for student–tutor and student–student interaction see Chapter 6.

Up-to-date presentations of media for distance education are given in Bates (1990a). Modern practice is illuminated in an international study by Doerfert and See-Bögehold (1991). The latter report that 114 distance-education organizations have set up separate media departments, 60 of which have provided detailed information about their work and problems.

THE CHOICE OF MEDIUM/MEDIA

In distance education the selection possibilities are often extremely limited for financial and other reasons. The printed and written word on the one hand and audio-recordings on the other sometimes exhaust the selection opportunities. Suitable combinations of these offer additional choices. For instance, it may be useful to provide recorded instructions on how to study charts and pictures that are presented in printed form, a procedure which has proved profitable for target groups with little reading skill. In other cases, however, the choice can be made among several of the media referred to above.

If, in the spirit of educational technology, course development is based on target-group analyses, specification of lucidly communicable objectives, and logical–psychological sequencing as elements of a system, it seems natural to include media selection for subject-matter presentation in this rational procedure. Several attempts have been made to create a standard taxonomy, ascribing specific functions and applications to each of the media available, so that a natural, logical choice could be made for each part of a course of study. See Reiser and Gagné (1983) on a media selection model of an algorithmic type. No such taxonomy has been shown to be generally useful or applicable, however. Ever since Wilbur Schramm published his now classical study *Big media, little media* in 1977, it has been generally admitted that any claim about the superiority of one medium over another has limited relevance. 'There is no cookbook of recipes for media selection that can be applied automatically in every educational system' (Schramm 1977: 263).

This admission does not mean that it does not make sense to consider the value of individual media in relation to functions desired. The availability must needs be the starting point for such considerations. Here the circumstances of social infrastructure, technical development, and cost may be decisive.

Of course, it is what a medium can do and not what it is like technically that is important in selection situations. This means that we must first pay attention to the relevant attributes of media rather than media themselves:

> The attributes of a medium ... are the capabilities of that medium to show objects in motion, objects in colour, objects in three dimensions; to provide printed words, spoken words, simultaneous visual and auditory stimuli.... Some attributes, such as the capacity to provide pictorial stimuli, are shared by many media. Other attributes, such as the capacity to show objects in three dimensions, are properties of relatively few media.
>
> (Levie and Dickie, as quoted by Clark 1975: 199)

Kathleen Forsythe, in developing her theory of conversation (pp. 54–5), directs her readers' attention to the 'generative' and 'degenerative' effects that a medium may have. 'A degenerative effect would be one that inhibited conversation. This could be effected by stifling the imagination or isolating the participant from conversation' (Forsythe 1986: 23). She refers to criticism of television in this context and underlines the necessity to choose and use media in a way that encourages creativity and to avoid 'feedback information in closed loops' (ibid., p. 24). This is particularly relevant to the use of computer technology, which often causes programming in advance. Forsythe rejects this as negative to 'the variety so necessary for learning' (ibid.).

Sparkes starts out from 'the assumption that the natural learning process is analogous to a conversational process' and 'emphasizes the teaching process of "educational conversation"' (Neil 1981: 112). See pp. 46–55. Sparkes

> draws particular attention to three communicational pathways, according to purpose. These are the primary forward path (teacher to student) and two feedback paths – problem identification and remedial tuition. He then goes on to relate each of fourteen media to the three pathways, indicating his opinion on how well each pathway is likely to be served by each medium, from a communicational technology point of view.... The fourteen media are related,

according to their degree of usefulness on a three-point scale, to the affective domain, to two levels in the cognitive domain, and to the domain of skills (following Bloom's Taxonomy). For example, Sparkes states: 'In general, teaching in the affective domain requires a form of communication with a strong appeal to the emotions. TV, radio, novels, drama, are particularly successful here. On the other hand, abstract concepts usually require verbal expressions rather than visual (abstract ideas cannot be photographed) although visual analogies and animation can be used to illuminate them. Tapes have the advantage over broadcasts for teaching the deeper concepts in the cognitive domain, since they can be replayed repeatedly, but texts seem the natural channel for teaching complex ideas.'

(Neil 1981: 113)

A theoretical approach, bearing on media selection, which has wide implications for distance education, has been presented by Chang et al. (1983), on the basis of Olson and Bruner's learning model. In a kind of taxonomy of educational objectives, they first make a general distinction between knowledge and skills. Skills to be learned through distance study are divided into operations on knowledge and operations with knowledge. The latter imply application of knowledge acquired and are concerned with 'results in the exterior world, reality' (Chang et al. 1983: 15). 'Operations on knowledge (critique may be a good example) apply to coded knowledge and result in new or new representations of knowledge, and in the skill of producing new forms of knowledge out of existing knowledge' (op. cit. p. 14). Distance educators following this approach must judge where these two types of operation are required and, as a guideline for selection, for each procedure and each medium must decide to what extent it helps students to acquire the operational capacities concerned.

Further suggestions helpful to distance educators were developed at an early stage by Gagné (1970 and 1977), in relation to the didactic functions he has described; by Handal (1973), who, apart from his own model, summarizes those of Bretz, Tosti and Ball, Briggs, Campeau, Gagné, and May; by Svensson (1973), who in his (Swedish) presentation with tables for the various media includes educational, technical and economic aspects; and by others.

A further approach that is undoubtedly interesting, although difficult to apply and exerting little influence on distance education, is the aptitude–treatment–interaction (ATI) research, which aims at relating the choice of media to students' personality characteristics. From these, and from the objectives of study, it should be possible to draw conclusions about the characteristics of the medium/media suitable in each case, which in their turn will decide the choice. Heidt (1976 and 1978) uses this and Salomon's 'supplantation' approach as bases for a careful study of media and learning processes. The ATI (or, as it is also called, TTI: trait–treatment–interaction) aims and procedures are well illuminated in Clark (1975) and Allen (1975). The latter makes specific suggestions for developers of learning materials and lists a number of tentative generalizations from research data available.

ATI (TTI) approaches to distance education, with their courses for large numbers of students, meet with great difficulties. They will require instruments developed for students, by means of which the students can diagnose their own structure of intellect, and facilities that will make it possible to offer a wide range of choices of both learning tasks (objectives) and course materials which are presented by means of different media related to specific learner characteristics.

Experiences from today's reality, with more or less mass-produced courses, indicate that varying media combinations can be equally successful as educational tools for the same learning matter. There are signs that it is the use made of the media rather than the media themselves that is decisive for learning outcomes.

In cases where there is a reasonably free choice of media, i.e. when cost considerations and other so-called frame factors do not limit the choice to a minimum, practitioners nevertheless had better adopt some systematic method to guide them in their choice of media. It has proved profitable to start the selection by listing first the media available for the course that is being planned and second, the criteria by means of which the selection among the available media can be made. Among the selection criteria belong such considerations as the time available, the attitudes of the students, the cost, the opportunity of profitable co-ordination with practical work, the degree of risk involved in experiments, etc. It is useful to judge the relative importance of the selection criteria. This can be done by awarding each of them a mark in the form of a number, e.g. from 1 to 3 in relation to their importance. With these two lists as instruments, an attempt can immediately be made to find out which medium/media meet the requirements of the most important criteria for each part and each group of objectives of the course. This approach, which I have developed elsewhere (Holmberg 1987: 19–21), is inspired by Lehmann, who himself stresses its evident weakness, namely that it hardly prevents bias from influencing the outcome (predetermined conclusions can be rationalized by idiosyncratic scoring systems). However, the approach offers a practicable guideline which, when used with judgement and discretion, seems to be of some use.

PRESENTING THE LEARNING MATTER

Sensible structuring of the learning matter, as well as the use of an appropriate medium or appropriate media, are prerequisites for the development of learner-friendly courses. The writing of texts will be our prime concern, not only because print is the basic medium of most distance teaching but also because presentations in other forms (broadcasting, films, audio and video recordings, etc.) are regularly based on scripts.

Style and language

As already indicated, any text to be used for teaching–learning purposes must be developed in a way to facilitate learning not only by providing information but also by helping the learner to relate newly acquired knowledge to what is already known, i.e. to anchor it in already existing knowledge structures (Ausubel, 1968: 107). This has been called coherence formation, which

> can be seen as an intentional strategical process where the reader constructs a mental representation of the topic matter by using not only text information but also his or her own prior knowledge. From a communicational perspective coherence formation results from a co-operation between the author and the reader.
>
> (Schnotz 1986: 2)

Distance-teaching courses thus can – and should – activate students so that, instead of being passive (and therefore possibly inattentive) receivers, students do real work in that they process information, compare new concepts with those already known, draw conclusions, apply and practise knowledge acquired, etc. It has proved useful to encourage them to make tables and summaries, to consider questions and solve suitable problems.

What this thinking further implies in practice is as matter for consideration and discussion. To the present author there can be no doubt that the conversational approaches discussed on pp. 46–55 effectively contribute to facilitating the acquisition and application of knowledge.

Texts used must organize and explain ideas and must be perfectly lucid (for a different opinion see Rowntree (1973) below). They should not only clarify concepts but, on the basis of the distance educator's experiences of teaching and learning, foresee probable errors, provide correction of these, confirm and reinforce fruitful thinking and correct solutions. Consolidation of essential contexts and items as well as necessary overlearning (see p. 36) must be catered for by revision exercises and references to relevant experiences.

The requirements concerning the lucidity of written presentations have been studied, in a way that is relevant to distance education, by scholars analysing the use of English and German printed texts. Langer *et al.* have shown, on the basis of German instructional prose, that the accessibility of texts – i.e. how intelligible ('verständlich') they are – mainly depends on four 'dimensions' of the text characteristics, as follows:

1 simplicity of sentence structure and vocabulary
2 structure and cohesion
3 succinctness and relevance
4 additional stimulation.

These dimensions are largely independent of one another. Nevertheless, the authors point out that 3 and 4 usually influence each other.

In the third dimension, a medium value (between extreme succinctness, making almost every word important, and long-windedness) seems preferable, whereas the other dimensions denote qualities of positive value for the readability of texts (Langer *et al.* 1974: 13–25). Another German study (Groeben 1972), which relies more on theoretical considerations than the one referred to and is concerned with learner–text interaction, largely supports these conclusions.

The importance of simple grammar for readability and understanding has been shown to be a decisive factor. The active form of verbs facilitates reading compared with the passive form. However, practice in the reading of passive sentences seems to eliminate this difficulty, which may be an important fact for presentations in German, for instance. Short clauses, many finite verbs, many pronouns, and short and well-known words are advantageous from the points of view of readability and understanding (Coleman 1965; Groeben 1972; 18–23). Readability problems are particularly great for courses written in German, as the German scholarly tradition favours rather a complicated style. A thorough study by Tergan (1983) of readibility, as related to success in distance education, confirms the importance of text accessibility in German. The problems are far from negligible in other languages. Research illustrating this, based on texts in English, has been succinctly summarized by Davies (1971: 140). Also compare the following extract from Taylor:

> Learners grasp affirmative more easily than negative statements. They understand the active voice more readily than the passive. Equally, a declarative sentence is more easily understood than an interrogative.
>
> Abstract nouns make continuous discourse harder to understand. They can, in most cases, be replaced by verbs. For example, 'Great emphasis must be placed on the importance of consultation of the attached plates in attempting the identification of a particular species', which can be rendered, 'We must emphasize how important it is to consult the attached plates when you are attempting to identify a particular species.' The use of personal pronouns facilitates the transformation from abstract nouns to verbs. Coleman (1971: 167), for example, feels that most of the abstractness in scientific writing can be attributed to the traditional avoidance of the words 'I' and 'we'. Verbs, on the other hand, increase the ease of presentation. A high proportion of verbs makes understanding easier. However, a difficult passage is not made easier by merely adding more verbs without taking into account the length of sentences or the frequency of occurrence of the verbs. A useful strat-

egy, as already indicated, is to change abstract nouns into verbs. By this means the communicator gains the double advantage of increasing the number of verbs and reducing the number of abstract nouns. Educational psychologists who insist on properly defined behavioural objectives usually make precisely this transformation. They exchange nouns like appreciation, understanding and knowledge for infinitives like to differentiate, to identify and to write (Mager 1962). Comprehension decreases as adjectives increase, but pronouns, on the contrary, make the message easier. Miller (1951) found that communications with more pronouns were easier to understand, and attributed that fact to the personal interest they stimulated. Apart from such psychological factors, however, other and more powerful linguistic variables may well be involved. Lastly, prepositions decrease comprehension. The more prepositions, the harder the communication.

These findings are broad generalizations derived from correlational studies and should be applied cautiously and intelligently. Until more rigorous and controlled experimental studies are designed, these are all we have.

(Taylor 1977: 115–16)

One of those who go far in their application of these and similar principles is Rowntree:

Write plainly:
— Cut out surplus words,
— Use short familiar words,
— Use precise words,
— Use strong, active verbs,
— Use specialist vocabulary – but with care,
— Write short, simple sentences.

(Rowntree 1986: 231–2)

Without detracting from the appreciation of the studies mentioned in the quotation from Taylor, at least one reservation should be voiced. We have to contend with some intervening variables influencing the results. Personal motivation, the standard of prior knowledge and cognitive structure of the students concerned, the time available, and other circumstances evidently influence the results of studies of this kind (Klare 1976). Further, we must consider which types of learning are concerned. What is relevant for purely reproductive learning and simple transfer achievements need not apply to problem learning and understanding. Some scholars are apt to regard formal text criteria as relatively unimportant in relation to individual cognitive structures and the learning activities of students endeavouring to solve problems. See Weingartz and Marton below.

Readability formulae using word length, word frequency, sentence length, and similar measures to predict reading difficulty have been used with success (Gilliland 1972). Naturally, the reservations regarding other formal criteria of understanding apply to readability formulae as well.

> Gilliland (1972: 96) points out, for example, that reading difficulty is not necessarily caused only by word and sentence length (e.g. 'grandfather' is a more familiar word than many shorter ones and short sentences of unusual structure may also be more difficult than longer ones).
>
> (Aitchison and Aitchison 1987: 23)

Nevertheless, like the guidelines provided by Langer *et al.* (1974), readability formulae can be quite useful. They are also usually easy to apply. In a critical study of language in texts, Macdonald-Ross comes to the conclusion that, in spite of the problems known, a 'readability "filter" is ... more reliable than the exercise of unaided human judgement' (Macdonald-Ross 1979: 5). He refers to what is known about

> the clear relationship between readability and learner acceptability (Klare *et al.* 1955), between readability and efficiency of reading (Klare *et al.* 1957). Klare and Smart (1973) found a rank-order correlation of 0.87 between the readability level of correspondence material and the probability that students would send in all their lessons (with length held constant). Such decisively clear-cut field results are not to be put aside lightly.
>
> (ibid. p. 4)

The compactness of a text, i.e. the degree of succinctness with which something is explained, also influences the readability to a great extent. In most cases, the compactness can be judged in relation to how many words are used per item of information. We may therefore speak of the density of information in a study text. In a scholarly paper the density of information can be extremely high, whereas in a conversation it is usually kept to a level that makes immediate comprehension possible. Faust and Anderson (1967) and Frase and Silbiger (1970) have shown the value for motivation and learning of moderate density of information in print. Langer *et al.* stress the importance of avoiding both extreme concentration and long-windedness, whereas other scholars show that marginal information of illustrative value both supports the learning of the main points and is itself incorporated in the knowledge acquired. Rothkopf and Kaplan (1972) report after an experiment that 'increases in density of instructional objectives resulted in decreases in the likelihood that any intentional item was learned' (Rothkopf and Kaplan 1972: 295).

Taylor (1977) expresses similar conclusions:

> The effective communicator elaborates his discourse. He identifies the novel and more difficult concepts. He gives examples, he rephrases his exposition and provides repetition. . . . When the amount of elaboration is low, the presentation is considered difficult. As elaboration increases, the discourse gets easier for the subject. Up to 30 per cent elaboration reduces presentation difficulty. When the amount of elaboration exceeds 30 per cent the presentation gets more difficult. A more general statement of this effect would be that redundancy improves ease of comprehension. This point has received ample experimental support.
>
> (Miller *et al.* 1951)

Taylor's 1953 study, using the 'cloze' technique, also illustrated how 'messages with a high level of redundancy convey their meaning more successfully than those low in redundancy' (Taylor 1977: 47).

The warning quoted against extreme concentration on the one hand and long-windedness on the other, as well as the reservations about formal text criteria as indicators of text effectiveness, may be taken to question how far the educational editing should go to make the reading palatable. Rowntree (1973), quoting Sanders, is quite categorical in rejecting the most readable texts as patterns to be followed:

> The more explanatory and 'clear' the exposition, the less

93

there is for the student to do. Some texts are so 'perfect' as to stifle all real thinking activity. Sanders (1966) has this to say about textbooks:

'Although many are attractive, accurate, readable and understandable, they are also one of the biggest deterrents to thinking in the classroom, because the writers assume that students learn best by studying a polished product. The key function of the writer is to explain, and a good explanation is interesting, orderly, accurate, and complete. The vocabulary suits the level of the student and complex ideas are clarified by dissection, integration, example and visual images. Thus, the textbook is weak in that it offers little opportunity for any mental activity except remembering. If there is an inference to be drawn, the author draws it, and if there is a significant relationship to be noted, the author points it out. There are no loose ends or incomplete analyses. The textbook is highly refined and as near perfection as a human mind is capable of making it – but the author does the thinking. The book never gives a clue that the author pondered (maybe even agonized) over hundreds of decisions.

The result is that the creative process and the controversy of competing ideas are hidden from the students.'

(Rowntree 1973: 2; Sanders 1966: 158)

When considering this warning against text perfection, we should ask whether, in case Rowntree and Sanders are correct in their assumptions, it is the clarity, the interesting presentation, the readability, the intelligibility, the perfection, or something else that makes the 'polished product' detrimental to thinking.

It is probable that a text that seems very simple and full of platitudes makes a reader inattentive. But is such a text to be described as attractive and interesting? Conversely, it is well known that a text that is not lucid, however important it is, makes some readers impatient and thus little motivated to learn.

It is my contention that clarity, readability, and forms of presentation that attract interest all promote reading and learning. The fault with the type of text criticized by Sanders and Rowntree lies elsewhere, i.e. in the presentation of learning matter as a ready-made system instead of as something to be looked into and considered. The texts described do not require the students to ask themselves questions, try possible solutions leading to conjectures and refutations, or search on their own. There can be no doubt that guiding students in this way is what must be required of study texts, unless they aim at providing material for memorizing only.

Groeben (1972) expresses views which closely agree with Sanders: 'Do not accept the principle that you must be entirely intelligible to the student.' Groeben recommends what he calls an intermediate degree of intelligibility. It appears probable, however, that what he objects to is not perfect lucidity but the presentation of knowledge as facts and ready-made systems instead of a series of complex problems: 'Do not lack in responsibility in that you enumerate the facts you know.' This could imply an interpretation that agrees with the one I have developed above. To attain a reasonable degree of intelligibility, the measures recommended by Groeben imply helping the students to structure concepts (Groeben 1972: 147).

Techniques have been developed to direct students' attention to important issues, to considering and searching for solutions. Rothkopf's questions aimed at promoting 'mathemagenic–positive' behaviour belong here. The use of questions as attention directors, along the line of Rothkopf, has been criticized. Whereas much research endorses this use and many agree with Macdonald-Ross in regarding this as supporting common sense, others are rather negative. This would seem to apply to Weingartz, who considers formal text criteria fairly insignificant in relation to the basic text design, which may either start out from problems to be solved and thus support problem learning, or simply present ready-made systems of knowledge for reproductive learning. Even more negatively inclined is Marton, who fears that all kinds of attention directors may avert students' interest from the content to the technical aspects of the reading process, thus encouraging surface learning and leading to neglect of deep-structure learning (see pp. 34–6).

Considering arguments for and against inserted questions, it would seem to be important what type of questions are asked. If they merely concern facts, wordings, and examples provided in the text, they may certainly encourage what Marton calls surface learning. Questions causing students to think independently, to formulate their thoughts and relate these to the text are not only radically different from the questions attached to the wordings of texts but also would seem to be useful instruments to encourage problem learning and deep-structure study as Marton and Saeljö define this concept. Research reviewed by Faw and Waller (1976) confirms this. See also Marland and Store (1982: 93). On students' reactions to inserted questions see above under *Self-checking exercises.*

It would be extremely interesting to know more about how students really use the various devices developed to facilitate their learning. Perc Marland recommends as investigation method the use of self-reporting techniques 'such as think-aloud, journal-keeping or stimulated-recall interviewing' (Marland 1989: 180).

If used with judgement and discretion, aids to making distance-study units and other texts accessible and instructive can no doubt be valuable instruments in the hands of sensible course developers. In my view, this applies to readability formulae; to the principles of intelligibility discovered by Langer *et al.*: to the research quoted on density of information and on questions based on texts to support mathemagenic–positive study. They all contribute to the character of didactic conversation that I have described as highly conducive to individual learning. Irrespective of the medium used, an argumentative presentation, which encourages problem learning in the spirit of Lehner and Wein-gartz, adapts itself in a natural way to the forms of didactic conversation that state and suggest, query, reconsider, search for additional information, improve the wording of a finding and use this as a basis for further deliberations. The style of didactic conversation no doubt has its rightful place in distance-study courses.

All this evidently means that there is a considerable difference between a distance-teaching course presented in print and a conventional book (see p. 68). Guidelines and activities of different kinds naturally belong to a course which has to train students to evaluate their study material at a more or less academic level. See Iley (1983: 76).

Typography and layout

It is usually assumed that the layout and general typography of a printed course may exert influence on its teaching effectiveness. Decisions on the graphic presentation of text usually rely predominantly on general assumptions about legibility, on intuition and personal taste. This does not mean that there is a lack of scholarly studies in this field.

> The history of typographic research is a lengthy one, going back to the 1880s and probably before. The research has been ably summarized by several workers, notably Tinker (1969), Spencer (1969), and Katzen (1977). Yet despite its long history, it is clear that much typographic research seems to have little practical relevance for writers, editors, typographers, publishers and printers.
>
> (Hartley 1980: 127)

Distance-education practice in this respect relies only to a very limited extent on research. Among the studies on typography that are relevant for distance educators, those of Hartley and Tinker seem particularly fruitful. The following guidelines, inspired by Tinker, would seem to be useful:

1 Two-point leading improves the legibility of 8-, 9-, 10-, 11- and (to some extent) 12-point type in lines of moderate width.
2 With 10-point type and 2-point leading, it seems to be possible to vary the line width between 13 and 28 picas without any significant change in legibility; however, readers seem to prefer approximately 20-pica line width.
3 With 11-point type, under the same conditions, line widths from about 14 to about 30 picas would seem to be practicable; for 12-point type the safety zone seems to be 15 to 34 picas.
4 Eleven-point type seems to be preferable to other sizes; with 2-point leading, line widths of about 22 picas are apparently optimal.

A slight modification by Hartley and Burnhill should be added:

> In general, however, a good all-purpose size is 10-point type on a 12-point line to line feed: 8-point on 10-points is possibly as small as one would want to go in the design of instructional materials.
>
> (Hartley and Burnhill 1977: 190)

Clarity rather than typographical elegance is usually stressed as important. Thus Hartley and Trueman (1979: 102) provide this recommendation:

1 Set the text unjustified (i.e. with equal word spacing and ragged right-hand margin, as in normal typescript).
2 End each line at a sensible place syntactically (e.g. at the ends of clauses). Avoid word breaks (hyphenation) at line ends.

Logical divisions of the text into reasonably short paragraphs, and generous spacing of chapters, sections, and paragraphs can evidently help the student considerably. A number of headlines and sub-heads are valuable not only in facilitating legibility but also in structuring the contents.

A valuable contribution to the theory of graphic elements has been offered by Waller, who has developed the notion of access structure (Waller 1977 a, b). His thinking is based on the insight that the normal way of reading is selective. We do not normally read every word or from the top to the bottom of the page, but look for what is relevant to us at the time of reading. What a reader needs, according to Waller, is help both to plan and execute his reading strategy. Lists of content, statements of objectives, surveys, and explicit suggestions may be helpful for planning. Graphical devices, e.g. headings, are useful for the execution in that, as Macdonald-Ross (1979: 30) says, they signal 'the status of the communication to the reader'.

Another relevant approach is presented by Doerfert (1980) on the basis of information theory and the so-called redundancy theory developed by von Cube. The formation of 'supersigns' is regarded as particularly important for learning efficiency. Supersigns are comprehensive concepts including 'signs' on a lower level, in the way that a word is a supersign in relation to the individual letters of which it is made up. According to von Cube, supersign formation is an effective means to bring about 'redundancy', as this concept is understood by him.

Von Cube's theory is based on a cybernetic approach, mathematically defining the probability of what a student can foresee. The gist of the redundancy theory can be described as follows. Each study task contains a certain amount of information that is to be absorbed. Each item of prior knowledge and each step on the path of learning leads to a reduction of the amount of information left, and so does the capacity to form supersigns with the inclusion of new knowledge matter in its proper context. To the individual student, the task then contains redundant information beside what remains to be learned. The more that is

learnt, the smaller the amount of remaining subjective information and the greater the redundancy. Felix von Cube explains
all learning processes by means of this theory. The fact that
meaningful material is learnt more quickly than meaningless
material is explained by the higher statistical redundancy in the
meaningful material: thus the amount of information per unit to
be learned is lower than in the meaningless material. Similar
illustrations are given of conditioning and learning by success.

Doerfert applies this thinking to the use of graphical elements
in distance-study courses. The use of structuring key-words in the
margin, to denote essential concepts in the course presentation,
has been tried with success: these key-words reproduce the content of the course unit as a kind of abstract and, according to
Doerfert, in this way facilitate the formation of supersigns favouring redundancy. Various typographical measures including the
use of italics, underlinings, etc., which aid the understanding of
relations between concepts and other items of a presentation,
are also seen as facilitators of supersign formation.

From another point of view, Waller tends to reject general
information theory as 'unhelpful and somewhat misleading'.
'Information theory while having a limited direct impact on the
study of graphic communication, left a metaphor for communication, reflecting the transient nature of electronics signals rather
than the permanence of the printed media' (Waller 1979: 213).
Following Hatt, Waller favours 'a taxonomy of communication
outcomes in which the rejection or partial use of a message is
seen as quite valid and not necessarily inconsistent with adequate
comprehension' (ibid., p. 216). He further argues that 'the construction of a text (or diagram) is itself part of the process of
organizing and structuring ideas' and discusses graphic devices
as aids to problem-solving. Here, in accordance with his selectivity
approach mentioned above, he refers to cases 'where the
sequence and strategy for obtaining information is determined
largely by the reader, and is conditional on, firstly, his goal and
secondly, on the outcome of various steps in the problem-solving
process' (ibid., p. 221).

The application of typography to distance education is investigated within the general framework of teaching strategies in
Marland and Store (1982).

Illustrations

Illustration of what is presented or discussed in a course is usually felt to be valuable from the points of view of both motivation and instruction. In a verbal presentation, whether printed, broadcast or recorded, illustrations take the form of visualizing through graphs, drawings, and pictures included in printed matter or offered separately (slides, films). If the presentation is based on printed material, illustrations may consist of both pictures and sound. How illustrations are to be used is partly a matter of selecting appropriate media and partly a matter of creating course units within the limits of a medium or media already chosen.

For printed courses, Kaufman *et al.* (1982) have developed a two-dimensional model for classifying visuals according to their function (instructional, motivational, and directional) and mode (drawing or photograph).

Weaving texts and pictures into what Sven Lidman calls one integrated lexivisual presentation, including explanatory drawings and text units, panoramic pictures and photographs of details, documentary illustration, etc., has been tried with success and is evidently a form of presentation that distance educators will have to investigate further (Lidman 1979; Lidman and Lund 1972).

According to Bock (1983), complementarity between text and illustration is a necessary condition for influence on learning, whereas mere repetition has been shown to be without effect, at least in some experiments. Lidman's lexivisual approach aims at complementarity, of course, in that text and picture each contributes its part to the whole. Applications of this principle can be found, independently of Lidman, in distance-teaching courses, for instance when processes and procedures are illustrated not by one picture but by a series of consecutive drawings or photos with verbal explanations. A Swedish example, from an elementary course of mathematics used in the early 1960s, is shown in Figure 6. Here learners are shown how to proceed consecutively to divide an angle into two angles of equal size. Pictures 2–4 demonstrate how an angle can be divided into two angles of exactly equal size by a pair of compasses, no protractor being used. The pictures show the consecutive positions of the compass leg and the marks made by the compass pencil.

Although any number of examples could be shown to illustrate the application of text–picture complementarity, few, if any, clear-

1

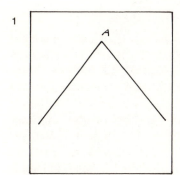

Den spetsiga vinkeln vid A ska delas
i två lika stora delar.

2

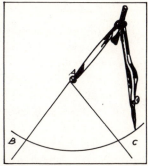

Sätt passarspetsen i A och slå en
cirkelbåge, som skär de båda
vinkelbenen. Vi kallar skärning-
spunkterna för B och C.

3

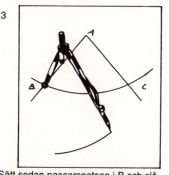

Sätt sedan passarspetsen i B och slå
en båge med godtycklig radie, som
dock inte får vara alltför liten.

4

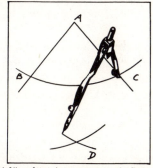

Behåll måttet i passaren och flytta
passarspetsen till punkten C. Slå en
cirkelbåge med lika stor radie som i
bild 3. Om de båda bågarna inte
skulle skära varandra, har Ni valt en
alltför liten radie i cirkelbågarna.

Figure 6 Series of drawings with explanatory texts
Source: Hermods

cut rules can be derived from studies of practice or experiments.
Not a little research has been done (Willows and Houghton
1987), but so far it is with little practical impact. Cognition psychology pays considerable attention to the issues concerned, however, also from the point of view of distance education. See, for
instance, *Fernstudium aktuell* 8, 3–4 (1986), the journal of the
German Institute for Distance Study (DIFF) at Tübingen University. In this Institute, painstaking research on learning from texts
and pictures has been done for several years (see Ballstaedt, *et
al.* 1987).

101

Non-contiguous oral and video presentation

Apart from the section on typography, most of what has been said so far also applies to the endeavours that are made non-contiguously to facilitate learning by oral means (radio or audio recordings) and by combined oral and visual means (television or video recordings).

The main difference between radio and TV on the one hand and recording on the other hand being the ephemeral character of broadcasts, the latter would seem to be relegated to new items and spontaneous supplements to pre-produced courses, at least in developed countries where recorders and cassettes are constantly available. This need by no means be an inferior function, however, as demonstrated in a number of question-box programmes applied, for instance, in the Swedish Delta project described on p. 151.

Audio and video cassettes or tapes, on the other hand, are parts of the pre-produced course which, like printed course units, students can refer to again and again. Combinations of spoken, recorded instructions with printed illustrations have proved very useful. Durbridge (1984) illuminates their use at the university level. In Sweden in the 1960s, Hermods worked with audio cassettes to guide the study of brochures containing illustrations and very brief printed comments. This was in the teaching of elementary physics and chemistry. In the latter case the target group consisted of textile workers being retrained for jobs in mechanical industry.

CONCLUSIONS ABOUT COURSE DESIGN

The above comments will have shown that a number of different but – as a rule – compatible approaches to subject-matter presentation have been developed and applied. I am convinced that the empathy approach is the most helpful guideline to course developers and should pervade the whole of the distance-education process. There will be reason to return to this in the part of this book devoted to distance-education theory.

In OTIC, the centre for distance-education research at the Dutch Open Universiteit, 'embedded support services' are being developed to facilitate learning from texts (Valcke and others in OTIC research reports). In Valcke *et al.* (1993) and Dochy (1988), a number of theories relevant to instructional design are looked into.

A report on an Australian research project is of particular interest to course developers considering the various methods discussed above:

> It was found that students valued and were aided by access structures, i.e. devices which gave them access to the author's argument, enabling them to gain an overview of the text and to locate the key elements of the subject. Although few used the terms 'access structures' or 'advance organizers' to describe these devices, they did mention the assistance given by tables of content, objectives, headings, introductory chapters, selective sampling and summarising. All this confirmed the importance of access structures . . . It also led to the conclusion that access structures are of greater help in studying than legibility features.
>
> The further conclusion was that the use of unambiguous and logical language, with appropriate sentence and paragraph sequences, can compensate for inadequate typographic signalling; that headings, illustrations and photographs that are not directly relevant can annoy those who seek connections between all elements of the textural presentation.
>
> (Parer 1988: 1)

This largely applies to course presentation also when other media than the printed word are used. There is always a text in the background. Dubin and Taveggia (1968: 47), underline the powerful impact of textbooks 'which cannot be washed out by any known methods of instruction'. Juler who refers to this quotation, concludes that 'text is basic to all education and that the interactions students have with their texts are just as important as the interactions they have with people' (Juler 1990: 28). This, of course, applies even more to distance education than to conventional modes of teaching and learning as distance students wholly or mainly rely on non-contiguous, i.e. mediated communication. It is the realization of this that is the reason for the emphasis above on the empathy approach, conversational style and the organization of learning matter presented in print.

6

INTERACTION BETWEEN STUDENTS AND THE SUPPORTING ORGANIZATION

The importance of a kind of simulated communication and conversation-like approach has been stressed above in the discussion of the first of the two constituent elements of distance education: learning-matter presentation. For the second constituent element, real communication in the form of interaction between tutors and students, much of what was said on pp. 45–55 is relevant.

Empathy and rapport between tutors and students remain important guidelines. This applies to both contiguous (i.e. face-to-face) interaction and non-contiguous (i.e. mediated communication).

THE FUNCTIONS OF COMMUNICATION

The purposes of two-way communication in distance education are generally as follows:

1 To support students' motivation and interest by contact with an encouraging tutor and counsellor.
2 To support and facilitate student learning by students applying knowledge and skills acquired to tasks to be checked by and discussed with tutors as well as by tutors' comments, explanations and suggestions.
3 To give students opportunities to develop their thinking while benefiting from tutors' criticism.
4 To assess students' progress in order to provide them with an instrument by means of which they can judge their educational situation and needs, and by means of which marks can be awarded; the assessment of students' progress and the contact with them are also evaluation elements used more or less sys-

104

tematically for the purposes of modifying courses on the basis of students' needs and wishes. This applies to assignments set for submission and then corrected and commented on as well as to unstructured communication.

That these are considered the most important tasks of mediated tutor–student interaction is borne out by a study by Bååth on the practices of thirty-four European distance-education institutions, including the British Open University, which were asked to rank fourteen functions in relation to their importance. By far the most important function of non-contiguous communication proved to be 'to give the students effective feedback – help them to correct their mistakes and control their progress' (Bååth 1980: 31). An educationally most important function is added by Perraton (1987: 5): 'to allow learner and teacher to take off in directions . . . not forecast'.

Let us first concentrate on the teaching-learning situation as such and then consider counselling, which is undoubtedly part of the educational endeavour, in a context of its own.

PROCEDURES AND MEDIA APPLIED TO STUDENT–TUTOR INTERACTION

In distance education there are three different types of tutoring to be considered, namely the one actually provided at a distance (by some kind of correspondence or over the telephone), the one offered in recurrent, more or less regular personal consultations or tutorials supplementing distance study, for instance in regional study centres, and finally tutoring at concentrated residential refresher courses.

The whole system of distance education is based on the insight that what is really important is the student activity, i.e. learning, and that tutoring distance students, rather than teaching them, implies paving the way for student activity. Distance education is concerned with attempts to develop autonomous learning. It is thus basically the task of tutors – as well as that of course developers, planners and administrators – to provide what Rothkopf and his school of thought call 'mathemagenic–positive' conditions, that is conditions, surroundings and measures that favour and facilitate learning. It may be worth our while looking into the application of this way of thinking to the kinds of tutoring referred to.

Tutoring at a distance

Tutoring at a distance is by far the most important form of tutoring activity in distance education. It derives its particular importance from the fact that it is a basic component of the system of distance education whereas all kinds of contact with tutors physically present are contingent on special conditions. It is the only form of contact with tutors that all students can make use of and benefit from.

It is customary for courses to provide questions, problems, and other tasks, the replies and solutions to which, including essays, reports, and other independent papers, are to be submitted for comment, evaluation, and correction. It is possible, though seldom practised, to provide an extensive battery of assignments, from among which students are encouraged to select those that they find particularly interesting or that coincide with their specific study objectives. This could be one way to bring about student autonomy in a way useful to students who realize what they need. If students were to select their own study objectives and, on the basis of this selection, were able to concentrate on the corresponding parts of the course and were offered assignments related to the parts chosen, then they would be provided with more appropriate opportunities for autonomous study than distance education is normally capable of offering.

A less satisfactory but more common method of individualization is to make assignments for submission voluntary without providing the students with selection instruments related to individual study objectives.

As a rule, a number of students submit replies to the same questions, solve the same problems and write essays on the same subjects. This provides an excellent basis for judging the relative merits of the work of each student.

It has been found practical in some cases to use so-called objective tests, which only require the student to mark his reply in the right place. Their advantages are that they can be judged wholly objectively (it is perfectly possible to have the marking done by means of a computer), whereas essay-test marking must be influenced by the tutor's subjective judgement. Objective tests can cover a great many items and save students' time.

The main types of objective tests which have been used with success in distance-study courses are as follows:

1 Multiple-choice tests in which the student marks which of several suggested answers is/are the correct one(s).

2 Re-arrangement tests in which the student numbers the various items of a series of events, a process of work, etc. to demonstrate the right order between the items.

3 Completion tests in which the student fills in gaps in sentences requiring figures, terms, or other indications of fact; or, in a sentence in a foreign language, words, phrases, missing endings, etc.

Tests of this kind are sometimes useful for checking factual knowledge, application, understanding, and even analysis. They may also serve instructional purposes, particularly if after the test the student receives model solutions with comments. Naturally, their limitation is that they do not encourage the students independently to express their insight into logical connections, etc. Normally, it is required that students should be able to express themselves verbally, and this is where objective tests are not appropriate. For that reason they can play only a limited part in education. However, they are entirely appropriate in all of the cases where an analysis of the desired result of a training programme shows that recognition (and not the ability to record something) is essential.

Communication initiated by students and based on the questions that they raise and want further comment on along with suggestions for further reading, implementation, and practice, would seem to be very desirable. However, few distance-study institutions have managed to inspire more than a minority of their students to make use of this facility, and others do not even offer it. Thus it occurs mainly as a supplementary form of communication, the normal procedure being based on assignments provided by the course. These assignments vary from bitty questions and answers to comprehensive project work leading to essays and theses (see p. 74).

Every student has a legitimate interest to know to what extent he is successful, if he meets recognized standards, what his strengths and weaknesses are. Also his school or university is interested in this both in order to evaluate the teaching–learning system as a whole and to judge the progress of individual students. Though legitimate, this interest in grading the work of students endangers the 'mathemagenic' character of the interaction between students and tutors. Thus to be able to be just in assessing students' work, tutors may wish as often as at all possible to work with a reasonably representative number of papers, to go through the replies of all the students concerned to a particular question at a time and to judge the relative merits of the individual assignments against one another, in other words to apply something of the procedure appropriate in grading examination papers.

This has two consequences detrimental to learning: it causes delay and it removes the focus of attention from the learning activities as such to assessment. This is a problem particularly in the cases when distance education programmes are administered by degree-giving institutions. In the highly commendable attempts to attain something of a continuous assessment system, thus avoiding dramatic examination procedures, such institutions often wish to include the achievements of students on ordinary submission assignments in the assessment on which classes of degrees and marks are based. This makes it important to make sure that each paper submitted is an individual achievement, which in its turn induces those in charge of tuition and assessment to insist on uniform pacing, co-ordinated correction and other types of rigidity that are more concerned with examining than with tutoring.

If – as I think we should – we give priority to tutoring, then we are compelled in many cases largely to refrain from using assignment results as bases for continuous assessment of students' achievements in the sense of awarding marks. The assessment will then be coupled with and support the tutoring. The question arises how best to motivate students, how to help them to overcome difficulties, how succinctly and effectively to explain what they have misunderstood and how to stimulate critical and comparative study of various sources. Evidently most of this must be done by the pre-produced self-instructional course itself, which has to anticipate most problems, but where the course fails it is up to the distance tutor, the one first to notice the failure, to help the student by explanations, references, advice, encouragement and suggestions, all of which should induce him or her to reconsider what has been studied and review factual presentation wherever necessary. Here we have little more than didactic intuition to guide us.

A quotation from Kenneth MacKenzie seems worth referring to in this context. He says that

> there is a clear need to wean assignments and course tutors away from mere testing and passive marking, as if the written exercise is intended to be the perfect once-and-for-all-time safe 'answer'. Course teams might make increasingly plain in their supplementary material that the assignments (can the word be altered?) compose an educative sequence and that the individual assignment is thought of as a creatively incomplete essay, in the original sense of a tentative and provisional effort. Similarly, the course tutor may increasingly learn how to pass through the assignment, like Alice through the looking-glass, into the reverse world of the student beyond, engaging there with the student's struggle to sort out, inform and expound his thinking. The student in turn needs to see himself and his assignments in this way too, each as a phase, cumulative and not transient, in his personal development. So that, as in a symphony, themes he has touched on at the outset return finally at the close of the course enhanced and developed in significance. The course tutor's advice is relative to that development: 'this is what you most need to attend to now, here is the way you might develop, have you thought of this forgotten aspect . . .'
>
> (MacKenzie 1974: 50)

A comment by Bruner is relevant here:

> Instruction is a provisional state that has as its object to make the learner or problem solver self-sufficient. Any regimen of correction carries the danger that the learner may become permanently dependent upon the tutor's correction. The tutor must correct the learner in a fashion that eventually makes it possible for the learner to take over the corrective function himself. Otherwise the result of instruction is to create a form of mastery that is contingent upon the perpetual presence of a teacher.
>
> (Bruner 1971: 53)

A difficulty most tutors come across is the question what to do when a student answers that he/she does not know or does not understand how the problem in question ought to be solved. It occurs particularly in mathematics and kindred subjects when the student asks for a complete solution without submitting any work of his/her own. There seems to be general agreement that in such cases the tutor should tell the student to try to start working on the problem and to send in an attempt so that the tutor may help him/her with particular difficulties. As a rule some suggestions or references to a lesson can – and should – be made to start the student off as he may otherwise be quite helpless. The idea behind this is that the student, to learn something, must do the work actively himself/herself and that it is the tutor's task to help him/her to learn and not to deliver ready-made solutions of problems. It is thus vital in distance education that the scrutiny that applies to any kind of test and exercise should be played down in favour of helpful communication.

Frequently the submission of assignments, with their opportunities for expressing interpretations, suggested solutions, doubts, and queries, are the students' only means for communicating with the tutor. This makes it imperative that the tutor should encourage spontaneous viewpoints from the students on relevant topics and provide stimulating and informative comments.

It is the tutor's task to support the motivation of students by engaging them in thinking, reading, and other activities that make sense, and to try to motivate them for what comes later in the course. A pleasant atmosphere and feelings of friendly contact are important when the tutor contributes to his students' learning by explanations, examples, suggestions and references. Most of this work consists of personal contributions by individual tutors who write, or record on tape, their comments on individual students' work and/or talks with their students on the telephone.

This work is challenging and time-consuming. As Elton says

> If tutoring is done by correspondence, then experience indicates that it requires far more time, skill and application on the part of the tutor than may normally be found in 'essay marking' on campus. However, if this is provided, then it can be more effective than either campus essay marking or the traditional group tutoring'.
>
> (Elton 1988: 12)

The support given to students in this way has several purposes.

Lebel (1989b) analyses this support as methodological, metacognitive (helping students to learn), motivational and administrative.

It is perfectly possible and often useful to pre-produce or pre-programme text modules for use by the individual tutor. In subjects where the students are not expected to submit creative essays, most tutors find that certain misunderstandings occur so frequently that they have standardized comments ready for them, either in their minds, written (printed) on paper or stored in a computer.

Some schools of distance education have found it practical to work with a battery of carefully prepared explanatory comments that tutors can use either in the form of appendices to the student's paper when this is returned with handwritten tutor comments, or as sections of typed letters. These sections are sometimes programmed for automatic typing, whereas other sections of the same letter are typed following dictation from the tutor (see pp. 121–2). The experiences of pre-produced tutor comments are favourable. (Rekkedal and Ljoså 1974 and Fritsch 1989).

Some distance-education organizations expect students to submit their assignments by dates prescribed and thus pace them in accordance with a timetable decided on by the teaching organization. This seems above all to apply to distance education within public education (such as many distance-teaching universities). Whether this is an acceptable procedure or not is a controversial question, see pp. 165–9. An international study of some 200 distance-teaching organizations (Graff and Holmberg 1988) showed that most of them refrain from pacing their students. Further, a correlation was found between success rates and approaches favouring student independence which included free pacing.

Students on the whole seem to appreciate student–tutor interaction highly (Beijer 1972; Kelly 1982). Open University studies indicate that project work in particular is regarded as helpful (Thorpe 1986: 41–5). So are tutor-marked assignments:

> Open University tutors are required to comment extensively on a student's work, as well as to grade it. These comments provide the student with the most substantial, often the only, feedback they will have during their studies of how their understanding of the course is progressing.
>
> (Thorpe 1986: 34)

111

For a discussion of project work, see p. 74.

An Open University survey of 1983 'provides conclusive evidence for the importance of correspondence tuition'. Thus

> almost all respondents (over 90 per cent) felt assignment comments were important for explaining errors and making helpful criticism. Students were also asked what they usually did with marked assignments... fewer than 10 per cent are only interested in the grade. Seventy-two per cent read comments carefully and tried to use them in subsequent assignments.
>
> (Thorpe 1988: 74)

Sometimes, however, distance educators have to contend with students' too respectful attitudes. Consider the following quotation:

> The assumption behind much of our distance education materials of an independent and self-confident learner who is willing to ask, to question and to risk being wrong, may be entirely inappropriate in many cultural settings. Further, we must be more conscious that many learners have attitudes towards knowledge and towards 'educated' individuals which minimise the potentiality of dialogue. One of the most common statements from learners about their hesitancy in talking to tutors was that their problem was not worthy of their tutor's attention, and they were unwilling to take up their tutor's time.
>
> (Haughey 1991: 20)

Difficulties of this kind illuminate the importance of the empathy approach leading to rapport between students and tutors.

Media for student–tutor and student–student interaction

Since, in the typical distance-education teaching–learning situation, tutors are not on the same premises as their students, non-contiguous communication is the type of interaction on which distance educators and students mainly have to rely. Correspondence in writing, by computer, telefax or electronic mail, and oral conversations on the telephone or on audio cassettes are the means that can be used to bring about this communication at a distance.

Face-to-face sessions

In many distance-education programmes there are also elements of face-to-face interaction between tutors and students. The second and third types of tutoring mentioned at the beginning of our discussion of teaching–learning communication belong here. The occurrence of such contiguous communication is dependent on the possibility, opportunity, and inclination of students to go to and take part in face-to-face meetings. Many distance-teaching organizations find meetings important either as a motivational device encouraging course completion or as a purely instructional element, or both. For that reason, regional and local study centres, offering tutorials, the use of technical equipment (computer terminals, recording apparatus, laboratory facilities), library service and other support, are set up. Students often appreciate measures of this kind; frequently, however, when attendance is not compulsory, most students seem to prefer or (for reasons of family, job, and social commitments) be/feel compelled to give priority to non-contiguous communication.

While there is often a case for supplementary communication in group and person-to-person meetings, there is no doubt that the use of face-to-face sessions is not exclusively based on rational decisions. It is also, to some extent, due to the power of tradition and to negative prejudices regarding the applicability of non-contiguous forms of study. As a basis for rational decisions in this respect, it would seem to be practical to consider the usefulness of distance study per se in the cognitive, psychomotor, and affective domains.

A number of studies have shown that both cognitive objectives in general and psychomotor objectives, which are aimed at skills in the fields of written achievement (in language and mathematics, for instance), are attained at least as well by distance study based on the written word as by conventional classes (Granholm 1971; Bajtelsmit 1990). There seem to be 'no studies of achievement which show that correspondence study students do less well than do classroom students, a number which show that they do as well, and a number which show that they do better' (Childs 1965: 81).

This, and the assumption that many psychomotor objectives and objectives in the affective domain, i.e. attitudes and emotions, are more effectively attained by personal contacts lead many

113

distance-study institutions and their students to use face-to-face sessions, if at all, less for subject-matter learning and more for the following purposes:

- practising psychomotor skills in laboratories and under similar conditions (Holmberg and Bakshi 1982; Kember 1982); also verbal skills belong here
- facilitating the understanding of the communication process and human behaviour
- encouraging attitudes and habits of relevance for the study
- mutual inspiration and stimulation of fellow students; training in co-operation.

Many students cannot or do not want to use their time for face-to-face sessions as long as they manage by means of non-contiguous communication. They prefer phoning (or writing to) their tutor to travelling, perhaps for an hour or more by car or train, to a tutorial. This is apparently the attitude of a majority of the students of the FernUniversität. Elsewhere, large groups of distance students seem to prefer working entirely at their own pace and privately and are not willing to adopt any time schedule or join any meeting or tutorial (Beijer 1972 and Wångdahl 1979). However, to others benefiting from the advantages of both distance-study and face-to-face sessions, tutoring in both forms is something found desirable. It is also in many cases practicable. (Fritsch and Ströhlein 1988). Combining oral tuition with distance study causes some difficulties that have not, however, always been coped with successfully.

Efficient tutors in a class or group are apt to take command and teach, instead of guiding or advising, and thereby deprive students of the initiative by taking over part of the function of the self-instructional course. This often leads to the students being given too much instruction (the tutor doubles the course). The students are also to some extent put in conflict because of differences of approach between the course and the tutor, a confusion which is always time-consuming (but may be productive in academic study). Further, in this way the planned guidance and consultation are sometimes converted into a kind of more or less conventional classroom teaching which requires considerably more time than can reasonably be set aside for the guidance and counselling that is intended to support the individual study of a distance-education course. This may be harmful, as such a course is meant to teach on its own, introducing new elements at the points where students are in a position to assimilate them, and consolidating newly acquired knowledge by means of illustrations, graphs, exercises of various kinds, summaries, etc.

Face-to-face interaction as a supplement to distance study can be applied in more profitable ways, however. Personal consultations along the lines of Oxbridge tutorials (i.e. periods of stimulating educational interchange between tutor and student) and discussions in groups, organized and formed spontaneously, appear to be the most valuable supporting functions of face-to-face sessions (apart from those that require special equipment, such as laboratories, machinery, computer terminals, etc.).

Another profitable way of integrating distance education with face-to-face sessions is running concentrated residential courses which support individual distance study. These can help students over previously insurmountable difficulties; they can introduce and thereby facilitate the study of new parts of the distance course; they can inspire co-operation with fellow students and provide a pleasant academic atmosphere with motivational potential. As they take place during concentrated periods, when an interruption is made in the individual distance study, they do not interfere with or disturb this.

A third successful combination of distance study and face-to-face sessions has been developed for 'supervised' distance study in schools and in companies and organizations, including military units. Students work in libraries or classrooms and have a teacher available there as a resource. The teacher is their individual adviser and helper rather than their instructor, and answers questions, explains when asked to, motivates, organizes group activities, and administrates. The learning matter is presented throughout by the course, which may be based on several media, and the didactic communication with the distance-study school remains an essential element. See Chapter 8.

A general conclusion seems to be that certain principles must be observed when combinations of distance and face-to-face methods are introduced. It is not a teacher but a resource person and moderator that is needed as the leader of supplementary oral class. The actual teaching is done by the distance course and the non-contiguous communication. There is every reason to plan any combination of contiguous and non-contiguous study with extreme care and then to respect the dearth of time available to most students.

Media for non-contiguous communication

The decisions to be made concerning media for two-way communication are still often limited to a choice between written, recorded, and telephone communication, though some use is made of radio for this purpose (McGuire 1973) and modern information technology offers new possibilities. Assignments may be given in a printed course, while the students are required to reply either in writing or, where oral achievements are a study objective, on audio-tape. Students may also listen to recordings and comment in writing; on tutor–student interaction by audio tape see, e.g., Valkyser (1981); Durbridge (1984); Evans (1984). Even phonetic discrimination exercises have been arranged in this way. The telephone is useful for direct and indirect communication; in the latter case, students dictate their questions on the telephone to a recording machine and receive phone calls from their tutors after the latter have listened to the questions and studied the problems raised.

Interesting studies of communication by telephone have been made by Flinck (1978), who also reports on content analysis of didactic telephone conversations, by Blom (1986); Moore (1981); Winders (1984); and others. The last two named examine telephone conferencing. Satellite communication can offer similar service (Williams and Gillard 1986).

A study by Torstein Rekkedal indicates student satisfaction with telephone communication although 'very few students actually phone their tutor(s)' (Rekkedal 1989: 35). Tutors were highly stimulated by telephone communication agreeing 'that the telephone conversations with the students had added a complete new dimension to their work as distance educators' (ibid., p. 38).

The use of the telephone for seminars has proved successful in a number of cases. This is what is usually called teleconferencing. It should perhaps be called audio teleconferencing, as it is possible to include video elements in the wider concept of teleconferencing. The cost of these does not always seem to correspond to the educational value added by them although visual cues are sometimes considered important in regulating discussion (Tuckey 1993: 601).

116

Teleconferencing makes discussions between students possible at the same time as it gives the tutor opportunities both to moderate the discussion and to make his/her own contributions. It can thus be a rewarding form of non-contiguous two-way communication.

Writing on Canadian conditions, Robertson reports that audio conferencing has a growing appeal to Canadian adult educators because

- many part-time adult students are widely scattered in communities that may be several hundred kilometres apart, with each centre having fewer than ten students in the same programme;
- the costs for starting and operating an audio teleconferencing system can be relatively low;
- the technology is readily available and is familiar to instructors and students;
- most systems can be adjusted quickly to serve large or small groups;
- the mode of instruction can be similar to that of an on-campus seminar with the instructor being in charge but able to stimulate multi-point interaction;
- scheduling adjustments can be made almost as readily as for on-campus classes;
- access to the instruction or programmes can be controlled through a limited number of centres;
- the quality of the instructional materials is often increased because of the need for careful preparation several weeks before presentation;
- properly organised, it has the potential for generating operating profits;
- immediate cost benefits can be shown;
- very useful working relationships can be developed with community groups having dispersed memberships.

(Robertson 1987: 121–2)

There are various technical methods for bringing about non-contiguous conferencing as an element in distance education. Computer-based communication occurs in several forms.

The discussion about the character and potential of computer-mediated communication sometimes appears somewhat confusing as on the one hand exaggerated claims about its potential, on the other hand misguided aversion to technology seem to obscure judgement. For that reason I begin this presentation of computer use in mediated communication by a lucid clarification of concepts written by Erling Ljoså and quoted here with his permission:

> Computer-mediated communication (CMC) is a notion used to describe a system of two-way communication based on the transmission of electronically written information. Basically, there are two types of CMC system:
>
> 1) Electronic mail systems
> 2) Computer conferencing systems.
>
> In an *electronic mail system* every user has his or her own mail box, and electronic letters are exchanged between these boxes. The physical communication takes place by forwarding the information from one computer to another until it reaches the mail boxes of the receivers.
>
> The main function in an electronic mail system is to carry out a dialogue between two persons. Group communication may be conducted if the same letter is sent to a group of people engaged in the same conversation. But if several hosts and messages are involved, the sense of group communication may be lost. This is due to the fact that each of the participants has to save the letters in his or her personal mail box to review them later. And there is no function numbering the letters in a way that easily identifies them and relates them to each other. Therefore, to facilitate group communication, computer conferencing systems are preferable.
>
> The notion *computer conferencing system* (CCS) is an internationally recognised metaphor used to describe a text database usually located on a central computer. This is in contrast to electronic mail systems, where the conversation is stored in individual mail boxes. When using a CCS, the sender transmits information from his personal computer (PC), terminal or whatever to the database, and the receiver gets the information when connecting to the database. The communication is asynchronous, that is, the messages are transmitted and received at different times.

A computer conferencing system may carry out three different forms of communication:

1) Dialogue or one-to-one communication: the electronic mail function.
2) One-to-many communication: the electronic bulletin board function.
3) Group discussion or many-to-many communication: the electronic meeting function.

The *electronic meeting function* is the essential element in a CCS, and it is mainly this function that makes it different from an electronic mail system. Electronic meetings or conferences are metaphors. They may also have different properties in different systems. But many systems on the market today offer the possibility of arranging both open and closed conferences. In an open or public conference, everyone with access to the system has the possibility of joining the conference and taking part in discussions. Closed conferences have restricted access.

(Ljoså 1992b: 44–5)

Use of the computer along these lines occurs to an increasing extent (Mason and Kaye 1989; Ortner 1992). Combinations of computer technology and telephone communication appear particularly promising, such as electronic mail, telefax systems and modern text processing of the type used by newspapers (when a contribution is typed by a correspondent at a distance from the printing-office to where it is transmitted electronically and where it may be changed or edited).

Computer networks play an important part. Cf. Mason 1989. Connecting students' personal computers (PCs) with a host computer in such a way that – as indicated by Ljoså – students can communicate asynchronously not only with tutors but also with fellow students is often seen as a great advantage and is being increasingly practised. On Deaking University work of this kind, see Castro (1987). A valuable presentation of applications, potential and problems occurs in Rekkadal (1992).

An interesting type of non-contiguous conferencing heralding so-called telewriter systems was developed at an early stage at the British Open University under the name of CYCLOPS. This is

an extremely versatile audio-visual teaching system based on

119

the conventional television set, standard audio cassettes, and microcomputer technology. In face-to-face teaching CYCLOPS can be used as an audio-visual aid, for displaying pre-prepared diagrams and other graphics which have been produced in the CYCLOPS studio at Walton Hall and stored on one channel of a stereo audio cassette. By synchronizing sequences of pictures with a spoken track, a self-instructional package can be produced for students' personal use.

However, it is when CYCLOPS is linked to telephones and used for distance tutoring that its versatility as a teaching tool becomes most apparent. The CYCLOPS television screen can be used for writing and drawing on by both tutor and students, the telephone lines being used to relay the writing between the various participants in the tutorial who each have a similar set of CYCLOPS equipment.

The writing is achieved by using either a light-sensitive pen to draw directly on to the television screen or a 'scribbled pad' which displays drawing on the screen.

(McConnell 1982: 21)

This and other telewriter systems implying audio-visual two-way communication have mainly served groups of students rather than individual tutoring (Shale and Garrison 1989; Tuckey 1993). There are interesting exceptions, however, as shown by Rekkedal and Vigander (1990).

We have reason to look forward to further useful developments of computer communication in distance education. Simple off-line procedures, first developed in the early 1970s to serve individual learners are still being applied and appreciated. Fully developed systems of this kind, such as CADE (Hermods, Sweden), make use of a computer off line for the correction of and commenting on replies to multiple-choice questions with carefully selected distractors. In the CADE system, an optical reader 'corrects' the solution of the students, after which the computer selects relevant comments and explanations from among a great number of those programmed and stored for the purpose. The computer also checks and refers to the individual students' earlier achievements, when parallel or similar problems have been solved. A mistake or unsatisfactory solution of a problem is given different comments according to which of the incorrect distractors the student has chosen, i.e. in relation to the way in which he or she has misunderstood or wrongly combined items. The computer program see to it that sometimes even correct replies are commented on to underline something important or to support the motivation of the students. Encouraging and counselling comments, based on the total result of students' papers, are also provided by the computer. All this is typed out by the computer on to a personal letter addressed to the individual student (Bååth and Månsson 1977). A similar system, LOTSE (FernUniversität), was developed in Germany (Wilmersdoerfer 1978; Kueffner 1979).

A computer system which allows the free rendering of replies in the form of numbers has been developed at the FernUniversität (CMA). The numbers are 'read' by the computer by means of markings in columns of numbers provided. Thus, there is no choice between different solutions suggested (Graff 1977; Möllers 1981). The students create their own answers (numbers).

These off-line systems are usually regarded as very useful. In an empirical study, Bååth found strong indications that even off-line computer-assisted versions functioned better 'as far as starting behaviour, completion and attitude toward the tutorial work was concerned' than tutor-marked versions of the same courses. These findings are, as stressed by Bååth, well in accordance with the results obtained from the evaluation of the CADE system' (Bååth 1980). Andrews and Strain (1985) offer further evidence supporting Bååth's conclusions. This may reflect unsatisfactory tutor work.

Whatever technological progress is made, however, two-way communication in writing, which leads to instructional comments, suggestions, and, at an advanced level, scholarly analysis, remains a core medium. Ordinary reading and writing remain the basic means of student–tutor instruction with audio recordings and telephone interaction as the most important supplementary media. Sensible use of the computer can be very helpful also in traditional written student–tutor interaction. As indicated above under *Tutoring at a distance*, text modules commenting on expected errors and misunderstandings can be programmed for use by individual tutors in their communications with individual students along with personal comments, notes, explanations and suggestions. For detailed reports on an application of such a procedure see Hartmann-Anthes and Ebbeke (1991) and Fritsch 1989.

This kind of individual student–tutor interaction is also well served by telefax and electronic mail, which should perhaps be regarded less as products of media development than as means to speed up written communication.

The speed and frequency of communication

Speeding up communication is very important. A great weakness of distance education has in most cases been the slowness of the communication process caused by the correspondence method dominating this kind of education. For a student assignment to be sent by the student, received by the supporting organization, corrected, commented on and returned to the student so that he/she receives it within a week is considered remarkably quick and represents a turn-around time that many distance-education institutions (and post offices) seem unable to achieve. This weakness applies also to computerized correction of and comment on students' assignments, unless students can go to a terminal or use a home computer (Jones 1984).

Applications of electronic mail have a potential for solving this problem. The principle is that students submit assignments and papers of various kinds by typing the text into their personal computers (or terminals). By means of the telephone and a modem, these communications are tele-transmitted to the computers of the individual tutors or that of the supporting organization; there they are stored in the tutors' mailboxes (teleboxes) where the tutors pick them up to comment on and return them by telecommunication. With special equipment, so-called printers, both students and tutors can have the complete messages typed out on paper. This is usually necessary. Vicky Vivian reports on experiments with electronic mail in New South Wales, which among other things show that the 'turnaround time of lessons was dramatically reduced from 2–4 weeks to a matter of days, hours or occasionally even minutes' (Vivian 1986: 246).

Undelayed communication can also be brought about by the use of telefax when students fax their assignments to tutors and these also fax them back with their comments. Many tutors actually prefer telefax to electronic mail as it allows them to mark and comment on papers by hand in the traditional way, writing notes in the margin and between lines etc.

Electronic mail and telefax are very important innovations as they remove the weakness inherent in normal correspondence, its slowness. That this is essential has been shown by empirical studies. There is evidence to show that while students seem to accept and profit from comments and corrections given within a week after an assignment has been completed, they are usually dissatisfied if the delay is of longer duration. Students expect full comments on their submitted work within as few days as possible. Completion rates have been shown to correlate with turn-around time (and also with encouraging, 'reminding' letters on the occasions when students have been passive for a period; Rekkedal 1983).

Some reservations as to the general validity of Rekkedal's findings have been expressed after cross-cultural studies carried out in Australia and other empirical research in the USA (Barker *et al.* 1986, Diehl 1989). When the value of short turn-round times is judged, it is important on the one hand to consider the diminished need of prompt mediated feedback in the cases when supplementary face-to-face tuition is also provided, which is relevant in the Barker study, and on the other hand to make clear what is meant by short turn-round times and delayed feedback, which must be taken into account in relation to Diehl's research, in which immediate scoring is studied, whereas Rekkedal's short turn-round times allow up to a week for a student's assignment to be returned with the tutor's comments. Rekkedal's conclusions no doubt apply to normal distance education.

Turn-around time is closely related to the question of how often students are made to submit assignments for correction and comments. Studies of current practices have shown that the frequency of student–tutor interaction varies to an apparently extreme extent. As in most cases, this interaction is brought about by assignments for submission that are placed at the end of each unit, the length of the units is usually decisive for the frequency of course-inspired communication (see p. 69).

Bååth reports from a comprehensive study of this that in Europe the size of course units varies between as little as eight pages and more than 100 pages. Students have declared their study time per unit to range from about half an hour to 117 hours. The number of study hours per unit is estimated by representative European schools to range between 2 and 25 (Bååth 1980). In addition, an early FernUniversität study showed that for one particular unit the declared study time varied between 1 and 80 hours (Bartels and Wurster 1975: 4).

The frequency with which communication occurs would seem to be an important issue if it actually serves the supportive functions discussed on pp. 104–5. The relevant question is which frequency exerts the most favourable influence on students' success and satisfaction with their study. This area was first approached in a scholarly way by Ulla Rosberg-Johnson as early as 1966. She designed a plan for an empirical investigation which, however, was never undertaken (Rosberg 1966). A systematic study of the same problem was undertaken by Bååth, who made some interesting experiments (Bååth 1980). He examined three different groups studying the same course material, with a view to finding indications about what could be considered an ideal frequency of assignments ('submission density'). On the basis of the same instructional text one group was required to submit two assignments, a second group four assignments, and a third group eight assignments. (In one experiment, however, the number of submissions required of the three groups was three, six, and twelve respectively.) The total number of assignment questions was constant and the questions were identical.

One of Bååth's hypotheses was that frequent communication opportunities, i.e. what he called submission density, favour learning. While his study, which was carried out with great acumen, showed that more students who were in the groups offered a greater number of submission opportunities than in the low-frequency group started sending in assignment solutions and that higher submission density correlated with 'more positive attitudes to the assignments for submission' (Bååth 1980: 151), no consistent differences were found with regard to course completion or test results. A replicating study (Holmberg and Schuemer 1989) proved no more conclusive. There is thus no empirical evidence to show that the frequency of student–tutor interaction exerts any influence on the learning. This has been found surprising as contact with a tutor is assumed to be helpful. The question arises to what extent tutor contacts have been really helpful in the cases studied – and, of course, in distance education generally. It is probable that the surprising outcome of Bååth's study and the replication mentioned should be interpreted as an indication that it is the quality of the student–tutor interaction rather than its frequency that is decisive for its effectiveness and/or that high interaction frequency can be expected to be helpful on condition that the interaction is of high quality. Revising the research done on this a decade after his original empirical study Bååth expressed himself as follows: 'If the work of the tutors in the postal two-way communication is of great value to the students, then it would seem highly probable that the density of postal contacts between students and tutor(s) is important' (Bååth 1989: 85). The impact of frequent student–tutor interaction and of the length of turn-round times has been studied by several scholars. For a collection of relevant papers, see Holmberg (1989b). An aspect to which so far little attention has been paid is the motivational value of assignment submission following the completion of a course unit.

Most educators probably agree that goals close at hand (i.e. goals that can be attained in a reasonably short time) are motivating, in that they demonstrate to the student that he or she is making progress. If motivation is taken to promote success, this would seem to indicate that a suitably high submission frequency should be expected to lead to greater success than low submission frequency, provided, of course, that the assignments and the units leading to them are felt to represent steps on the path to the desired competency. This proviso again directs our attention to the types of assignment tasks used and the quality of the interaction.

In advanced study it is on the other hand important to ensure that frequent two-way communication does not lead to a large collection of only small, bitty pieces of work. Students at this level must be given tasks that train them to master, digest, and reorganize large quantities of facts, reading matter, rules, theories, etc. and to integrate and interpret them in a way that indicates learning in a scholarly manner.

Personal approaches to student–tutor interaction

Common sense as well as the empirical studies discussed above make it clear that student–tutor interaction to be useful has to be of such a character that students feel it is really helpful to them personally. This means, among other things, that tutors must comment on each individual student's approaches, understandings and misunderstandings, queries and mistakes, and relate such comments to the overall picture emerging from the study. They can well be combined with pre-produced comments as described on pp. 111 and 121–2 above.

Distance education is unique in providing a one-to-one relationship between student and tutor throughout the teaching–learning process. This facilitates personal approaches. The feelings of personal rapport, which are likely to be brought about by the style of didactic conversation in learning-matter presentation, can be strongly promoted in tutor–student interaction by the personality and tone of the tutor and can have evidently favourable consequences for study achievements. This is borne out by many experiences, for example in a report by Stein on a course with originally low completion rates. After a change of tutors 'from a cold subject-oriented man to someone equally competent in the context who also liked people', the 'percentage of completers was . . . doubled'. Stein writes: 'A warm, friendly attitude by the instructor leads to higher completion rates and a stronger feeling of satisfaction by the learner; the reverse is also true' (Stein 1960: 165–6). The favourable impact of personal approaches is further demonstrated in research reports by Posz (1963) and Brady (1976).

An empirical study by Torstein Rekkedal is of particular interest in this context. Rekkedal based his investigation on such administrative arrangements as can be seen to promote impersonal approaches; the separation of tutoring from counselling belongs here and so does contact with several tutors rather than one.

> Students studying a course composition will normally have to communicate with a number of different tutors, who all feel responsible mainly for their own subject(s). Lack of insight into the students' total situation and the total teaching system may be an obstacle to giving maximum support.
>
> (Rekkedal 1985: 9)

By comparing a (control) group taught in this more or less impersonal way with an experimental group given more personal service, Rekkedal tested the influence of the latter. The personal service included a personal tutor-counsellor system including introductory letters in which the tutor-counsellors introduce themselves to their students, short turn-around times for assignments, and frequent telephone contacts with students. 'The main difference between the treatment of the experimental group and the control group was that the experimental students communicated with one personal tutor integrating administrative, teaching and counselling functions, which normally are separated' (ibid.).

Statistically significant differences were found between the two groups. 'The students in the experimental group had a higher completion rate, they were more active in their studies and completed a larger number of study units and courses during the experimental period' (Rekkedal, 1985: 13). Research at the Open University also indicates the importance of a personal approach to tutor-student interaction. Gibbs and Durbridge (1976), in a report on the use of audio cassettes, explicitly testify to the importance of a personal style.

> Student feedback on Open University courses for example (Durbridge, 1982) suggests that tutors who adopt a friendly, personal approach in their cassette teaching are very highly regarded. Such a style appears to be educationally effective for the way it can evoke the sense of a one-to-one tutorial for many listeners, and appears to draw even the distant student towards active and participative work rather than passive and unthinking listening.
>
> (Durbridge 1984: 99–100)

There is thus evidence testifying to the favourable influence of personal approaches not only to course presentation, as discussed above, but also to tutor–student interaction, whether in writing or recorded on audio cassettes. Undoubtedly the same applies to telephone conversations and other types of non-contiguous interaction.

Whatever organization procedure is applied, there is always a risk that tutoring on the basis of assignments may degenerate into mere matter-of-fact correction and comment without any really personal element. This is a waste of valuable opportunities. It is important, indeed, to be fully 'aware of the potential depersonalization of the individual student and the danger of subordination of the real needs of students to the bureaucratic requirements of the institution' (Roberts 1986: 34) and to counteract this by personal approaches. If personal rapport is established, students are likely to enjoy the learning more and to be more successful than otherwise. Empathy remains a highly desirable distance-educator quality.

COUNSELLING

Counselling has been described as a 'systematic exploration of self and/or environment by a client with the aid of a counsellor to clarify self-understanding and/or environmental alternatives so that behaviour modifications or decisions are made on the basis of greater cognitive and affective understanding' (Maslow, as quoted by Thornton and Mitchell 1978: 2–3).

From the counsellor's point of view, Sewart divides the counselling function into four different groups of tasks: referral (to the proper agency), vocational (career planning), information provision, and coping with students' personal study problems (Sewart 1984: 9–11). For the last-mentioned task, counsellors 'must be close enough to the student to have a thorough knowledge of the student's domestic, work and study circumstances' (ibid., p. 11). Students need support that helps them 'to address problems that are not only practical and organizational but also educational and intellectual' (Kirkwood 1989: 39).

There is much experience to show the importance of counselling services both of the types mentioned and frequently in the form of moral encouragement. Students need information about the paths of study that interest them, where they lead, and what they are like. In many cases they also wish to have access to personal advice both before their study decision and during their studies. The fact that distance students are usually on their own in their study, with the anxiety and problems that they encounter, makes it important for distance-teaching organizations to find ways to offer counselling service. As a rule, students are adults who have a job, social responsibilities, and often a family. A number of everyday circumstances influence their study. Many of them may need help to master difficulties that crop up as a result of their endeavours to combine study with their other commitments. Combinations of study difficulties and personal problems sometimes become so considerable that psychotherapeutic advice is necessary. Few distance-study organizations, unlike many conventional universities, are equipped to deal with difficulties of this kind. However, most try to help their students by counselling of a more general character.

Thus, while counselling in distance education is not immediately concerned with 'problems which are of a serious physical or mental nature . . . , counsellors advise and support students' (rather than 'patients'; Sewart 1984: 8).

Supporting study skills

Helping students to develop effective study skills is one important counselling aim. A number of rules have been worded for what is sometimes called study technique. One rule of this kind tells students to read with pencils in their hands, to underline what seems important, to list key words, etc. This applies on condition that students are deep-level readers (see pp. 34–6); it is evident that it makes no sense to someone concentrating on the superficial characteristics of the text and on memorizing its words rather than understanding the message.

The general rules that are frequently given about hygienic conditions for learning, for example requirements for sufficient sleep and exercise, healthy food, and fresh air, as well as reasonably undisturbed study (not too much noise, say) are uncontroversial. This also applies to the well-known suggestions about planning self-checking procedures and short breaks during spells of study.

But what about repetition and over-learning? Have we reason to fear that stressing deep learning and problem-solving may lead to neglect of the learning of facts? As mentioned on p. 36 it has been argued that, when students' retention of facts is weak, the sacrifice should be considered small as long as they understand and can apply principles. This, as shown on pp. 60–1, is a questionable conclusion. The two approaches can well be combined with each other.

It is far from easy to lay down universally applicable principles for the teaching of learning strategies and study skills, particularly as these appear to depend to a considerable extent on personal idiosyncrasies. Nevertheless, it seems safe to include in counselling activities the following recommendations:

1 Inspire deep-learning strategies by suitable types of testing, as students' choice of learning strategy has been found to be influenced by what is expected of them in examinations.
2 Direct students' attention to both the subsumability of new concepts under wider concepts already known and to the

interrelationships of concepts; cause students to practise subsuming and interrelating (see p. 33).

3 Use approaches conducive to problem-oriented learning (see pp. 23 and 35).

4 Apply teaching methods that support individual study and students' own responsibility (see pp. 44 and 71–5).

5 Present learning matter (see pp. 93–5) lucidly and in a thought-provoking way.

6 Encourage activity including internalized conversations, interaction with study material and with tutors along the lines of guided didactic conversation (see pp. 47–50 and 125–7).

Organizing counselling

The British Open University and the Australian 'dual-mode' institutions, such as the University of New England, have, among others, well-known and evidently successful counselling services.

The Open University counselling is characterized by 'continuity of concern for students' (Sewart) and integrates counselling and tutoring in this concern. During the early stage of their degree studies, students benefit from the support of so-called tutor-counsellors who unite the roles of tutor and counsellor and look after a group of individual students assigned to them. Cf. Rekkedal (1985), as discussed on pp. 126–7.

These tutor-counsellors do not wait for students to ask for help but themselves approach those who seems to have difficulties or do not submit assignments for correction and comment. The importance of continuous support of this kind for students' satisfaction and for completion rates has been forcefully stressed by Sewart (1981). See also Sewart (1984); Coltman (1984); Paine (1984).

There are, however, different views of how counsellors should work. Simpson (1977) identifies two clearly recognizable approaches, the GP approach and the interventionist approach.

The 'GP' counsellor operates on the surgery principle. Having established initial contact . . . he or she assumes by and large that if problems arise the student will contact him or her. It is assumed that students do not wish to be contacted by the counsellor unless there is some very good reason. The 'interventionist' tends to initiate rather more contact with students'.

(Simpson 1977: 61)

Simpson's description applies to counselling at higher levels of university study at the Open University in the UK. The German tradition as represented by the FernUniversität favours the GP approach at all levels of university study (which in my opinion has contributed to very high German drop-out rates). See Thorpe (1988: 97) and on an underlying ideological issue p. 170 below.

Methods and media for counselling

Counselling is usually provided by correspondence, on the telephone and, where possible, face to face. The telephone plays a particularly important part in counselling at a distance. Proper advice must be based on knowledge not only of study paths and study methods but also of students' prerequisites, their formal and informal but real qualifications, and their hopes and wishes. Thus there is normally a written element in such counselling, even in the cases where students and counsellors communicate orally.

A very simple, frequently used form of counselling that has proved to be of great importance is sending encouraging letters to those students who have not submitted papers for a period or who have otherwise deviated from their plan of study (Rekkedal 1972b). Such letters both express concern and ask pertinent questions.

The computer is also used in counselling. An application of this kind is to be found in a pre-study advisory system developed at the FernUniversität in Germany. In connection with an informative booklet, a number of questions are asked. The foreseen replies to these, in their various configurations, are commented on by computer through the automatic selection and use of pre-programmed text modules (Fritsch, Küffner, and Schuch 1979).

In fact, counselling presentations in print, which inform would-be students (making them realize what their study situation, requirements, benefits, advantages, and problems are likely to be, if and when they register), have proved to be very valuable. There is much experience testifying to this in all parts of the world.

'Based on the assumption that students will take responsibility for self-counselling', such a presentation 'provides "a structure, a technique which enables a student to engage in that process" (Moran and Croker 1981)' (Coltman 1984: 47, commenting on the Deakin University counselling package). Counselling by correspondence based on printed materials has been subjected to an illuminating study by Gaskel, Gibbons and Simpson (1990).

Offering students facilities to contact fellow-students through membership of associations (Qvist-Eriksen 1986), students' journals, or in other ways may be part of counselling. On a student-operated support network, see Williams and Williams (1987).

Whichever medium is applied, counselling must evidently 'promote a sense of close rapport between the student and the counsellor'. The latter 'needs to demonstrate empathy' and 'be sensitive to the needs, spoken or unspoken, of the student' (Thornton and Mitchell 1978: 23). These requirements are fully compatible with the personal approaches advocated on the basis of theory and empirical evidence for course development (see pp. 45–55) and tutor–student interaction (see pp. 125–7). Thornton and Mitchell further stress that

> the counsellor in his relation with the student should try to work himself out of, rather than into, a job, by promoting and encouraging student self-help. The student will become increasingly more confident about seeking and finding his own answers and solutions to problems and less dependent on the counsellor.
>
> (ibid.)

The processes and outcomes of counselling in distance education have been studied in a way helpful to practitioners by Thorpe (1988), who looks into a number of case studies.

7

THE ORGANIZATION AND ADMINISTRATION OF DISTANCE EDUCATION

Distance education as a private arrangement between a student and a tutor is possible and occurs occasionally. In most cases known, however, there is an organization responsible for the teaching and a student body making use of its services. Following Delling I have referred to the former as a supporting organization. This reflects a view of teaching as facilitating learning (see the synonym 'facilitating institute' used by Mitchell 1975). The facilitation includes a great number of tasks, such as information about study paths and study opportunities, pre-enrolment counselling, instructive and advisory interaction with students, provision of learning materials and other activities that help students to learn and reach their goals. Work of this kind requires an organization co-ordinating the work of various specialists and administration of the processes necessary and desirable.

SERVICES REQUIRED

The services that are required in practically all distance-teaching organizations are as follows:

1 The development and technical production (or, possibly, the selection and purchase) of printed courses for distance study and supplementary media; the development work requires special facilities for editing, visualizing, audio recording, and for the work of project leaders, editors etc.
2 Warehousing.

3 The distribution of course materials.
4 Mediated tutorial interaction between students and tutors.
5 Information and publicity about study opportunities offered.
6 Counselling.
7 Course evaluation.

See Öster, who at an early stage defined distance-education administration as 'service to students and care of students (tutorial advice service before and during the course of studies, handling and despatching of submitted solutions, direction of the course of studies by means of timetables, etc.)' (Öster 1965: 71).

In many cases, services are also required for one or more of the following activities:

1 Library services.
2 Video recording.
3 Laboratory work for developing prototypes of experimental kits.
4 Supplementary face-to-face contacts between students and tutors/counsellors.
5 Student-to-student contact.
6 Awarding scholarships and administering financial support of students.
7 Issuing course certificates.
8 Administration of examinations and degrees.
9 Institutional research (systems evaluation) and general research into the conditions and methodology of distance education.

ADMINISTERING COURSE DEVELOPMENT

The development of course materials requires an establishment that is a combination of a research institute and a publisher's editorial office, providing facilities for course developers to work with various media. The organization can, but need not, include faculties of specialist course authors. Such specialists can also be engaged externally. Further, the technical production of print, audio-tapes or cassettes, films, etc. can be provided for by external bodies.

The internal organization for course development can thus be limited to an editorial body with educational subject-based and

134

technical expertise that enables it to develop courses and to control and administer co-operation with external organizations.

Different types of organization occur for course development. The simplest consists of a subject specialist as author and an editor. A large course team for each course with authors, other subject specialists, media specialists (for print, radio, television, etc.), artists, editors, etc., constitutes a different approach. This latter type of organization is advantageous in providing for the best expertise available for all of the various tasks involved. See Walter Perry on the beginnings of the Open University course teams:

> To produce the drafts on the various 'course materials' that would enable an adult, working in isolation, to reach a predetermined standard of performance in a given area of study, called for the combined skills of a number of groups of people. First we had to have not just one university teacher, with his thoughts and ideas about the objectives, contents and methods of presentation of the course, but several, because our courses were to be multi-disciplinary as well as multimedia in nature. This, in turn, meant that each teacher would have different and inevitably conflicting thoughts and ideas which would somehow have to be re-conciled with each other to lead to an agreed final version. Second, since the university teachers that we could recruit would mostly be unfamiliar with the special problems both of educating adults and of teaching at a distance, we would need the advice of other experts, in particular educational technologists and television and radio producers, in order to determine the method of presentation of the course.
>
> (Walter Perry 1976: 77)

This course-team model has been very influential. Its main advantage is that the various tasks are divided between a group of highly specialized team members, among them subject specialists, specialists on instructional design, media, technical production etc. and editors. The professional standard can then be very high. The drawbacks of the course-team model are that it may impede personal approaches and may tend towards knowledge being presented more as a finished product than as a complex of problems under development (Weingartz 1980: 167–9).

Distance-teaching organizations which cannot or do not want

to work with course teams usually support their course writers by the services of an editor with experience of distance education. Sometimes an outstanding subject specialist is asked to write a draft only from which an editor produces a course. Some organizations entrust practically all course development to subject specialists. The University of Waterloo in Ontario can be mentioned as an example (Seaborne and Zuckernick 1986).

The co-operation between authors and editors varies with the organizations concerned and the individuals engaged. There are reasons based on experiences to describe the co-operation as particularly profitable when author and editor work together from the very beginning. In such cases they plan the course together, exchange drafts of objectives, items of contents, and plans for sequencing. When they have agreed on this, the author develops a preliminary draft of one or part of one unit at a time, on which the editor comments and suggests improvement. This leads to detailed discussions between the two before any attempt is made to create the version to be produced. The motto here is constant contact between author and editor, perhaps almost daily telephone contact between meetings and exchanges of drafts and emendations.

In a paper about course development procedures, Kevin Smith classifies the approaches to course development 'into five broad categories' (Smith 1980: 61)

1 The course team model.
2 The author/editor model.
3 The author/faculty model.
4 The educational adviser model.
5 The intuition model.

The 'author/faculty model' which is to my mind just a variety of the author/editor model, is said to be unique to the FernUniversität and is characterized by outside experts being 'contracted to write the courses but the material is vetted by the full-time faculty of the University' (Smith 1980: 65). Also, the so-called educational adviser model seems to be a kind of author/editor approach. Smith has in mind the practices of Murdoch University and the Darling Down Institute of Advanced Education in Australia. They include the use of educational advisers whose services are advisory only, which means that 'each author is the final arbiter of content, standards and format' (Smith 1980: 66). The 'intuition model', on the other hand, is based on no other principle than letting the work be guided by academic intuition rather than systematic procedures. On the whole we thus seem to be entitled to distinguish between two separate approaches, the author/editor model and the course-team model.

The author/editor model has the advantages that a personal tone and suggestions for problem-solving come naturally to the presentation as one person guides his/her students through a kind of mediated conversation. The weakness of this model is that, at least in a small organization, the author and editor may not have sufficient specialist support available for all of the course development tasks. They can usually have recourse to external advisers, however, which can compensate for lacking support within the organization.

Neither the advantages nor the disadvantages of the two models are inevitable corollaries, however. Awareness of the potentials and dangers of the models can overcome the weakness of both of them, whereas lack of such awareness may make both models weak. In reality there are several intermediaries between them. If the course author does not work completely alone, the difference between the author/editor model and the course-team model is often more a difference of degree than of character. Nevertheless, important principles are involved.

The choice between the two models is related to a large-scale and a small-scale approach and to the discussion about distance education as an industrialized type of teaching and learning. See pp. 7 and 16, where Peters' approach, relevant to this, is discussed. In both models there are, to different degrees, elements of industrialization, for instance, division of labour, mechanization through the use of modern technical equipment, and quality control. Mass production may also be a characteristic of both models. The aspect of industrialization in course development has been studied by Kaufman (1982). The person-to-person approach, the style of didactic conversation, can also be provided for in both models. As always in education there is no categorical reply to the question of which is the best procedure; it all depends . . .

The present writer's favourite model is this: one course author is made ultimately responsible for the course development after decisions have been made about target group, broad aims, and contents. The author addresses the students in a personal style reflecting his or her approaches and values. The course author is supported by editors for written and recorded, radio and television presentations, by advisers who may be educational technologists, subject and media specialists, by illustrators, print, and other production specialists, etc. While benefiting from the co-operation of all of these, the author consistently writes for (and may speak to) the students in his or her own way. Only those authors who are capable of establishing a personal rapport with students by means of their presentation (the simulated, mediated conversation), and who are reliable subject specialists can be made the final arbiters of what a course should eventually be like. The influence of others (editors, course co-ordinators, designers, or whatever they may be called) will have to vary with the experience, knowledge, and empathy of the authors.

An Australian study by David Ross of project management in the development of courses is worth mentioning in the present context (Ross 1991).

DISTRIBUTION OF COURSE MATERIALS

Course units and other learning materials for distribution to students are handled in practice in three basically different ways.

A few distance-teaching organizations send packages containing complete courses at the beginning of the study. This is usually felt to be a questionable procedure, as many students are likely to be intimidated by the large quantity of learning material to be worked through. It is also bad economy, as even modest drop-out rates lead to smaller editions of later units being required if course materials are distributed in batches along with students' progress.

A much more common practice is to send study material on pre-determined dates. However, sending course units without paying attention to individual students' needs seems to be counter-productive; such a great number of course units may then be amassed on the desk of a slow-working student that the person feels frustrated and may be discouraged. Students in this position have complained that they have felt it to be hopeless to tackle the course as they have been intimidated by 'the mountain of course material' in front of them (a FernUniversität evaluation; Bartels and Fritsch 1976: 62). See also Graff *et al.* (1977: 21). The rigidity on which such pre-planned distribution is based is usually due to a firm desire to make students conform to a time schedule. It may also reflect lack of imagination, i.e. failure to realize what students' work situations may be like when they have to combine study with professional, social, and family commitments.

A third way is to adapt the distribution of course materials to what is desirable from the points of view of motivation support and the non-contiguous two-way communication. Proper adaptation to the conditions of distance students makes it desirable that course units should be distributed in relation to the individual study pace of each student. One way of doing this, which has proved valuable, is to provide the student at the outset with a small number of (say three) units of each course enrolled in and then to send out a new unit with each assignment that is returned with corrections and comments. Having initially received three course units, the student can work on unit 2 when unit 1 has been submitted to the supporting organization for correction and comment. Unit 3 acts as a buffer in case the student works so quickly that unit 1 has not been returned when unit 2 is submitted. With the return of the first assignment, unit 4 arrives. This system works well if it is possible for students who work fast to receive more units on request.

ADMINISTRATION OF STUDENT–TUTOR INTERACTION

There are a number of different aspects of communication between the students and the supporting organization that influence the administrative procedures. Thus pre-registration counselling and routine correspondence with potential students requesting factual information require effective organization, and so do counselling and other correspondence with enrolled students and would-be students. Correction of and comment on students' papers must be organized so that the right tutor receives without delay the right students' papers and any necessary background information. Procedures are necessary for application and enrolment, registration and statistics. Warehouse and dispatch arrangements have to be made for the course materials, and quick turn-round must be provided for all communication with the students.

As made clear on pp. 122–5, speed is a high-priority concerns for the administration of tutor–student interaction. Thus it is important to arrange record-keeping and distribution in such a way that it causes no delay in the communication process. The relevance of this is evident from the fact that most distance-education institutions apparently use the services of external tutors to whom students' assignments are submitted.

This is how Renée Erdos described the administrative procedure in the 1960s when the work was still usually done manually:

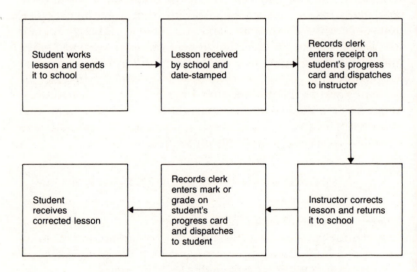

Figure 7 Movement of a correspondence lesson
Source: Erdos 1967: 26

While with the almost universal use of the computer this description is out of date, the tasks to be carried out remain. Students' papers, assignment solutions or other communications may arrive by post, by telefax or by electronic mail, tutors may comment on them in writing, using the post, the fax or electronic mail when forwarding them with marks to the administration of the supporting organization and returning them to students. The whole administrative work is usually computerized today.

The computer has, indeed, proved a very useful and economical instrument for both the distribution of course material and the handling of students' assignments, inclusive of record-keeping. There is a danger inherent in its use, however. Some administrators tend to adapt the system to the computer instead of developing computer programs that cater for what is educationally desirable. Valuable computer systems have been developed for the administration of distance education; one pioneering model description occurs in Merup (1968). Computers can, above all, provide (without mistakes) individual dispatch of study material and perfect record-keeping for several different purposes simultaneously, at very high speed, and at very low cost. The Merup study describes a large-scale application of such computerized administration of distance education with particular emphasis on the communication element.

The use of the computer may lead to depersonalized service which makes students feel that they interact with an institution or authority rather than with human beings. The computer is a versatile instrument, however, which can instead be used to bring about feelings of personal contact with tutors, counsellors and others representing the supporting organization. It is important that the empathy approach characterizes also the administrative parts of the distance-education processes.

TYPES OF ORGANIZATION

The type of the organizations offering distance-education facilities varies with cultural and social contexts, with national and other traditions as well as with the target groups and educational levels of study. It is possible to identify four prototypes as follows:

1 Single-mode universities and schools.
2 Dual-mode universities and schools.
3 Specialized service organizations.
4 Networks.

(1) Single-mode universities and schools committed to the special purpose of providing distance education

The single-mode organizations employ their own academic and administrative staff to take responsibility for (develop or vet) printed courses, audio and video tapes and/or radio and television programmes, kits for laboratory work, and other study materials. They organize and provide advisory and didactic mediated two-way communication with their students as well as some supplementary face-to-face tuition. Counselling, examining, issuing certificates, running research projects, etc. are other concerns for these organizations. For their course development, tutoring and counselling, special organization units have been set up. Procedures conducive to the administration of distance education have been developed.

(2) Dual-mode universities and schools offering distance education as well as on-campus study

Well-known examples are extension departments of universities, which provide distance study opportunities for their own extramural and on-campus students. The distance-education departments of dual-mode organizations rarely have their own teaching staff. Usually no attempt is made to cover whole countries or to cater for large populations. This implies, on the one hand, small-scale course development with modest resources for pre-producing study material and, on the other hand, far-reaching parallelism with residential study.

See White (1982) and the presentation of the Australian University of New England model on pp. 7 and 202–3.

(3) Specialized service organizations

Examples of service organizations are correspondence schools with expertise in distance-education methodology and administration which administer distance education on behalf of universities or other bodies awarding degrees or examination certificates. These organizations, while drawing on freelance expertise, provide editorial services, development of printed courses and other media, they organize and run tutorial and counselling services, and take responsibility for warehousing, distribution and all administration. Usually they also evaluate their own work as part of the development process (formative evaluation).

When the possible founding of a distance-teaching university or school is discussed, co-operation with or setting up such a service organization may be an alternative as it is much less costly than creating a full distance-teaching university or school with academics representing each discipline.

(4) Networks

Networking bodies, the fourth type, co-ordinate and supplement the course offer of other distance-education organizations. Norsk Fjernundervisning in Norway and Deutsches Institut für Fernstudien at Tübingen University in Germany are cases in point. The latter is a somewhat special kind of network. It has developed courses for use by other organizations, and runs a department for distance-education research as well as a documentation centre. This institute in the summer of 1993 changed its name to Deutsches Institut für Fernstudienforschung (The German Institute for Distance-Education Research).

Contributions to an organizational typology are presented in Keegan (1990). A remarkable classification based on educational criteria has been developed by Schuemer (1988). It is an empirical study which, in a statistically manageable way, identifies a student-friendliness concept including the recognition of the importance of student–tutor interaction and the need for student support, a further flexibility concept (regarding individual choices of submission frequency vs. imposed pacing, e.g.), an autonomy concept, the place (use and role) of supplementary face-to-face sessions and similar characteristics. This results in a classification of distance-education organizations in six fairly homogeneous groups listed with relevant data.

THE STUDY OF DISTANCE-EDUCATION ORGANIZATION AND ADMINISTRATION

The principles and practice of distance-education administration have been investigated by several authors. The management of distance education, in practical terms and against the background of basic theoretical approaches, is a concern discussed in Graff

(1981) One of the earliest and still most important contributions to the administration of distance education is Öster (1965). This paper was ably supplemented, as regards the application of computer methods, by Merup (1968), also still of relevance. They both based their analyses on the practice of a very large and prestigious correspondence school with courses from university level to elementary stages, with professional and occupational training, etc.

A model for distance-study institutions in developing countries has been developed by Erdos (1975a), who, as shown above, has also elaborated her theoretical bases in the form of a systems presentation (Erdos 1975b). The organization of small private correspondence schools has been discussed by A. F. Saxe (1965), and the management of public, small distance-education systems is investigated by Snowden and Daniel (1980).

Among later studies, strongly influenced by the work of distance-teaching universities, is Kaye and Rumble (1981: 13). They identify two key features:

1 A *courses subsystem*, concerned with the creation, production and distribution of learning materials.
2 A *student subsystem* concerned with enrolment, support and assessment of distance students, and their learning needs.

Keegan (1986) develops this further:

> The *course development sub-system* comprises the planning, designing, crystallizing and recording of the teaching (together with the proposed methodologies and structures for presenting the teaching at a future date) in mechanical or electronic form. The *student support sub-system* comprises the activities designed by the institution to focus on the student's home (or institutional centre near the student's home) that will provide a private and individualized presentation of the pre-recorded course content together with the stimulation of teacher and peer-group clarification, analysis, motivation and non-verbal atmosphere that normally accompany the presentation of the course in oral, group-based educational provision.
>
> (Keegan 1986: 197)

Rumble (1986) describes this approach as 'rather technocratic' (p. 17) and compares it with a 'holistic model' of Perraton's

144

(1981) and a 'transactional model' developed by Henri and Kaye (1985). Why Keegan's systems model is not called holistic, whereas Perraton's is, seems to be because the latter starts out from more comprehensive, external, social requirements, whereas the former's system is limited to specific distance-education concerns. The transactional model views distance education from the different perspectives of its principal agents.

At the time of writing, Rumble (1986 and 1992) are the most comprehensive and best documented presentations available of distance-education administration. Economic and political perspectives are given due prominence and the organization, staffing, planning, budgeting, management, and evaluation of distance education are thoroughly and competently discussed. Institution-centred, person-centred, and society-centred organizations are studied in this monograph.

Interesting presentations of the operative aspects of distance education from Latin American points of view are to be found in Villarroel (1987). They include, but are not limited to, organizational and administrative concerns as to tutoring, course production, media use, student assessment, and course evaluation.

An administrative function of particular importance to distance study at the university level and to project work generally (see p. 72) concerns library facilities, on which some important studies have been published (Brockman and Klobas (1983); Winter and Cameron 1983).

8

SPECIAL APPLICATIONS OF DISTANCE EDUCATION

Distance education as usually applied and thus described in the preceding chapters is aimed at individual students in developed parts of the world who are mainly working in the privacy of their homes, in libraries, or in rooms made available in clubs or places of work. However, there are other types of application of distance education: those in which students are continuously supported by advisers to tutors present with them for much of the time of the learning, and those where students work under primitive conditions. Some applications of special interest will be discussed here.

SUPERVISED DISTANCE STUDY FOR YOUNG PEOPLE

Supervised distance study occurs in schools in sparsely inhabited areas or where there is a lack of qualified teachers. Usually one teacher/supervisor looks after a number of young people undertaking distance study of various subjects at varying levels. Supervised distance study also occurs as entirely individual study when isolated children are taught by distance methods at home, usually with one of the parents as supervisor. Most supervised distance study of the former kind is concerned with secondary education; Australia in particular has much experience of primary distance education of isolated children.

What has been said above about methods and media is largely applicable to supervised distance education. Although the term 'supervised correspondence study' may still be more common than 'supervised distance study', written communication seems to be less dominant here than in other types of distance education. This is mostly because of the face-to-face support inherent

146

in this type. Further, for many years radio has been a most important communication means in primary education of this kind, both for one-way traffic and for two-way communication (see McGuire (1973) and Fitzpatrick (1982) on Australia's schools of the air). Electronic mail will, of course, be of great importance to supervised distance education of any kind. Taylor and Tomlinson hold that it could even 'signal a new approach to primary distance education' by involving 'the distance education teacher more closely with the isolated child' (Taylor and Tomlinson 1985: iv). See also Vivian (1986).

Obviously, it is extremely difficult fully to describe the practice of supervised primary distance education and the roles of the supervisors in the many individual families where this type of education occurs. Harley (1985) argues in favour of the home as an effective learning environment for children at the primary level. Although there is also much variation in the practice of supervised secondary distance education in classrooms, typically the greater part of each pupil's day at school is devoted to individual learning. This involves reading correspondence courses, consulting reference books, doing exercises, and doing assignments (solving problems, writing essays, etc.), which are to be sent to the distance-teaching organization for correction and comment. The exercises may be done either in writing or, following the instructions of the distance course, by listening in little booths to recordings and/or by the pupil likewise recording his or her own pronunciation in foreign languages. If a pupil doing individual work feels uncertain, he or she consults the supervisor. In addition to individual work, the pupils work in groups. While individual work is done in the classroom, where the relative silence of a library is observed, there are usually special group rooms. The pupils are also given some tuition orally in the traditional way by the supervisor, normally in a group of about five pupils at a time in a group room. The division of pupils into groups is based on what they have in common in their individual learning. They may, to some extent, read different things depending on what choice of subjects they have made, they represent different stages and age groups, and they invariably work at different speeds. The Australian so-called hub class is an interesting, evidently valuable further development. 'In the hub class approach to distance education a classroom teacher has, in addition, other students linked to the class by a telephone link' (C. J. Dawson 1985: 3). See also Dunnett (1985).

The supervisors' task is to help their pupils in every conceivable way. It is up to them to motivate their pupils and keep them aware of their goals. Completion of each course unit marks the reaching of one goal. If some pupils find it difficult to follow the exposition of the pre-produced course, the supervisor explains it to them, either individually or in groups. Sometimes pupils hesitate over what conclusions to draw from corrections when their assignments are returned from the distance-teaching organization with a specialist-teacher's comments. Here again the supervisor must provide the necessary explanations. The supervisor also has important administrative tasks. He or she must organize the work, which makes it necessary to keep in close contact with not only the individual learners but also the distance-teaching organization. The local timetable must be planned; as must the use of auxiliaries (such as tape-recorders, projectors, and demonstration material) and the arrangements for tests and for record-keeping. Unavoidably, the supervisor must also do some teaching of a more traditional kind because there are things that youngsters usually cannot learn entirely by distance methods, such as pronunciation in foreign languages. Laboratory exercises also require active teaching.

As it is impossible for one supervisor to acquire teaching competence in all of the subjects being learned by the pupils, the advisory and supporting roles are more important than the purely teaching roles. Nevertheless, specific training is required for the types of teaching that the supervisors are expected to give. This is particularly tricky as far as foreign languages are concerned, but it is a problem that can be solved in countries where the choice of foreign languages is limited. In Sweden, where schools insist on reasonable accuracy in English and basic knowlege of at least one other language (German or French), the methods of supervised distance education have proved to be successful also for the acquisition of linguistic proficiency. This is, of course, the result of much attention being paid to language learning, to the training of supervisors, and to consistent use of phonetic transcriptions and recordings.

All this necessarily means that the distance-teaching organizations running supervised distance-study schemes in schools have very special tasks. They include the development of suitable

courses in writing and by other media, the non-contiguous tutoring of the individual pupils, the training and continuous support
of the supervisors, and regular contacts with the local schools.
Although much can be done by telephone, fairly frequent visits
to the schools where supervised distance study is carried out
seem to be unavoidable.

Much experience has been gained of supervised distance education and some of it has been duly documented. On work done
in this area in Australia, see Rayner (1949); Taylor and Tomlinson
(1985); Tomlinson *et al.* (1985); in North America, see Mitchell
(1962); Childs (1953); Woodley (1986a); in Israel, see Weissbrot
(1969); in Sweden, see Holmberg (1973a).

DISTANCE EDUCATION IN PERSONNEL TRAINING: STAFF DEVELOPMENT

Supervised distance education is frequently applied to personnel
training. As a rule a distance-teaching school provides pre-produced courses and non-contiguous tutorial service, whereas the
company or professional body concerned offers face-to-face support, classes, laboratory or workshop exercises, personal counselling, and other kinds of on-site service. Many traditional
correspondence schools devote much of their work to this kind of
training and provide advice to the training officers of companies,
organizations, and authorities on the planning and carrying out
of personnel training projects. Military units also make use of
this kind of service (B. Saxe 1965); some correspondence schools
attached to the armed forces of individual nations are also known
(such as the United States Armed Forces Institute and Forsvarets
Brevskole in Norway).

However, distance education of a more individualized type is
also applied in personnel training and staff development. Thus
the Centre for Medical Education of the University of Dundee
in Scotland runs distance-learning programmes for hospital staff,
for instance one on palliation in advanced cancer. It is 'interactive and includes personalised feedback from experts in palli-
ative care' (from University of Dundee pamphlet). Doctors and
others active in the health-care professions are also offered a
distance-education training programme for a diploma in medical
education and a master's degree programme.

There are distance-teaching organizations that (almost)

149

exclusively serve personnel training in companies. In these cases contracts are made with the companies, not with individual students. An organization of special interest in this context is the Universidad La Salle de Sud América (ULSA) in Argentina, which serves twenty-two Spanish-speaking countries. The non-contiguous tutorial work is done in the central office in Buenos Aires, which insists on a remarkably short turn-around time; every assignment submitted is returned with corrections and full comments within 24 hours of its arrival. Resident directors are in charge of contacts with the client companies in the various Latin American countries. Counselling and study support are offered locally on the basis of agreements between ULSA and the companies concerned (Milanesi 1978).

Sometimes distance education is combined with so-called sandwich courses, i.e. introductory face-to-face courses at the beginning of the study and face-to-face summing up courses after individual study of distance courses, during which students have benefited from non-contiguous tutoring (assignment submission, correction, and comment). An example of this type of training is a course 'Resurs' in personnel management, organization, and rationalization for the various categories of staff in Swedish hospitals, which were studied by several thousand people in the early 1970s. It was a correspondence course of 14 study units with assignments for submission, preceded and followed by two three-day seminars. This distance-education programme was introduced with a view both to reducing costs and to raising the quality of the training. Not only was the first aim reached, but the course output also proved highly satisfactory. It was judged by those in charge of the hospital personnel training to be superior to a previous training programme. Explicit mention of direct practical applications of what had been learnt was made in connection with the evaluation of the course (Staaf 1973: 28 and appendix: 7).

In other cases, similar approaches are applied to the use of distance courses at the same time as face-to-face sessions are inserted into the individual study of the distance courses, sometimes in the form of weekend courses once a month or once every two months. Other variations also occur.

Uppsala University in Sweden trains teachers for nursing, care of old people and allied subjects using printed material, correspondence, telephone contacts and short residential courses. This has proved a successful training attractive to students (Hellkvist 1981 and 1982, Kjellman 1985).

A number of comprehensive, rather sophisticated staff-development programmes occur in various parts of the world. One such is the Swedish so-called Delta project mentioned on p. 102 (Hermods and the Swedish Broadcasting Corporation). This was a training programme for teachers for mathematics in the so-called new maths. It ran from 1969 to 1971 and was used by about 50,000 teachers. It consisted of a correspondence course with assignments for submission (evaluated mechanically), radio and television (alternatively audio- and video-recorded programmes), and group work. The groups consisted of the teachers involved in the training in individual schools and their meetings were usually held in the staff rooms. The result of this training was deemed to be satisfactory by both the National Board of Education and the students. There was a drop-out rate of slightly under 30 per cent and it was a very economical training programme.

A British (University of Surrey) small-scale programme for staff development, aimed at university lecturers in Southern Asia, illuminates a further special application of distance education. The purpose is

> to provide training opportunities for academic staff who wish to acquire a more professional orientation towards their function as teachers. The course is provided entirely at a distance and leads to a Diploma and MSc with the possibility of continuation to MPhil/PhD.
>
> (Elton *et al.* 1986: 29)

The course consists of both compulsory and optional modules, it includes a fairly comprehensive project on a theme chosen by the individual course participants, and there is a strong element of interaction in the form of correspondence between tutors and students. There is consistent individualization, as the aim is to make 'the course particular for each member' (op. cit. p. 31). This is brought about by assignments which induce students 'to relate the general to their particular experience' (op. cit. p. 30). In this way each student strongly influences the content of the study; cf. pp. 15 and 168. In spite of this individualization, the cost 'is less than one-third of the cost for an equivalent full-time course' (op. cit. p. 35). It is particularly interesting to see that

151

the ratio of fixed and proportional costs is about 1:3, i.e. the opposite of the balance found at the large distance-teaching universities, for whose costs economies of scale are decisive (see p. 203).

On German experiences see Kammerer-Jöbges (1992) and Schwalbe and Zander 1984.

COMBINATIONS OF DISTANCE AND FACE-TO-FACE TUTORING

There are numerous examples of other arrangements including both distance and face-to-face elements other than those mentioned. Some occur as guided study arranged by schools, colleges, or other bodies on the basis of courses provided by distance-teaching organizations. The West German Funkkollegs, combining radio programmes, correspondence texts, and group work, represent one application of this kind. Basically the same approach is applied in a number of British so-called flexistudy programmes.

The 'Open Tech Programme' in the UK, adopted by the Manpower Services Commission (now called The Training Agency) for personnel training, can be mentioned in this context. In the last issue (February 1987) of a newsletter called *Open Tech News* were published the results of two surveys of the experiences resulting from the use of distance-study courses. From the first, a 'readership survey', here are three illuminating quotations:

> The main reason given for choosing open learning was work commitments, or the difficulty of releasing staff for college courses with set timetables. Several users said that there was no suitable college course available, and that open learning offered more relevant training.
>
> There was a fairly even split between people studying at home, at work or in a college or training centre.
>
> There was no 'favourite' time for study – users studied during the daytime, evenings and weekends (showing open learning to be flexible!).
>
> (*Open Tech News* 13: 3)

The second survey, undertaken by an evaluation branch of the Manpower Services Commission, showed among other things that only six per cent of the respondents who trained to improve their promotion prospects felt that they were not satisfied. Reasons for using open learning included updating/acquiring skills, improved job performance, to gain a better job, or being encouraged by an employer to train.

(op. cit. p. 6)

In some of the combined programmes the distance-learning element dominates, in others face-to-face tutorials or group work dominate. The well-known Scandinavian study circles to some extent use combinations of distance and group learning. The groups concerned may, or may not, engage a subject specialist as a tutor to help them. Great numbers of other mixed-method applications occur. Among new developments towards the end of the 1980s should be mentioned the British Open College.

The term 'fleximode' refers to flexible arrangements not only for individual (often self-paced) learning based on pre-produced course materials but also for teacher-contact time and the use of resources (Ashhurst 1985). Administrative and financial concerns related to fleximode and its use of computers have been studied by Bowles (1987).

DISTANCE EDUCATION IN DEVELOPING COUNTRIES

In principle, distance education as described and discussed in the preceding chapters may be applied not only in the developed part of the world but also in developing and underdeveloped regions. However, the most common needs, the distribution problems, and the possibilities for using technology are different. See Young *et al* (1980); Ansere (1978, 1982).

In most developing countries, literacy programmes are needed for large numbers of people who, as children, had little or no formal schooling. Some forms of distance education can be applied in these programmes, for example instruction on audio cassettes (if available) on how to work with simple printed materials. However, literacy programmes primarily benefit from distance education in that adult educators are trained at a distance.

The further training of men and women who are active as teachers of young people and who themselves have little formal educational background is another field of activity that is typical of distance education in developing countries, where the need for teachers is usually much greater than the availability.

Health education and family planning are other needs for which distance education is mainly applied to the training of supporting staff rather than those with poor health or too frequent pregnancies. It is not unknown for paramedics successfully to undertake urgent, quite advanced surgical measures, to give injections, and to prescribe medicine, besides their advisory tasks concerned with child care, breast feeding, nutrition, and looking after the infirm, as well as teaching contraceptive methods. Their training is successfully updated by distance education. Basic training in business administration and technology, for example for the needs of producer and/or consumer co-operative societies, is yet another application of distance education in developing countries. Much experience of activities of the kinds so far mentioned has been gained in East Africa (Holmberg 1985b), other parts of Africa, Asia, and Latin America.

Rural development and various kinds of occupational training are often served by distance-education methods. Higher education is a concern of distance education in some developing countries, such as India (Singh 1979; Khoul and Jenkins 1990); likewise secondary education.

Reference to sophisticated 'schools of the air' and television series combined with classes are quite common in discussions of adult education in developing countries. They do occur, and have been known to make essential contributions to education (Young *et al.* 1980: 48ff.), but represent only a modest part of the educational situation in Africa and other developing regions. Distance education in these areas can make little use of sophisticated media. Lack of resources strictly limits the number of methods and media available to distance education. Conventional correspondence study, relying entirely on the written word, has proved its mettle, however, and serves those for whom reading and writing constitute no problems excellently. A problem that occurs is scarcity of light for reading after daylight hours.

Inexpensive and frequently applicable media that can support correspondence study are broadcasts and audio recordings. However, radio receivers and cassette players are often expensive in developing countries, in relation to not only average wages or salaries but also North American and European prices. Lack of batteries, which may for long periods be irreplaceable, sometimes prevents the use of these media for oral presentations. Nevertheless, radio broadcasting is a potentially effective and inexpensive medium that lends itself to supporting pure correspondence study, not only in developing countries (Halliwell 1987).

Postal services are unreliable and irregular in some areas of Africa and Latin America, which is a major drawback in correspondence study. Various distribution methods are applied to overcome this difficulty; these very often rely on students walking long distances to centres of distribution.

In spite of all this, distance education functions well in developing countries among both students who are strongly motivated and dedicated and those of more average educational inclinations who are given sufficient support. Group work plays a considerable part in the support services that are offered, particularly in Africa, under the influence of those who not only wish to make individual learning effective but also have an ideological concern with 'Nyere's vision of education as a prerequisite for group action for social development' (Young *et al.* 1980: 61–2) in preference to education for personal advancement. However, it would not be correct to describe African distance education as generally less careerist than its counterparts in Europe, America, Asia, or Australia.

While distance education in developing countries functions under much more difficult circumstances than in the industrialized world and has fewer choices as to methods and media available, it is basically identical with the latter. Printed course materials and student–tutor interaction in writing are the foundations upon which most distance education in the world relies. They have proved to work well.

9

THEORETICAL APPROACHES TO DISTANCE EDUCATION AND THEIR PRACTICAL CONSEQUENCES

Theoretical considerations, whether explicit or implicit, guide actions and procedures applied to education – as will have been shown in the preceding chapters of this book. Writers often refer to theory, but what is really meant is not always evident. Attempts have been made to classify theories into different categories, thus by Royce (1978), who was above all concerned with psychological theory. His contribution has been aptly summarized by Rumble in an interesting scrutiny of explanation, theory and practice as related to distance education (Rumble 1992: 115–16).

The term theory is problematic, indeed. In scholarly literature it is used to denote different concepts. It is frequently used to identify any systematic ordering of ideas about the phenomena of a field of inquiry (Gage 1963: 102) – as sometimes when reference is made to the theory of distance education. This is evidently meant when the disciplinary areas of chairs at, for instance, German universities are described as 'theory of education' or 'theory of the school'. Theories are sometimes, in Royce's terminology, analogical. Examples already discussed in Chapter 2 (p. 19) are Fox's metaphors for four different views of learning (the transfer, shaping, travelling and growing theories). In other scholarly contexts a theory represents a structure of reasoned explanations, for which intersubjective testability is a sine qua non. As shown in the general discussion of the impact of theory on practice in Chapter 2 a theory in this sense may be expressed as a set of hypotheses logically related to one another in explaining and predicting occurrences. Empirical data can – in principle – corroborate, refute or leave unresolved hypotheses of this kind. The normal starting point in a so far unresolved problem, for instance that of the influence of varying frequencies of opportunities for assignment submission (discussed in Chapter 6 p. 123ff.). An hypothesis is formulated. Relevant data are then traced, collected and evaluated to help to solve the problem, i.e. to support or falsify the hypothesis.

Some theoretical approaches aimed at identifying essential characteristics of distance education are well known, including Charles Wedemeyer's liberal, individualizing 'independent study' (see p. 8); Manfred Delling's process model (Delling 1987b; Graff 1970: 44), which may be compared with Kathleen Forsythe's learning system (see pp. 54–5 and 85); Otto Peters' view of distance education as an industrialized form of teaching and learning (see pp. 7 and 16); Michael Moore's theory of independent study, classifying educational programmes on the two dimensions of autonomy and distance (to be considered below); David Sewart's support model, called 'continuity of concern' (see p. 130); and the student-centred, small-scale approach (see pp. 7 and 137).

These and other theoretical analyses illuminate the basic character and varying applications of distance education. Only in part, however, do they meet the well-grounded requirements expressed by Desmond Keegan:

> A theory is something that eventually can be reduced to a phrase, a sentence or a paragraph and which, while subsuming all the practical research, gives the foundation on which the structures of need, purpose and administration can be erected. A firmly based theory of distance education will be one which can provide the touchstone against which decisions – political, financial, educational, social – when they have to be taken, can be taken with confidence. This would replace the ad hoc response to a set of conditions that arises in some 'crisis' situation of problem solving, which normally characterizes this field of education.
>
> (Keegan 1983: 3)

Attempts have been made to meet these tough requirements. As early as 1970, Kurt Graff developed a decision model on the basis of a study of the structure and process of distance education, but concluded that the great problems are beyond calculation (Graff 1970: 54).

Hilary Perraton (1981, 1987) has ventured other suggestions as steps on the path toward a theory of distance education, and so has the present author. See under 'A theory of learning and teaching in distance education' below pp. 172–9.

DISTANCE EDUCATION AS RELATED TO GENERAL THEORIES OF TEACHING AND LEARNING

If we relate the appreciation of what constitutes distance education, as discussed in the preceding chapters, to current teaching and learning theories, we inevitably come to the conclusion that several of those theories are relevant to distance education. John Bååth has made systematic searches in this respect and has analysed the following 'models' with a view to discovering to what extent they are applicable to distance education:

1 Skinner's behaviour-control model.
2 Rothkopf's model for written instruction.
3 Ausubel's organizer model.
4 The model of Structural Communication.
5 Bruner's discovery-learning model.
6 Rogers' model for facilitation of learning.
7 Gagné's general teaching model.

Structural communication, so far not mentioned in this book, is an exceptional type of programmed learning which is unrelated to the behaviourist stimulus-response theory and based on Gestalt thinking. It was originally developed by J. G. Bennett and A. M. Hodgson. This particular type of programmed learning is to all intents and purposes compatible with the problem-solving approaches discussed earlier in this book, whereas the behaviourist school of stimulus-response theory is not (Egan 1976).

Bååth has investigated the general applicability to distance study of each of the approaches listed and has analysed their implications for the development of course material, for non-contiguous two-way communication, and for supplementing this two-way communication by face-to-face contacts. Further, he has analysed some special relations between these various models and distance education.

The following would seem to be an accurate summary of Bååth's study:

- All models investigated are applicable to distance education.
- Some of them (Skinner, Gagné, Ausubel, Structural Communication) seem particularly adaptable to distance education in its fairly strictly structured form.
- Bruner's more open model and even Rogers' model can be applied to distance education, though not without special measures, e.g. concerning simultaneous non-contiguous communication (telephone, etc.).
- Demands on distance-education systems which should inspire new developments can be inferred from the models studied.

(Bååth 1979b)

It is possible to describe some learning theories as more compatible with distance education than others. In this context it is tempting to refer to Nuthall and Snook's rational model with its view of students as 'rational agents' and its creed 'Learning . . . should not be a process to which the student is subjected but an activity which he performs' (Nuthall and Snook 1973: 67), and also to two theoretical works by Lehner, which develop, on the basis of Popper's philosophy, a so-called genetic teaching strategy aiming at problem-solving learning. Lehner regards all learning as problem-solving in that it consists of constructing hypotheses or theories and trying these out. In the sense of Popper's 'Conjectures and Refutations', the rejection of a false hypothesis in favour of a better one is seen as progress in learning. Causing students to follow the development of theories and research, inclusive of the steps that have been found to be wrong, is a method of introducing them to both a subject and critical, independent thinking (Lehner 1978, 1979). See also pp. 35 and 64.

Ausubel's theory of reception learning has proved particularly influential in the general domain of written instruction. It is interesting to note (taking one well-informed educationalist as an example) that Hudgins on the one hand says that only 'rarely have investigations of instructional media been guided by an overarching theory or conceptual structure about the nature of communication, teaching, or learning', and on the other hand explicitly takes 'advantage of the basic concept of Ausubel's system' (Hudgins 1971: 177). On Ausubel's advance organizers see pp. 59–60.

Among the Ausubel arguments that Hudgins considers 'particularly relevant to a consideration of text materials for instruction' the following seem specially noteworthy:

- Text materials should follow the principles of progressive differentiation and integrative reconciliation. In turn, these two concepts demand that the text writer begin by introducing a selected set of the most general concepts from the domain of knowledge about which he is writing.... The principle of progressive differentiation demands that the writer subsequently introduces less important concepts, and continues to indicate the ways in which they differ from each other and from the more overarching concepts previously introduced. Ausubel argues that those major concepts provide a kind of ideational anchoring, a clarity, and a stability for the learner to hold on to as he learns lower order and less general elements of the lesson.

  Integrative reconciliation is a term used by Ausubel to refer to the repeated reference to the same concepts as the discussion of an area of knowledge proceeds. It is his contention that textbook writers compartmentalize knowledge and write as though one topic, once it has been presented and developed, need never again be thought about, and has no relationship to other concepts or topics within the same domain of knowledge. On the contrary, as Ausubel points out, knowledge is not typically so compartmentalized, and textbook writers would perform a more effective service to learners if they attempted to avoid the fragmentation of isolated chapters and utilized the principle of integrative reconciliation more frequently and more appropriately...

- Text materials should be written so as to stimulate the active, critical, reflective, and analytic involvement of the learner.

(Hudgins 1971: 178–80)

The theories mentioned by Bååth, Hudgins' highlighting of some concepts of Ausubel's, Lehner's genetic approach, and Nuthall and Snook's rational model would all seem to show conclusively that distance education and thinking about distance education are firmly based in general educational theory although distance education represents a separate type of education with special target groups, methods, media, and other circumstances in which it differs from other kinds of education. It is, writes Desmond Keegan, 'a coherent and distinct field of educational endeavour', it 'is more than a teaching mode or method. It is a complete system of education' (Keegan 1986: 6). Not everybody would agree, however.

DISTANCE EDUCATION: A MODE OF EDUCATION IN ITS OWN RIGHT OR A SUBSTITUTE FOR FACE-TO-FACE EDUCATION?

The applications of distance education already referred to in this book will have shown that there are important basic differences in the appreciation of its character. To some it is merely a means of distribution that can sometimes replace oral distribution of subject matter for learning, to others it is a mode of education that exists beside and is equal to education offered face to face.

While the latter view is, on the whole, represented by the large correspondence schools, the distance-teaching universities, and similar organizations (see pp. 9–12), the former view is implicit in, for example, the comparative studies of the effectiveness of distance-education methods and that of face-to-face methods that were common at a time when distance education (correspondence education, home study) fought for recognition as a useful approach to teaching and learning (Childs 1971: 238ff.). The usual design of such studies was an arrangement with two comparable groups of students made to learn the same subject matter, one by working through a correspondence course, the other by taking part in ordinary classroom teaching; the achievements of the two groups were then compared statistically. Peters refers to research of this kind as relatively advanced statistical work combined with a complete lack of theory ('ein relativ fortgeschrittenes statistiches Treatment bei völliger Theorielosigkeit'; Peters 1973; 17). This kind of comparison illuminates a view of distance education which entirely neglects the inherent potential for both individual and mass education (rather than the education of organized classes of students), for reaching students irrespective of geographical distance, and for the 'multiplication of advanced expert achievements' (ibid.).

Something of the same approach to distance education emerges in cases where, for technical reasons (such as the impossibility of co-ordinating in an acceptable way periods for classroom activities for gainfully employed adults, or the lack of teachers), courses are offered at a distance as a substitute for ordinary face-to-face courses. While there can be no objection to this use of distance-education procedures, they utilize only a small part of the potential of distance education. This can also be said about some small-scale applications. A striking example is the Canadian University of Waterloo:

> we have fixed starting times for a course, a fixed schedule of assignments, a fixed duration of a course, and a fixed examination schedule. Our approach is to treat students as members of a class, although that class is distributed geographically. Thus our students start a course together at the same time and have to submit assignments and write examinations on a schedule in exactly the same way as a class on campus is required to do.
>
> (Leslie 1979: 36)

The insistence on classes and pacing seems to represent a typical characteristic of the view of distance education that regards it as a substitute for education face to face. Conventional views of educational planning and organization induce protagonists of this school of thought to impose the same restrictions on distance study as are usually unavoidable in traditional study: limited geographical coverage, classes of limited size, regular meetings, pacing, division of the year into terms of study, prescribed examination dates, vacations, etc. To the extent that, in systems adopting these limitations, the type of distance education applied is felt to be innovative, it is what Ross (1976) calls innovation within the accepted paradigm.

Once distance education is applied outside the organizational and administrative framework of conventional schools and universities, its potential for extra-paradigmatic innovation becomes evident. Its claim to be a mode of education in its own right is based on this potential.

The innovatory character of distance education in this sense emanates from the following:

1 The underlying ideas that learning can occur without the presence of a teacher and that the support given to students can

be adapted to their standards of knowledge (instead of insisting on formal entrance qualifications).

2 The consistent use of non-contiguous media both for the presentation of learning matter and for the ensuing communication.

3 The methods used to exploit the non-contiguous teaching/ learning situation so as to attain the highest possible effectiveness for the individual learner: structure and style of presentation and communication (didactic conversation), appropriate use of media available, adaptation to students' conditions of life, etc.

4 The particular organization which makes it possible to provide for both independent individual learning and mass education through personal tutoring and more or less 'industrialized' working methods.

5 The liberation from organizational and administrative restrictions usually inevitable in face-to-face education: geographical limitations, school or university terms, keeping prescribed pace etc.

6 The possibilities it offers for economies of scale.

7 The influence distance education exerts on adult education, further training, and labour-market conditions, by opening new study opportunities as well as through its methods and organization.

In distance-education systems using these characteristics to the full, it is possible for each student to begin, interrupt, and complete the study as it suits him/her or as work, health, and family conditions allow, to work at his/her own pace, and to disregard all the restrictions that apply to classroom teaching or group learning.

Thus there are at least two different schools of thought on distance education: one stressing individual study and individual, non-contiguous tutoring, the other aiming at parallelism with resident study and usually including class or group teaching face to face as a regular element. The former can and does serve mass education. It is in this context that the industrial approach is important. It stresses rationalization and division of labour in the interest of quality and economy. This view is widely accepted as shown in this Canadian statement:

The extra effort required in the development of distance

education courses pays off when the same materials can be used to teach any number of students at any number of different institutions. The creator of the course need not be involved in delivery, and the tutor who deals with students 'ceases to be the master of the content and must become the guide, mentor and catalyst to aid the student's journey through a pre-structured or open-ended learning experience'.... Communicating with distant students requires special skills for which training may be provided ... This is an area that would benefit from further attention by researchers.

(Calvert 1986: 102)

Industrialization in this sense implies using first-class specialist authors, editors, media specialists, designers, etc. for the development of courses to be produced in large editions, and other specialists for counselling, tutoring, assessment, administrating the work, etc. High quality is attained by the division of the work among specialists for each individual task.

This approach is fully or partly applied by the large distance-education organizations, whereas (as shown on p. 162) small-scale distance education in many cases favours procedures more in line with traditional face-to-face education. Sometimes there is no other choice, as only large-scale organizations are in a position to benefit fully from this 'industrial' approach. Both usually aim at individualizing their tuition. Thorpe (1979a) says about one large-scale organization, the British Open University, that 'the course teams provide the reading material (texts, broadcasts, kits) for hundreds or thousands of students in general and the course tutors and tutor-counsellors teach the students as individuals' (p. 1).

It is evident that the industrial approach in this sense does not preclude individualization or personal communication. It is thus quite compatible with the attempts to create rapport between tutors and students, characterizing the conversation concepts discussed on pp. 45–55.

Distance education, using its full potential as indicated, must necessarily be regarded as a separate kind of education which can only to a limited extent be described, understood, and explained in terms of conventional education. This is one of the main conclusions of Otto Peters' analysis of the 'industrial' character of distance teaching as compared with traditional teaching (Peters 1973: 309–10).

STUDENT AUTONOMY V. CONTROL OF STUDENTS

As shown above, distance education can be extremely flexible. It is adaptable to students' conditions in that they can learn anywhere and at any time. There are no lecture or lesson periods to be observed and concepts such as terms of study and vacations need have no importance. It is inherent in distance education that organized learning can occur whenever students have opportunities and inclinations to study. In principle it leaves the student entirely in command.

If consistently applied, this flexibility allows students to begin and finish courses, submit assignments, make interruptions in their study, and register for examinations, if any, whenever they wish. A great many distance-teaching organizations, in particular correspondence schools, adopt this flexibility. Other distance-teaching organizations, among them most distance-teaching universities, compromise in that they do not make full use of the inherent potential of their mode of teaching: they tend to apply a term-vacation system like conventional schools and universities, they insist on a certain amount of pacing, and are often prepared to handle, correct, and comment on students' assignments, essays, etc. only during periods that they prescribe for this type of work.

Michael Moore has developed an interesting theory of independent study, classifying educational programmes on the two dimensions of autonomy and transactional distance, the latter expressed in terms of dialogue and structure, which he describes in the following way:

> Autonomy is the extent to which the learner in an educational programme is able to determine the selection of objectives, resources and evaluation procedures.... Distance in an educational programme is a function of dialogue and structure. Structure is the extent to which the objectives, implementation procedures and evaluation procedures of the teaching programme can be adapted to meet the specific objectives, implementation plans and evaluation methods of a particular student's learning

programme. Dialogue is the extent to which interaction between learners and teacher is possible. . . .

. . . To the extent that a programme consists of pre-produced parts, at least in the form of particularized plans listing item by item the knowledge and skills to be covered by the programme, the programme may not be responsive to learners' idiosyncrasies, and structure is said to be high. . . .

When dialogue is difficult, or impossible, and when structure is high, 'admonitary acts' become difficult or impossible. In a programmed text, such as Mager's, a minimum of dialogue between teacher and learner is obtained by use of the branching technique. The admonitary acts, such as 'Oops! You didn't follow instructions', are weak by contrast to the power such statements would carry in a highly dialogic interaction. In telemathic teaching [= distance teaching in Moore's terminology] 'directive action' is more easily communicated than admonition, but the teacher must assume that a large part of direction, as well as admonition, will be self-administered by the learner. The less distance, the more direction will be feasible. Even the most distant teachers are able to communicate 'logical operations'. Whether a particular learner will benefit from a programme low in distance, or from a highly telemathic programme is determined by the extent to which he benefits or is impaired by direction and admonition. This is determined by his competence as an autonomous, or 'self-directed' learner.

(M. Moore 1977: 33 and 20)

[Telemathic (teaching) equals distance (teaching) in Moore's terminology.]

The highest degree of distance occurs when a person studies without any support at all, which Moore describes as 'programmes with no dialogue, and no structure' and exemplifies by 'independent reading-study programmes of the "self-directed" kind'. A normal distance-study course provides facilities for interaction ('dialogue') as well as structure in Moore's sense. He has made an empirical study of the hypothesis that autonomous persons are particularly attracted to distant methods of learning and teaching. On the whole, this has been confirmed although it has also been found that distance students do not reject guidance (M. Moore 1976).

166

This thinking has been developed further by Farhad Saba, as summarized by Moore:

> Saba has confronted the problems presented to distance education theory by interactive telecommunications and expanded the concept of transactional distance by using system dynamics (Saba 1989). Through this methodology he has produced a fine model of the dynamic inter-relationship of dialogue and structure. He refers to 'integrated systems' of telecommunication media and explains that maximization of dialogue via integrated systems minimizes transactional distance. He proposes that a significant feature of integrated telecommunications is that it achieves what he calls virtual contiguity by sight and sound, as well as by sharing and exchanging printed documents. This virtual contiguity more than equals face-to-face instruction.
>
> (Moore 1989: 161–2)

Full student autonomy would imply not only complete flexibility and independence for students in the process of study but also the right and possibility to decide entirely independently and individually on the learning content. This freedom is usually a fact only in so far as students can choose broad courses of study. Only in exceptional cases is it possible for a student to select his or her own study objectives, although modular systems can make this possible. See pp. 15, 44 and 70–1. Down-to-earth suggestions for dealing with this problem are given in Ljoså and Sandvold (1983).

Growing awareness of the role of learners in the construction of knowledge makes considerations of this kind come to the fore.

> Knowledge does not exist independently of those who possess it. It cannot be transmitted unchanged to the learner. It always fits into the existing framework of understanding of the learner and is shaped by this framework . . . Learning for meaning and tight teacher control sit uneasily together. Learners must make their own maps of knowledge.
>
> (Boud 1990: 6)

In an interesting staff-development course, leading to degrees in education for university lecturers (also referred to on p. 151), Lewis Elton and his co-workers have managed to cater for far-reaching student autonomy by 'presenting material in a general manner and expecting course members to relate this to their own experience and current work' (Elton *et al.* 1986: 30). As it was impossible to create a course directly relevant to all participants, a course was developed 'which each member could make directly relevant to his own experience. To do this, we kept the course purposely general, but expected participants in each assignment which they submitted to relate the general to their particular experience' (ibid.).

This approach (characterized by much dialogue and limited structure in Moore's sense) proved successful and can be regarded as a prototype of autonomy-supporting and autonomy-expecting academic distance teaching (cf. Holmberg 1986: 87–94).

The arguments both for and against complete flexibility, allowing students full autonomy, are based on ideological principles as well as on practical considerations. Those in favour of full student autonomy feel that any uninvited intervention in adult students' work (sometimes even offers of assistance in coping with specific problems) encroach on the personal integrity of students, whereas those prepared to limit students' independence by various control measures consider it a moral and social duty as far as possible to prevent failure.

The practical arguments in favour of student autonomy are based on adult students' general situation, which usually means that family and job commitments and social obligations must be given first priority. Study occurs when these duties allow and students are physically and emotionally prepared for it. This is taken to mean that no timetable that is arranged by others than the students themselves is to be followed. Complete flexibility and full student autonomy create a very open system attractive to many but hardly likely to lead to course completion in a majority of cases. It cannot be denied that here we often have reason to refer to the survival of the fittest, a kind of 'natural selection'.

If a system has, as its chief priority, respect for the freedom and autonomy of the individual student, it will allow him to begin a course whenever he chooses and to finish it at his convenience. The student paces himself and there are no external constraints although the good correspondence school, whose model this is, will have a system of written

168

reminders, encouraging phone calls and even financial incentives to incite him to keep at it. Nevertheless the drop out, or non-completion rate, with such a free approach is usually horrendous (over 50 per cent) if the students are humans rather than angels.

(Daniel and Marquis 1979: 34)

The practical arguments in favour of control are usually based on anxiety to avoid wastage. It is felt to be essential that course completion should be attained in as many cases as at all possible. See Coldeway (1986), who stresses the influence of pacing on completion rates: 'Students are less likely to procrastinate when deadlines are clear. Getting behind schedule makes it even more difficult to generate energy to continue' (Coldeway 1986: 89). This leads to somewhat restrictive practices which exclude would-be students unable to adapt themselves to them. Irregular working periods, travel on duty, poor health requiring occasional hospitalization, pregnancy, care of sick children, etc. are conditions which may prevent students from following a timetable but yet may allow periods of concentrated study, for example during normal vacation time. Control measures of the kind mentioned inevitably cause a kind of pre-active natural selection, supposedly more merciful than failure after enrolment and a period of organized learning, but perhaps unnecessarily obstructing study that promotes personal development.

In practice the potential of distance education, as discussed on pp. 161–4, is exploited more or less fully also in relation to student autonomy vs. institutional control of students. A careful study of student autonomy and its limits in distance education was carried out in 1990 by Monika Weingartz. Using as her empirical basis the data collected in a FernUniversität international study comprising some 200 distance-teaching organizations (see Graff and Holmberg 1988) she identified an autonomy score, a score of individual control, one of goal-oriented control and one of control by additional media. Her study shows that almost 25 per cent of the organizations studied endeavour to promote a high degree of autonomy, whereas some 70 per cent of them apply highly individualized control methods, i.e. personal tutoring and counselling. Weingartz' analysis includes contract learning (p. 73). She concludes that selected individual control measures of the kind mentioned are essential for student autonomy, that independent study does not imply unlimited freedom but a differentiated guidance of learners engaging students and tutors together and that the need for tutoring and counselling diminishes as students become more independent (Weingartz 1990: 81). Isaacs writing on computer-assisted learning comes to a similar conclusion: 'In courses aimed at making students more independent as learners a degree of control is placed in their hands; students learn control by practising control' (Isaacs 1990: 86). On the independence and control concepts see Boud (1988); Baynton (1992); Candy (1987) and Elton (1988).

Occasionally the value of attempts to promote student auton-omy is queried. Garrison and Shale ask 'whether autonomy is desirable, realistic, or even possible to attain', and believe that 'the usual notion of independence runs a serious risk of obscur-ing the true nature of education' (Garrison and Shale 1990: 124). They state their position as 'independence is not an essential characteristic of distance education' (p. 129). See also Willén 1981: 249–50.

In higher education and adult education, those in favour of student autonomy can find themselves in a dilemma. Should stu-dent autonomy be promoted by intervention (advice, suggestions, offers of support), which is possibly unacceptable to autonomous learners who consider study their private concern and decline what they regard as well-meant officiousness? Alternatively, should students be left alone to fight for survival, i.e. completion and/ or success in their study? This dilemma is aggravated in adult education, as its students can hardly ever give first priority to their study.

Adult students can reasonably be expected to be mature. Maturity seems to go well with autonomy. Thus, on the one hand, should adult students not be expected to be (and thus be treated as) autonomous learners, so that the responsibility for searching for solutions and asking for support when needed should be left to them alone? On the other hand, does their difficult situation with heavy commitments other than study not warrant special support? Distance educators and adult educators generally have to navigate between Scylla and Charybdis here (Holmberg 1986: 64–71).

From what has been said in the preceding chapters, it is evident that we can identify at least the following degrees of student autonomy in distance-education practice:

1 Voluntary study and free choice of course.
2 Autonomous execution of study based on prescribed curricula.
3 Free choice of optional elements as part of autonomous learning according to 2.
4 Possibilities to add to and reduce curricula, by including course units from other curricula and omitting units from the curriculum to be studied, as part of autonomous learning according to 2.
5 Free choice of learning objectives, course units, optional supplements etc. combined with autonomous execution of the study.
6 Autonomous work under the guidance of tutors (representing interdependence).
7 Autonomous project work.

If students are to be treated as mature people, and if student autonomy is to be promoted, this must have methodological consequences. The following principles belong here:

1 Student participation in the planning of the study is to be aimed at in order to secure its lasting relevance to the individual students.
2 Students' individual interests and/or experiences should influence the study content and process.
3 Flexibility in the structure and use of pre-produced courses is an indispensable condition: modular principles, study-guide approaches, student-initiated deep study of selected subject areas are applicable.
4 Problem-oriented discussion of subject matter should supplement and guide endeavours to impart knowledge; as an alternative to presenting 'ready-made' systems of knowledge, courses can start out from particular problems (an approach investigated by Weingartz 1980; see pp. 35 and 64).
5 Conversation-like, pre-produced presentations of subject matter, inviting students to query, check, investigate on their own, and pose explicit questions, are to be aimed at (see pp. 45–55).
6 Dialogue, contiguous or non-contiguous (the latter dominating in distance education), causing awareness of problems and attempts to solve them and making students consider and try to reach positions of their own, must be catered for (see

pp. 19–20 and the above remarks on course development and teaching–learning communication).

7 General empathy in relation to students' autonomy orientation should characterize the work of the supporting organization in subject-matter presentation, tutoring, and counselling.

A THEORY OF LEARNING AND TEACHING IN DISTANCE EDUCATION

The facts, issues and arguments discussed provide background matter for a possible general theory of distance education. Hilary Perraton's approach, mentioned above (p. 158), is pertinent. Perraton (1981) bases his arguments on a view of education as connected with power and makes a case both for expanding education as an egalitarian requirement and for stressing the importance of dialogue. His contribution to a theory of distance education is in the form of fourteen hypotheses or statements.

The dependence on political contexts is stressed by Perraton, as are the possibilities inherent in distance education for economies of scale and the expansion of education. This is evident from his statements:

No 2   Distance teaching can break the integuments of fixed staffing ratios which limited the expansion of education when teacher and student had to be in the same place at the same time.

No 3   There are circumstances under which distance teaching can be cheaper than orthodox education, whether measured in terms of audience reached or of learning.

No 5   Distance teaching can reach audiences who would not be reached by orthodox means.

These points have been covered above. So have the following, purely educational statements, which also partly coincide with my theory attempt on pp. 175–81:

No 6   It is possible to organize distance teaching in such a way that there is dialogue.

No 10 A multi-media programme is likely to be more effective than one which relies on a single medium.

No 11 A systems approach is helpful in planning distance education.

No 12 Feedback is a necessary part of a distance-learning system.

No 13 To be effective, distance-teaching materials should ensure that students undertake frequent and regular activities over and above reading, watching, or listening.

Perraton finishes his theory paper by asking if his formulation of hypotheses suggests 'ways of testing them which would yield useful knowledge for practical educators' (p. 24). This is exactly the concern that has caused me to attempt a theory, as presented below. Presentations of other theoretical approaches to distance education occur in Keegan (1990) and Holmberg (1985a).

A really comprehensive theory of distance education including all relevant and social aspects seems out of reach. The situation may well be different if theorising is limited to the teaching–learning process. A teaching–learning theory of distance education could consist of a mainly descriptive part, dealing with learning, and a more prescriptive part concerned with teaching. Whereas the former would expound the assumptions about learning, how and under what circumstances it occurs at a distance, the latter would attempt to gather into a coherent. inclusive exposition the principles for action supposed to cause effective teaching, i.e. facilitation of learning. Organizational, administrative, and financial conditions are relevant to both these parts.

It should be possible, at least to some extent, to express these assumptions as logico-deductive hypotheses (if A, then/then not B; or, the more/less A, the more/less B), which can be transformed into prescriptive rules of the type discussed on p. 24. If the hypotheses are based on (generated from) a consistent view of what is probable (a logically coherent but, at the outset, possibly only implicit theory), the testing of the hypotheses would then imply an attempt to falsify or corroborate the underlying theory.

Search for theory

In my search for an inclusive theory of this kind, I have for many years been concerned with the personal and the conversational as characterizing distance learning and teaching, have paid attention to the influence of emotions and have in this spirit developed (and published) attempts to base theory wholly or partly on this approach. My theory of the guided didactic conversation, first outlined in 1960 and later formalized and subjected to empirical testing (reported on in 1982 and 1983), has been summarized in the discussion of overarching principles for course development (see pp. 45–55). The relevance of personal approaches also to mediated communication has further been demonstrated (see pp. 126–7) and shown to be in agreement with empirical research findings (particularly Rekkedal 1985).

A more comprehensive theory of teaching for distance education, including the former theory, was presented at the ICDE conference in Melbourne in 1985 and subsequently published (Holmberg 1985c). In my book of 1986, I developed the same thinking and tried to provide a general base for it in a series of descriptive statements (pp. 108–11) and a general view of distance education (p. 114). In this presentation it should be possible to forgo these two elements as in the preceding chapters the concept, system, potential, and practice of distance education, with its constituent elements, have been dealt with at some length. Here I prefer to explore a theory concerned with the purely educational aspects of learning and teaching with their surrounding circumstances and restrictions.

Decisive to my approach is the realization that, as David Boud puts it, 'feelings and emotions are part of learning of any kind' and that 'learning is holistic. Learners cannot separate . . . their understanding from the excitement of discovery' (Boud 1990: 7). Necessary foundations of theory construction in our field are the meanings attached to the concepts of independence, learning, and teaching. These have been discussed on pp. 18–20, 32–6 and 165–71. Meaningful learning, which anchors new learning matter in cognitive structures, not rote learning, is the centre of interest. Teaching is taken to mean facilitation of learning. Individualization of teaching and learning, encouragement of critical thinking, and far-reaching student autonomy are integrated with this view of learning and teaching. A basic presupposition is the reliance on a school or university to administer distance education, in the spirit of what Delling calls the supporting organization.

I thus try to build on my previous attempts, as indicated, and include learning, teaching, and their organizational/administrative frames in a theory of distance education capable of generating testable hypotheses.

Theory content

My theory can be worded as follows:

> Distance education is based on deep learning as an individual activity. Learning is guided and supported by non-contiguous means which activate students, i.e. by mediated communication, usually based on pre-produced courses. This constitutes the teaching component of distance education for which a supporting organization is responsible.
>
> As individual study requires a certain amount of maturity, self-discipline, and independence, distance education can be an application of independent learning at the same time as it is apt further to develop study autonomy. Central to the learning and teaching in distance education are personal relations, study pleasure, and empathy between students and those representing the supporting organization.
>
> Feelings of empathy and belonging promote students' motivation to learn and influence the learning favourably. Such feelings can be developed in the learning process independently of any face-to-face contact with tutors. They are conveyed by students' being engaged in decision making; by lucid, problem-oriented, conversation-like presentations of learning matter that may be anchored in existing knowledge; by friendly, non-contiguous interaction between students and tutors, counsellors, and other staff in the supporting organization; and by liberal organizational–administrative structures and processes.

This epitomizing theory presentation, the factual and argumentative substance of which has been developed in the preceding chapters, immediately generates the following hypotheses, all of which can be worded as if . . . then or the . . . the propositions, as indicated on p. 24, and can, at least in principle, be empirically tested.

Hypotheses derived about distance learning

1 Organized learning can occur without the presence of a teacher or tutor.
2 Intrinsic motivation is a crucial condition for learning.
3 Learning is promoted by students fitting subject matter into existing cognitive structures.
4 Warmth in human relations, bearing on the study situation, is conducive to emotional involvement.
5 Emotional involvement in the study promotes deep learning and goal attainment.
6 Feelings of rapport with tutors, counsellors, and the supporting organization generally strengthen and support study motivation as well as promote study pleasure.
7 Intellectual pleasure favours deep learning, the use of problem-oriented study processes, and the attainment of study goals.
8 Participation in goal considerations and study planning encourages personal commitment to the learning and feelings of responsibility for the attainment of study goals.
9 Learning is encouraged by frequent, helpful communication with others interested in the study.
10 Maturity makes for motivational stability and the capacity to master difficulties and is more likely than not to be combined with inclinations and ability for independence.

Hypotheses derived about distance teaching

Two overarching hypotheses are natural corollaries of the hypotheses about learning:

1 Teaching and counselling can be effectively carried out by non-contiguous means; real mediated communication and simulated communication, incorporated in distance-education courses by conversational style and other personal approaches, make dialogue possible.
2 Personal (not necessarily or primarily contiguous) contacts with tutors and other representatives of the supporting organization promote emotional involvement.

These overarching hypotheses, which could be regarded as a theory of teaching for distance education (i.e. as covering part of the theory formulated on p. 175), seem to have explanatory value in relating teaching effectiveness to the impact of feelings of belonging and co-operation as well as to the actual exchange of questions, answers, and arguments in mediated communication.

More specific and more easily tested teaching hypotheses, which are derived from the theory, are that the following phenomena are favourable to teaching (i.e. facilitation of learning):

3 A presentation of course goals or objectives which engages the student in the evaluation of their relevance and, if at all possible, in their selection.

4 A course structure carefully based on required earlier learning, which makes subsumptions in Ausubel's sense possible.

5 Pre-produced courses characterized by a conversational style with invitations to an exchange of views and with attempts to involve the student emotionally.

6 A style of presentation that is easily accessible; a high degree of readability of printed course materials.

7 Graphical and typographical presentations facilitating access to printed courses and selections of relevant subject matter.

8 Sequencing, a choice of media and other principles for course presentation adapted to student needs and to the requirements of subject areas studied, e.g. those of operations on knowledge and operations with knowledge (Chang *et al.* 1983: 14–16).

9 Communication facilities (in writing, by computer, on the telephone, and/or by audio tape) constantly open to students for questions and exchanges of opinions with tutors and counsellors.

10 Frequent submission of assignments requiring students to solve problems, evaluate texts or recordings; research findings indicate that this is valid if combined with 11.

11 Friendly, helpful, and extensive tutor comments on assignments submitted, with suggestions expressed in a way to promote personal rapport between student and tutor.

12 Quick handling of assignments so that students need not wait for more than a week to have their work returned with corrections and comments.

13 Self-checking exercises in pre-produced courses, through which students are encouraged to practise skills (in, for

instance, foreign languages, mathematics, statistics); not only model answers should be provided but also extensive comments based on course writers' experience of probable errors and misunderstandings.

Hypotheses about organization and administration

Empathy is an essential requirement of the way in which students' (also more peripheral) concerns are handled by the supporting organization. This applies not only to counselling (which is, of course, closely related to teaching) but also to correspondence, telephone contacts, dissemination of information on administrative matters, the dispatch of learning materials, assignments commented on, and warehousing procedures.

This thinking produces a first hypothesis concerning:

1 the impact of the empathy approach on administration.

Other hypotheses related to the organization of distance education are possible and plausible. They can, for example, concern:

2 The factors leading to different types of organizations, for example goals, target groups, social and cultural frame factors influencing learning and teaching.
3 The educational consequences or organizational structures.
4 Effectiveness and economics.

The factual background of these and similar hypotheses is to be found in the basic characteristics of distance-education institutions and the interrelationships of these characteristics. (Graff and Holmberg (1984: 10–11 and 37–57).

Generally applicable hypotheses are these, for example:

5 The less dependent the study is of societal control and of prescribed curricula and procedures, the greater the possibilities not only to individualize the work but also to support student autonomy.
6 If industrialized working methods are used, including systematic planning of courses, standardized procedures, and mechanization and division of labour, then the standard of pre-produced courses is likely to be high (and distance education will be particularly cost-effective for courses with large student numbers).

7 If a small-scale approach is applied, including course creation by individual tutors who also teach students at a distance by interacting with them non-contiguously, then adaptability to specific groups is facilitated (whereas no cost advantages in comparison with conventional education are to be foreseen).

The testability of the hypotheses

Most of the above hypotheses have been expressed as straight-forward statements. It is evidently easy to translate them into if... , then... or the... , the... hypotheses: if the conditions mentioned occur (the more they occur...), then (the more) learning will be promoted (teaching and administration will facilitate learning).

As far as the hypotheses about teaching are concerned, I have actually elsewhere suggested exact wordings of this kind (Holmberg 1985c). Proper, non-ambiguous operationalization of concepts is required to make testing meaningful.

The teaching and administrative hypotheses derived from the theory are easier to operationalize than those of learning. If we assume that emotional involvement, intellectual pleasure, and empathy exert influence on learning, we can test this assumption only if we specify which signs are taken to indicate the presence of these feelings. In our case, the outcome (as to attitudes and learning) of measures taken to bring about the desired phenomena (i.e. the teaching and administrative procedures mentioned above), the effect of which can more comfortably be tested, is the indirect means to check on the relevance of the assumptions about learning.

Quite a few of the hypotheses mentioned have directly or indirectly been tested. This applies to the hypotheses about subsumption (Ausubel 1968); conversational style (Holmberg, Schuemer and Obermeier 1982); readability (Langer *et al.* 1974); access structure (Doerfert 1980); frequency of assignment submission (Bååth 1980 and Holmberg and Schuener 1989); quick handling of assignments, i.e. turn-around time (Rekkedal 1983); and the allocation of personal tutor-counsellors (Rekkedal 1985). In similar ways the other hypotheses derived from the theory, as worded on p. 175, can be tested.

EPISTEMOLOGICAL CONCERNS

While I feel committed to much in Popper's rationalism, it must be admitted that my theory concept only partially agrees with his. The hypotheses derived can be submitted to falsification following Popper's epistemological principles, as quoted on p. 24. According to these, the task of scholarship is both theoretical, to bring about explanation, and practical, to provide for application of technology.

According to Popper the aim of the theoretician:

> is to find *explanatory theories* (if possible, true explanatory theories); that is to say, theories which describe certain structural properties of the world, and which permit us to deduce, with the help of initial conditions, the effects to be explained... My explanation of explanation has been adopted by certain positivists or 'instrumentalists' who saw in it an attempt to explain it away – as the assertion that explanatory theories are nothing but premises for deducing predictions. I therefore wish to make it quite clear that I consider the theorist's interest in explanation – that is, in discovering explanatory theories – as irreducible to the practical technological interest in the deduction of predictions. The theorist's interest in predictions, on the other hand, is explicable as due to his interest in the problem whether his theories are true; or in other words, as due to his interest in testing his theories – in trying to find out whether they cannot be shown to be false.
>
> (Popper 1980: 61)

My theory is not what the 'critical rationalists' in the spirit of Popper would call nomological, i.e. it cannot be said to apply everywhere and under all circumstances. It is 'impossible to determine an absolute set of instructional procedures that will be "best", for different learners, or for different learnings by one learner' (Hosford 1973: 114). Education as a research area is, of course, concerned with human beings with personalities, hopes, and wills of their own. If we are not determinists in the sense that we totally reject the assumption that human will is in any respect free, then it is impossible to postulate any automatic cause–effect principle in research that aims at optimizing educational methods and procedures. Here theories usually have to be limited to statements to the effect that if such and such a measure is taken under specific circumstances, then this is likely to facilitate learning.

The requirements which my theory is meant to satisfy are, with the reservations made, those usually expected of educational theories, i.e. that they should:

1 Have internal consistency as logical systems.
2 Establish functional relationships between the teaching and the outcomes of learning.
3 Be capable of generating specific hypotheses and predictions.
4 Be expressed in such a way that research data capable of possibly refuting (falsifying) the theory can be collected.

My theory with its hypotheses in this spirit may stress prediction more than a truly Popperian theory would do. However, it has some explanatory power, as it implies a consistent view of effective learning and teaching in distance education which identifies a general approach favourable to learning and to the teaching efforts conducive to learning.

SUMMARY OF THE DISTANCE-EDUCATION CONCEPT AND THEORY

The principles, facts, and arguments developed above lead to the following conclusion. Distance education is a concept that covers the learning–teaching activities in the cognitive and/or psycho-motor and affective domains of an individual learner and a supporting organization. It is characterized by non-contiguous communication and can be carried out anywhere and at any time, which makes it attractive to adults with professional and social commitments.

Through distance education a course of study can be offered to very large numbers of students. This implies possibilities for division of labour in the supporting organization between counsellors, course writers, instructional designers, editors, developers of audio-visual materials, tutors, administrators, etc. This leads to a varying amount of mass-communication and industrialization and to economies of scale.

Distance education requires a degree of maturity in its students, as they usually carry out the study activity autonomously. While expecting a certain amount of student autonomy, distance education can also promote the further development of autonomy as far as the choice of study objectives, critical appraisal of competing schools of thought, and problem-solving are concerned. It includes individualizing procedures conducive to student autonomy and academic socialization.

Special methods have been developed for use in non-contiguous communication, including counselling, course development, the application of media, and administrative work, which rely on principles of instructional design and dialogue. Conversational approaches and general empathy have been shown to be conducive to students' satisfaction and goal attainment. On the basis of investigations of empathy approaches and other aspects I, on the one hand, conclude that predictive theories of distance education are possible and that a beginning has been made, yet, on the other hand, concede that empirical studies testing theories/hypotheses may cause both interpretative difficulties and modifications of assumptions without necessarily categorically refuting (falsifying) them. Rumble may well be right when he says that they are unlikely to be 'conclusively falsifiable in the same way that, for example, the discovery of a black swan falsified the theory "All swans are white" ' (Rumble 1992: 112).

Theoretical approaches more concerned with the economic, social, political and cultural contexts of distance education are sometimes asked for and are no doubt possible. Attempts in this direction occur in Campion and Guiton (1991), Edwards (1991), Evans and King (1991), Evans and Nation (1992) and elsewhere. See further pp. 212–13 below. Theorizing in this area faces problems regarding the separation of scholarship from value judgements (Holmberg 1992 and Ljoså 1991).

Finally, it is important to recognize that distance education is a separate kind of education, which cannot be regarded as a substitute for conventional schooling because of its openness to adults gainfully employed and/or fully occupied with family life, its independence of face-to-face meetings, classes, and generally of time and place, its combination of mass-communication and individualization, its potential for student autonomy, and its special methodology.

Chapter 10

THE ROLE AND CONCEPT OF EVALUATION

Educators and society at large find it increasingly important to evaluate the various contributions made to education. This is because of the general desire to safeguard the highest possible educational quality and also to ensure that money is invested in a way that yields the highest possible educational output. Evaluation is a general educational concern with some special implications for distance education. The purpose is usually to find out to what extent teaching and learning lead to expected results and acceptable standards. The knowledge acquired by evaluation studies can be used as a basis for improving the teaching–learning system as well as for describing and judging it.

The term 'evaluation' denotes different things in different contexts. Sometimes it refers to the assessment of students for the purpose of awarding marks, sometimes to the judgement of complete educational systems. Evaluating these implies an appraisal of their status in society, the relevance, quality, quantity, and results of their teaching and their impact on education, training, and the labour-market (Tate 1986) including in many cases consideration of their accessibility to various social groups, i.e. equality. This appraisal of the contribution of educational systems is usually related to the costs that they incur. Examples of such evaluation of distance-education systems are given in Keegan (1990 Part IV).

Particularly in the Anglo-Saxon parts of the world, evaluation of educational activities has been to some extent spurred on

> by the barbs of an accountability movement which attempts
> to respond to economic adversity through 'rationalization'
> of higher education provision and the promises of an

183

emerging technology of evaluation that it can provide the means by which 'rationalization' of – if not rationality in – educational provision can be achieved.

(Kemmis and Hughes 1979: 7)

The dangers inherent in this rationalizing approach are evidently that the complexity of the educational tasks may be underestimated and that academic concerns are replaced by administrative ones. Kemmis has developed a series of principles that are meant to 'create an image of evaluation as the process of marshalling information and arguments which enables interested individuals and groups to participate in the critical debate (the process of self-reflection) about a program' (Kemmis 1980: 4).

The principles and practices of distance-education organizations applied to evaluation at the beginning of the 1990s are described and analysed in Schuemer (1991).

PRINCIPLES OF DISTANCE-EDUCATION EVALUATION

Any appraisal of educational quality must be at least partly based on a micro level, i.e. individual and specific educational endeavours. In distance education, courses can be taken as starting points. Course is here taken to mean a defined part of a curriculum in one particular subject, for example a course of basic algebra for university students of mathematics or a course of English grammar for the upper stage of grammar schools. In this context I use the term 'course' to denote not only the course materials but also the whole process of interaction between the course materials, the students, the tutors, and the supporting organization as a whole (Thorpe 1979b).

Course evaluation as discussed here is related to, but narrower than, curriculum evaluation. Course evaluation is meant to provide evidence as to whether or not a given course or course draft is reasonable and effective.

The evaluation of distance-study courses includes various attempts to obtain a good grasp of how courses function, how effective they are, and how they are received by students and others concerned. One type of course evaluation concerns the assessment of students' progress; another that of the teaching effects of the system.

Assessing students

Studying the processes of students' learning is a prerequisite for helping them (see pp. 32–6). The assessment of students' progress is needed both to give students feedback so that they know how they succeed, and, in all cases where diplomas or graded certificates are required, to provide the basis for marks. In all examination systems it is important that tests should be both valid and reliable. If continuous assessment (rather than final examining only) is to some extent applied by distance-education institutions, it does not follow that these demands can be neglected. In the light of the literature available on psychometric and other considerations applicable to testing generally Lewis shows the importance of paying due attention to the development of exercises and tests:

> Let us suppose we took the trouble to analyse the co-occurrence of mistakes on (say) our computer-marked assignments; students who get question 1 wrong also tend to get questions 3, 8, 17 and 24 wrong. This suggests that the five questions are all actually tapping the same underlying dimension of confusion. This being so, we may be marking the student down five times over for having made just one mistake.

> (Lewis 1972: 119–20)

In one respect testing has special relevance for distance education. If students are offered the possibility to start, interrupt, and finish their study when they wish, to pace themselves, and generally to organize their study as they see fit, there must be a great demand for frequent examination opportunities in all subjects in which formal qualifications are required. A mastery-learning system allowing individual students to be examined when they feel they are ready for an examination (as according to the Keller Plan) would seem to be called for. This requires a bank of validated test items. On the Keller Plan, as related to distance education, see Holmberg (1981a); Coldeway and Spencer (1982).

In other respects, examination problems can be disregarded here; distance education causes no problems for assessment other than those occurring in all examination situations. The exceptions are those of an organizational and administrative type, for instance arranging decentralized written and oral examinations in special study centres, under the auspices of other educational bodies, embassies, consulates, etc. Nevertheless, assessing students' progress is an important matter to distance educators and has been thoroughly examined in this context (Lewis op. cit.).

A special form of student assessment is required when completely individualized study programmes are investigated. The PERC approach (Program Effectiveness and Related Costs) developed at the Empire State College in the US State of New York is a case in point. The individualization is brought about by individually designed degree curricula and learning contracts. The basic evaluation question studied is 'What kinds of students working with what kinds of faculty in what kinds of learning programs change in what ways at what costs?' (Lehmann and Granger 1991: 104). See further Palola *et al.* (1977) and Lehmann and Holtan (1988).

Evaluating courses

Educators may be interested in evaluating a distance-study course in order to be able to describe it properly, to provide a declaration about its characteristics and known effectiveness. This may serve as a guide either for people considering taking a course on the subject concerned or for study counsellors who are looking for detailed information about study opportunities that might be useful to students whom they are advising. This type of evaluation has been called summative and is a kind of product evaluation. It is a task for unbiased researchers, not for those who are engaged or have been engaged in the development of the course concerned.

Distance educators are not usually primarily interested in summative evaluation, however. They are, above all, concerned with evaluating how well a course can and does help students to attain their objectives of study and how it corresponds to their requirements and expectations. They usually want to investigate courses with a view to improving them. This is what is known as formative evaluation. Formative evaluation does not aim at passing judgement but is to be seen as a component of the development work. The findings of the evaluation are meant to influence, modify, or radically change the course presentation and the study procedures. Formative evaluation can have different functions, however.

One function of formative evaluation is to make the presentation coincide as closely as possible with the purposes which have led to the creation of the course. This 'ends-dominated' approach seems to prevail. It is primarily concerned with making learning more efficient. However, a learner-centred approach claims to regard the function of formative evaluation differently. The learner-centred approach stresses the desirability of finding out

> whether the concepts, procedures and criteria of a subject (have) been made sufficiently accessible, whether the problems involved could have been presented more cogently or clearly, whether the exercises or aids to thinking employed in the course really helped students to appreciate the concerns of the course makers. An evaluator would also want to know to what extent students had been able to pursue their purposes and interests through the course, what habits of thought or ways of seeing the world they might already have that may be getting in the way of aiding their understanding – and so on.
>
> (Mace 1976: 27)

The question is whether there is really a conflict between the two aims: effectiveness and adaptation to the student's situation. The latter appears to be a prerequisite for the former.

It is important to evaluate not only the pre-produced course as a product but also the tutoring and counselling belonging to it. This process evaluation is looked into in Thorpe (1988), Ganor (1991) and Naylor, Cowie and Stevenson (1990).

BASES OF EVALUATION

Comparing achievement with objectives and performance standards

How well students achieve in relation to the purposes of the course is a common basis for the judgement of the merits of the course. The effectiveness is then often measured by the use of pre- and post-tests. This type of evaluation may concern not only whole courses or course units but also individual parts of the presentation which concern specified items of knowledge and proficiency and for which desired performance standards have been laid down. The degree of attainment of each individual study objective is measured. If a sufficient majority of the students attain the performance standard, all is well. If not, either the course (the printed and/or recorded or broadcast presentation), the non-contiguous two-way communication, or some other course component must be revised on the point or points concerned. Alternatively, the objectives must be revised on the basis of the assumption or conclusion that they are not realistic.

This approach relies to a great extent on the definition of so-called behavioural objectives, i.e. study objectives which express what the student is expected to be able to do after he has completed a course or a course unit. These objectives can be derived from the known requirements of a job, from an analysis of what will be necessary for a new type of task, or from existing curricula and/or examination requirements. Since the 1970s distance educators have tended to go in for (or pay lip-service to) consistent endeavours to determine in advance what the students should be able to achieve and have expressed in quantitative terms how well they should be able to do it. The degree of objective attainment is then assessed with a view to improving the course.

Performance standards are not always specified in advance. Some evaluation based on defined learning objectives measures students' achievements after the course to find out what the performance standard is for each objective and does so without any pre-conceived requirement levels.

Consulting experts

An entirely different basis for the judgement of distance-study courses is the opinions of experts. This evaluation procedure means that the course is submitted to criticism by subject specialists recognized as educational authorities. No less than 29 out of 33 respondents to a questionnaire sent to 79 European distance educators in 1980 declared that they use this type of evaluation (Holmberg 1981b). There can be no doubt that expert opinions can influence courses in a very useful way by testing the intelligibility of texts, identifying difficulties and suggesting improvements. There are certain dangers connected with this procedure, however. First, it is very probable that only the course materials rather than the whole learning experience, inclusive of the two-way communication, is studied and commented on and that the course text is criticized on the basis of the criteria of a traditional educational text, without due attention being paid to the particular requirements of distance-learning students. Second, the experts who are consulted may well be regarded by course authors as a new target group; authors may write with a view to satisfying the expected opinions of the experts rather than the needs of students. This may lead to overloading and to unnecessarily scholarly presentations.

The use of internal experts is less problematic. Tutors' comments on course presentation, after they have graded and commented on a number of assignments, have proved very helpful. Some distance-education institutions expect their course authors to function as tutors of their courses for at least some months. This leads to useful feedback for course-improvement purposes and facilitates using student feedback (on which see Nathenson and Henderson 1980).

Consulting future employers and/or teaching bodies

Those employers or teachers in universities or institutes of further training who are to receive students may also be used as evaluators. It is then their task to relate the course and what it teaches to the requirements of the job or the further study at which the student is aiming. It is probably true to say that this group of evaluators have influenced course development in connection with the introduction of large-scale curriculum reform rather than by suggestions relevant to individual courses. In my experience it is difficult to induce the evaluators to specify the actual requirements of the job or further study concerned. They are more likely to express conventional views and say what is expected of them on the basis of academic traditions and other conventions. Whether this is due to a deficient awareness of the actual needs or merely to difficulties in articulating them seems uncertain. However, if this snag, which largely concerns finding the right representatives of the recipient organizations for the evaluation tasks, can be overcome, the procedure should be very valuable.

Investigating students' views

The students' own opinions of the course that they are taking are, of course, of paramount importance. Studies of students' attitudes to courses have been undertaken by a great number of institutions. Students may be asked what they think about a course generally, how motivating and interesting it is; they may be requested to comment on specified course items, on a particular method, etc. Very often questions are asked with a view to improving both the course presentation and the procedures that are applied to the interaction between students and the supporting organization. In some cases, as well as indicating where there is a problem, students may contribute to diagnosing the difficulty. An early example from the Open University illustrates such questions (see Fig. 8).

Twenty-six of the 33 European respondents referred to studies of students' opinions as a type of evaluation that they applied.

EVALUATION METHODS

Distance educators all over the world base their evaluation on one or more of the types of criteria discussed above (and others). While most seem to consider a comparison of students' achievements with the course objectives to be an essential type of evaluation, they adopt this procedure less often than that of asking the parties concerned about their opinions. Students' attitudes and expert opinions seem to play a very important part in the evaluation activities of distance-education institutions.

For obvious reasons the publicly funded, large distance-education institutions are able to apply more sophisticated evaluation procedures than most of the institutions that have to finance their work by means of students' fees only. As expected, the Open University has contributed much to the art of distance-course evaluation, not least to a method of early formative evaluation, referred to as developmental testing.

Developmental testing

This is a term that denotes try-out procedures characterized by small experimental groups taking courses in preliminary versions before these are offered for more general use. Developmental

a. Was section X clear to you?

$$\text{Yes ( )}$$
$$\text{No ( )}$$

b. If not, please say briefly exactly what was not clear. (Space for answer)

c. Can you suggest any way in which section X could be improved?
(Space for answer)

d. Without referring back to section X, what do you think it is important for you to remember? (Space for answer)

e. Were the examples on pp 00–00 clear to you?

| Example 1 | Yes ( ) | Example 2 | Yes ( ) | Example 3 | Yes ( ) |
| | No ( ) | | No ( ) | | No ( ) |

f. If not, please say briefly exactly what was not clear. (Space for answer)

g. Were there: too many examples? ( )
about the right number of examples? ( )
too few examples? ( )

h. Did you do exercise Y? Yes( )
No ( )

i. If you did, which parts did you get wrong?
(a) ( )   (b) ( )   (c) ( )   (d) ( )   (e) ( )

j. Did exercise Y have: too many parts? ( )
about the right number of parts? ( )
too few parts? ( )

k. If you did get any parts of exercise Y wrong, what did you do about it?
(Space for answer)

Your comments: (Space for answer)

Figure 8 Open University example of specified questioning of
students' attitudes
Source: Henderson and Nathenson 1976: 37

testing is thus a type of preliminary formative evaluation. In literature on programmed learning, formative evaluation very often means the same thing as developmental testing, as described here. For distance-education institutions, however, it may be practical to limit the latter term to evaluation work done before the course is offered to students as part of a syllabus and to use Scriven's term 'formative evaluation' for the investigation, with a view to modifying later editions, of how a course already on the market functions.

Inducing experimental groups to take a preliminary version of a course naturally offers many possibilities to try out alternative presentations, to ask the experimental students for their views, and to check on their attainments in relation to the objectives specified. There are difficulties, however, in that these experimental students do not work under the same conditions as normal students do, that their use of the course may differ from that of the normal students, and that they may pay less attention to the course than regular students do. Experiences of developmental testing in the Open University seem, at least partly, to bear out these objections whereas, to my knowledge, no traditional correspondence schools which apply developmental testing have reported on difficulties of this kind. An OU study showed that experimental students spent 30 to 50 per cent less time studying than actual students who later studied the same units (Henderson and Nathenson 1976: 33; see also Bartels and Wurster 1979: 2).

It seems to be fairly common practice in general educational evaluation to pay a fee to experimental students for their contribution to developmental testing. This may motivate them to do a reasonable job; on the other hand, it may lead to differences in attitudes and requirements between them and the regular students. Any such differences, of course, detract from the relevance of the findings to which they contribute. It is interesting to note that only one of the 33 above-mentioned respondents to my questionnaire pays their experimental students, whereas both the Open University and the FernUniversität compensate theirs for their work. Nine of my 33 respondents declared that they do developmental testing. The number of experimental students engaged varies between two to five and 300 to 500.

Some interesting studies of developmental testing were published at an early stage, among them Henderson and Nathenson (1976) and Henderson *et al.* (1977). The former find it important in developmental testing

> that a complete educational package . . . should be tested;
> that the evaluation should combine both objective and sub-
> jective data and be capable of identifying faults in the

material and generating potential solutions; that testers, and the conditions under which they study, should closely approximate the target student population; and that the developmental testing programme should operate strictly within the constraints of the . . . course production system.

(Henderson and Nathenson 1976: 33)
[They call testers those whom I call experimental students.]

Evaluation as illumination

The information acquired, through questionnaires and through analyses of students' achievements evidently does not give a complete picture of the students' situation, their interaction with the course, and their particular difficulties. For this reason, attempts have been made to find out not only what students' learning conditions are but also what their life in general is like in relation to their studies. This approach, which thus pays particular attention to the study milieu, is sometimes referred to as 'evaluation as illumination'. Typically 'in illuminative evaluation there are three characteristic stages: investigators observe, inquire further, and then seek to explain' (Parlett and Hamilton 1972).

In-depth interviews with individual students are made, with a view to understanding what happens to them, to their life while they study, rather than sampling the general reactions of the students to the course under study, which is what happens when questionnaires are used.

Work of this kind is sometimes combined with efforts to make students participate in the evaluation. It is considered important that the students should not be objects of study only but should be subjects themselves. Participative work of this kind can lead to a method of action research, as stressed in a FernUniversität study of the lives of distance students (Abels et al. 1977). It should be stressed that Parlett and Hamilton themselves do not combine their approach with action research. The evaluator, as they see him,

makes no attempt to manipulate, control or eliminate situational variables, but takes as given the complex scene he encounters. His chief task is to unravel it; isolate its significant features; delineate cycles of cause and effect; and comprehend relationships between belief and practices, and between organizational patterns and the responses of individuals.

(Parlett and Hamilton 1972: 16)

Quantitative analyses for formative and summative evaluation

Course development and tuition (the latter word being used in its British sense, meaning tutoring, teaching, not in its American sense) are based on assumptions of what will work. These assumptions are tested more or less systematically. Statistical methods to test their validity are commonly applied by educationists in terms of experiments and studies of what has actually happened in relevant situations. This applies to distance education as well as to traditional forms of education.

If the purpose of course evaluation is to improve the courses evaluated, and that is evidently the main purpose behind distance-course evaluation, then what is being sought is a theory of what the optimal procedure is in each case. Such a theory will enable the consequences of measures taken to be predicted, that is methods and/or media to be used in a particular way, etc. Further, it may be possible to indicate what can be done to attain certain purposes, i.e. to prescribe a technology. The evaluation may or may not falsify the theory.

Course evaluation includes both the description of what works and the search for causal relations. For both functions there are useful quantitative, statistical methods. Descriptive statistics may organize the findings in a handy form, including graphical forms of presentation (e.g. the histogram) and frequency distribution.

When testing predictions, i.e. statements that a change in one respect (the so-called independent variable) will lead to change in another respect (the dependent variable), it is of vital importance that no seemingly irrelevant variable is allowed to change systematically with the independent variable. This could happen if, for instance, in the division of students into an experimental group and a control group gainfully employed students were allocated to one condition and full-time students to another, or, if in a study of instructional design or communication frequency one group were made to consist of students taking part in supplementary face-to-face sessions, whereas those belonging to another group, with which the former is to be compared, benefit exclusively from mediated teaching. Here we are concerned with statistical inference trying to establish the cause of differences between findings. Conclusions of this type can evidently influence course development radically. Procedures for various types of quantitative investigations are in use. They include scales for measuring the attitudes of students (and evaluators), such as the Likert scale (Likert 1932) and Osgood's semantic differential leading to 'polarity profiles' (Osgood 1952).

Quantitative methods are chiefly used for analyses of students' achievements. They may concern the assessment of students for examination purposes, but seem especially important in formative evaluation for the purposes of testing the effectiveness of procedures, methods, and media. As this is related to the objectives of the course under examination, it has been found useful sometimes to formulate the objectives in the form of end-of-course examination questions and problems: 'By defining the objectives of a course in terms of the tests that the student should ultimately be able to pass, we do much to ensure that our tests are both relevant and equitable' (Lewis 1972: 119).

Measurement techniques have been developed for the assessment of students' achievements and the evaluation of courses and programmes. A study of the practices in this respect of sixteen distance-teaching organizations occurs in Chia (1990).

A very interesting – and evidently highly rewarding – approach is applied at the Open University of Israel. It is based on Guttman's facet theory. 'Specification of course content and its instructional objectives in "course maps" serve as a basis for preparing a teaching syllabus, establishing a computerized bank of questions and assessing all course components' (Ganor 1991: 80). Not only pre-produced courses but also student support and the assessment of students' achievements are subject to this evaluation. The information collected through the evaluation work is used as a foundation for staff development in the sense of didactic training. The technique used implies specifying what is to be investigated in a so-called mapping sentence. An example is shown in Figure 9. Descriptions of this approach occur in Ganor (1988, 1990 and 1991).

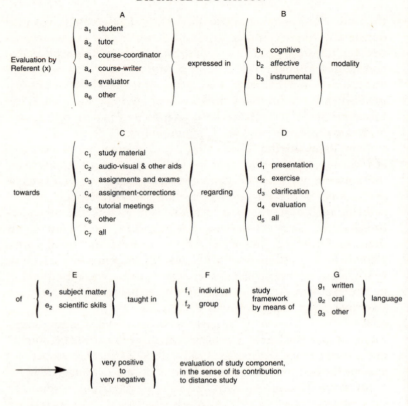

Reference (A) expresses attitudes in modality (B) towards study component (C) regarding didactic aspect (D) of course material (E) taught in study framework (F) by means of language (G). Range of evaluation (R) is from very positive to negative, in the sense of study component contribution to distance study.

Figure 9 An example of the 'mapping sentence' applied to course evaluation at the Open University of Israel
Source: Ganor 1991: 83

COMPLETION AND DROP-OUT RATES

Course completion is usually taken to imply success, whereas drop out is interpreted as failure. In distance education this understanding is valid only to a limited extent, at least if by course completion is meant the submission of all of the assignments of the course concerned. If by success we mean goal attainment, then only knowledge of individual students' goals can help us to decide if a student and a course of study have been successful or not. Céline Lebel illuminates the relations between dropping out and failure after an initial well-considered declaration that when a student – for whatever reason – does not complete a course 'il ne s'agit pas d'un échec académique mais d'un abandon transformé en échec' (Lebel 1989a: 51).

Distance-education programmes are often used by individual students who do not declare either their ultimate goals (self-actualization rather than the acquisition of competence may be their aim) or the period over which they intend to spread their study. Thus it is often impossible to say for certain, unless the students are conscious of their ultimate goals and have made their study intentions known, whether non-completion means interruption, or drop out in the sense of failure, or if it accords with their intentions or plans. The well-established accountant who takes a course in automatic data processing in order to get to know its basic principles and terminology so that he may be able to communicate with computer staff may well reach his goal by thoroughly reading the first few course units, submitting solutions of assignment problems based on these and, as far as the rest of the course is concerned, limiting himself to browsing and looking up items of special interest to him. From a statistical point of view, however, he will appear to be one of the drop outs. This situation is highlighted by a reply given by a successful inventor to a question as to why he had not completed his course:'I am a busy man. I took this course to learn how to solve a certain problem in advanced physics. When I learned that, I stopped sending in lessons' (James and Wedemeyer 1959: 93).

As all practitioners are aware, many successful graduates and students who have successfully passed professional and school or university examinations have refrained from submitting all of the assignments that belong to the courses preparing them for examination. They cannot possibly be referred to as drop outs since they have reached their goals, not only from their subjective point of view but also in the sense of examining bodies. They simply have not made use of all of the assistance offered by their distance-teaching organizations. This may, as explained to the author by a great number of successful former distance students, be due to pressure of time or to personal confidence of adequate examination standards before course completion. Data from a comprehensive research project confirm 'that submission of assignments is not perfectly indicative of how far a student has reached in his studies' (Bååth 1984b: 31; see also Bååth 1980: 87ff). Bååth here confirms a conclusion of Wedemeyer's (Wedemeyer 1971: 556).

The above-quoted paper by Bååth gives a short but balanced, and in my view accurate, summarizing picture of completion and drop out. After recognizing that it is difficult 'to determine exactly when a slow student should be considered a drop-out' ... 'as in a distinct majority of correspondence schools students are enrolled continuously and are often allowed to keep a very flexible time schedule' (p. 31), and after discussing the completion concept, Bååth sums up:

> Although there are some uncertainties connected with the notions of completion and discontinuation in the distance education context, it is fairly safe to say that the completion rate in this type of study is often fairly low ... When non-starters (i.e. students who have registered for the course but who have not sent in one single assignment for correction and comment) are included among non-completers, drop-out rates round 50 per cent are not unusual. The variation between schools and even between courses at the same school is, however, considerable. As an extreme, from 0 per cent to 100 per cent completers have been found in different courses of the same Institution (Ward 1954).
>
> Non-starters are sometimes as frequent as – or even more frequent than – 'real' drop outs. On the whole, most of the dropping out normally happens during the very first part of a correspondence course.
>
> (Bååth 1984b: 32)

The completion issue has been investigated by a great many scholars. Up-to-date reviews of the completion/drop-out problem are provided in Cookson (1990) and Schuemer and Ströhlein (1991).

A general characteristic is that dropping out, when it occurs, usually happens at the beginning of the study. Sometimes the first few months of study should evidently be regarded as a trial period. In agreement with this thinking, the British Open University requires an introductory period of study and, after this period, a reconfirmation of study intentions before a student is regularly registered. Those who drop out during the introductory period are not included in the university statistics.

Considering the typical students of distance-teaching organizations (adults with families, jobs, and various commitments), it is not surprising to find that the reasons given for discontinuation are in the majority of all cases the pressure of duties, work commitments, travel, illness, lack of time, and similar circumstances.

Some attempts to explain the occurrence of drop out in higher education are well known. Tinto (1975) refers on the one hand to such self-evident causes as lack of interest, academic ability and goal commitment, on the other hand to poor social and academic integration, i.e. to feelings of not belonging. Bajtelsmith (1988), who pays special attention to distance education, modifies this approach and stresses the influence of circumstances outside the study situation, such as family and work. Schuemer and Ströhlein (1991), partly with reference to research done in Germany, also query the applicability of Tinto's approach to dropping out in distance education. In a careful study of drop-out occurrence in university distance education Peters (1992) implies a need for active student support to counteract the drop out problem. However, he does not regard its introduction into the German distance teaching university, the FernUniversität, as feasible, the reason being that the 'active support of students to reduce the drop-out level has no tradition in German universities' (Peters 1992: 258).

Nevertheless in all of the cases where dropping out occurs without goal attainment, counter-measures are evidently desirable (which is also stressed by Peters). In my view the best possible assistance that can be given to students, and thus an antidote against unwished-for discontinuation, is the empathy approach that produces conversation-like real and simulated communication (see p. 55) and personal relations between students and tutors (see pp. 125–7). The findings that Stein, Posz, and Brady (quoted on p. 126) report on support this strongly. Encouraging reminding letters have also proved to be helpful, as shown by Rekkedal (1972b) and others. Further, as discussed on pp. 122–5, both a short turn-around time of assignments that are submitted for correction and comment and a suitable frequency of non-contiguous communication can be of great importance.

However helpful counter-measures may be, the really decisive factor for course completion is the student's personality. Data culled from three German studies carried out in the 1980s show that:

1 The agreement between personal interest and course offer (degree structure) is the most decisive factor for success (continuation of study) and failure (drop out) (Bartels 1982: 11; Bartels 1983: 16).

2 Students inclined to work on their own rather than collectively, i.e. those who do not feel any handicap of isolation but rely on their own initiatives to establish contacts when desired, tend to be successful (Bartels 1982: 18), whereas most drop outs suffer from learning in isolation (Bartels 1983: 24–5).

3 A certain amount of resignation concerning the chances of professional promotion is common among the drop-outs (Bartels 1983: 7).

4 The drop outs have 'greater problems co-ordinating the requirements of their jobs, families and study than those continuing their study and are less capable of sustaining heavy workloads and changes in job situation; the latter are more prepared to accept that their personal lives suffer during their time of study' (Bartels *et al.* 1984: 94).

Apart from the last characteristic, which is concerned with physical and mental strength, and, partly, the general level of satisfaction with the study facilities, this summary indicates the dependence of success on strong study motivation generally and motivation for distance study in particular. As to the handicap of isolation, it is interesting that a Swedish study showed that 24 per cent of the drop outs considered their failure to be due to 'incapacity to study on one's own' (Wångdahl 1980: 54).

That strong study motivation is decisive for success is confirmed by experiences in many different contexts (thus explicitly in Sewart (1983: 168); see McIntosh *et al.* (1980: 51) on the first intake at the Open University). It should be noted, however, that there are different kinds of motivation and that the study motivation of each individual is likely to be rather complex.

A study by Rekkedal already referred to indicates, on the basis of statistical evidence, that:

1 Practically no relationship could be established between

students' domestic background and discontinuance (Rekkedal 1972a: 17); this is remarkable, as distance students generally stress the importance of encouraging support from husband/wife and other family members (see Bartels 1982: 14 and 1983: 20, confirming this).

2 Older students 'survived' to a greater extent and achieved better results than younger students (ibid. p. 26), which, as far as the first statement is concerned, agrees with Donehower's study of 1968; as to the second statement, Donehower 'found that the oldest group (only 9 students more than 60 years old) received the lowest marks; except for these oldest students, the achievement rose with increasing age of group at least up to about 45 years of age' (Rekkedal 1972a: 26).

3 Not unexpectedly, there were positive correlations between the levels of previous education and both survival and achievement.

The greater success of older and better qualified students and of students already familiar with intellectual work of some kind, as well as the lack of influence of the domestic background, can all be related to motivation. Older, mature, and well-informed students may be assumed to be less likely than younger students to enrol unless they are strongly motivated. Good basic education, relevant prior knowledge, reading habits, and similar background conditions naturally confer advantages and make for initial good results; the maxim 'Nothing succeeds like success' interprets the motivational influence of this. Strength of will, self-discipline, and similar qualities are evidently connected with motivation.

The decisive influence of motivation for goal attainment in distance education is stressed by Sewart in a statement that puts other aspects referred to in perspective:

> In the final analysis, we are left with the conclusions that neither age nor distance nor domestic environment nor any other quantifiable term stands out as a salient feature. It is motivation above all else which, despite physical and general social and environmental problems, brings success.
>
> (Sewart 1983: 168)

THE ECONOMICS OF DISTANCE EDUCATION

Sweeping statements about the economics of distance education are hardly possible. Such statements must be differentiated. They may represent the factual situation that applies in most cases (the private correspondence schools), in well-defined extensive areas (such as the distance-teaching universities), or in applications of distance education to specific functions only (as is often the case in personnel training).

There are different kinds of distance education, and it is important to realize that even seemingly parallel systems include different components and media. The British Open University includes the use of television and radio for its teaching, whereas the German FernUniversität does not. Both these universities run a number of study centres where students are continuously offered tutorials and various media facilities. This is a type of service that is not provided by probably the vast majority of distance-study institutions in various parts of the world, the publicly funded and private correspondence schools. These in their turn may or may not make use of the telephone for oral tutorials. Some distance-teaching institutions provide video-recordings and films to be used during face-to-face sessions or individually in study centres; others limit their media provision to printed material and audio-tapes (cassettes) and/or discs. Whereas some insist on bringing students together for concentrated residential courses, others do not organize any activities of this kind. Some institutions work with student bodies limited to a few hundred or even fewer students. Others are mass-education institutions with many thousands of students. The differences in relation to economics between the two last-mentioned types of providers of distance education are illuminating.

In one application of the former at the university level, the Australian New England system, parallelism with on-campus study is considered valuable and even of vital importance. Periods of residential teaching play an important part. Further, distance 'students are taught and examined by the same staff that teach internal students. . . . They study the same courses as those offered internally. . . . They take the same examinations at the same time as internal students in examination centres' (Smith 1975: 163).

This parallelism has been extended to a requirement that distance study and on-campus study should have the same student/staff ratio.

It has been found at New England that one lecturer can

satisfactorily teach 50 students in one course, where three courses provide a full-time year of study. In other words, three lecturers are required to teach 50 students full-time, producing a student/staff ratio of about 16:1. Allowing for a drop out of about 20 per cent for external students, this produces a student/staff ratio of about 13:1, which is very close to the ratio considered reasonable for Australian universities generally.

(Sheath 1972: 288–9)

This is a very different approach from the one applied by the large correspondence schools and sometimes by the distance-teaching universities, when courses are developed for thousands of students and various kinds of technology, labour-saving devices, and division of labour are used to attain economies of scale.

The differences mentioned, and others, show that any reference to the costs of distance education must be qualified by a description of what kind is meant. Evidently, pure correspondence study, relying exclusively on the written word as its medium, can be very inexpensive if it is offered on a large scale, so that the cost of each course can be spread out over several thousand students. More sophisticated systems require higher costs per student, even if large numbers of students are provided for. The problem area concerned with the economics of distance education is surveyed in a profitable way in Perraton (1982); Kaye and Rumble (1981); Rumble (1986). Much discussion on economic issues has taken place. A summary with comments relevant to publicly funded tertiary-level institutions is given in Keegan (1990: Part IV).

In order to come to grips with the economics of distance education, comparisons with other forms of study may be helpful. If we compare the costs of reaching a particular educational goal, for instance a degree, by distance education with the cost of attaining the same qualification by conventional study, we should be able to draw important conclusions. Then it is essential to compare both input and output. The input would be the total cost (students' fees, government or other financing and subsidies, the loss of income incurred by students who give up work for study, etc.), whereas the output would be the degree or other study goal reached and possibly even its economic value.

Let us from these points of view look at the most sophisticated distance-education system known, that of the Open University in the UK. Its size in the UK and importance as a pattern for other distance-education institutions makes such a study particularly interesting. The economics of The Open University was thoroughly investigated at an early stage.

A study by Wagner in 1972 of the costs of the Open University in relation to conventional British universities showed the following results:

1 The average recurrent cost per equivalent undergraduate in the Open University was found to be a little more than a quarter of what it was in conventional universities.
2 The capital cost per student place in the Open University was found to be only six per cent of what it was in conventional universities.
3 The average recurrent cost per graduate in the Open University was found to be equal to that in conventional universities, provided that the Open University had a drop-out rate of 85 per cent. (It is actually less than 50 per cent).
4 The resource cost per equivalent undergraduate in the Open University was found to be about one-sixth of that in conventional universities.

A later study by Wagner (in 1977) confirmed the findings of his first study:

If the drop-out rate in the future does not differ significantly from the past then the average cost per graduate is likely to be below half that at conventional universities.

Finally the resource costs measure the cost to the economy and include therefore the output lost by full-time students not being in employment. This of course increases the Open University's advantage because all its students are part-time. The figures indicate a ratio of 5:1 in the Open University's favour.

(Wagner 1977: 365)

The fact that the highly sophisticated multi-media system of the Open University compares very favourably with conventional universities would seem to indicate that distance education generally can be very economical. To what extent this applies to all procedures and media applied is less certain. What we do not know, for instance, is whether the costs of study-centre activities or television programmes or various kinds of face-to-face support, all very expensive in relation to the use of printed and written communication, contribute to the effects of the system in relation to their costs. This is a subject well worth investigating. It has been the subject of some research but there is no conclusive evidence available.

In large-scale systems, the costs per student are normally low. However, some small-scale projects have also proved highly cost effective. A remarkable example is the University of Surrey staff-development programme for university lecturers in Southern Asia (see pp. 151 and 167–8).

Perraton, who has carefully studied the economics of distance education on the basis largely, but by no means exclusively, of experiences of teaching in developing countries, cautiously summarizes his findings by saying that

> it is possible only to claim that there are circumstances in which distance teaching looks attractive from an economic point of view. Economies of scale are possible. But distance education characteristically has high fixed costs and, with relatively low student numbers, its costs can be higher than those of conventional education.
>
> (Perraton 1982: 61)

For someone who, like the present author, is mainly concerned with the applications that make full use of the potential of distance education as referred to on pp. 161–5, it is possible to go a little further than Perraton. There can be no doubt that distance education, as applied to large student bodies, is characterized by very favourable cost-benefit relations provided that the distance-teaching element consistently predominates. A number of case studies illustrating this are reported on in an earlier book of mine (Holmberg 1985a) and also in the first edition of the present work. It is primarily the arrangements for face-to-face sessions, such as study centres, residential schools, and classes of various kinds, that modify or negate the validity of this statement, i.e. non-distance supplements. It is true that use of sophisticated and costly media and technology also in some cases detracts from the favourable cost-benefit relations, but this does not change the overall picture of distance education as economical.

A CONCLUDING GENERAL APPRAISAL OF DISTANCE EDUCATION

This chapter on distance-education evaluation has been concerned both with how this type of education is evaluated and with the outcomes of evaluating studies. The latter concern would seem to warrant a concluding remark.

There are different types of distance education which make more or less consistent use of the potential of its special characteristics. Within these types there are also more or less successful practices. Like conventional types of education, distance education cannot be described as intrinsically either effective or ineffective, good or bad. It opens up a number of possibilities, however, and it does so in ways that are different from those of conventional education.

The preceding chapters will have shown that distance education is applicable, and has been successfully and economically applied, to many educational tasks and many different target groups. It mainly serves adult students, the secondary and tertiary stages of formal education, vocational and professional basic and further training, and self-actualizing study with or without purposes connected with academic credit or labour-market interest. Methods have been developed that strengthen its personal relevance to individual students and make it effective from the aspects of goal attainment, intellectual and emotional development, and involvement in serious study, as well as from those of energy, time, and financial resources invested. Distance education can safely be described as a useful and flexible kind of education with special potential for student autonomy.

Distance education has been shown to have generated theoretical considerations, which are concerned with its particular character, and hypothetico-deductive approaches to its educational effectiveness. After early attempts at distance education in the eighteenth and nineteenth centuries, followed by about a hundred years of experiences with organized distance education and a great number of scholarly studies into its theory and practice, we are entitled to describe it as an established mode of education in its own right.

11

THE ACADEMIC DISCIPLINE
OF DISTANCE EDUCATION

Considering the integration of educational, psychological, organizational–administrative, sociological, philosophical, technological
and economical aspects of the study of distance education it is
possible to regard it as an interdisciplinary field of study. It can
also be assigned a place under the comprehensive discipline of
education. It has been shown to be a separate entity, however,
which can only to a limited extent be described, understood, and
explained in terms of conventional school or university education, classroom teaching, or group activities (see pp. 164–5),
and so it makes sense to describe it as a special discipline with
its roots in education, which, in its turn, is rooted in philosophy.
The criteria for a university discipline are usually that there is a
body of research encompassing and defining it and that it is
taught as a university subject. 'Obviously, an academic discipline
is an area of academic interest, and one that poses sufficient
problems to stimulate research, and one that leads to the publication of journals in the subject area' (Sparkes 1983: 179).

RESEARCH ON DISTANCE EDUCATION

That there is a body of published research on distance education
will have been made manifestly clear by this book with both its
constant references to research and its bibliography. However,
the study of distance education is evidently benefiting from
knowledge and theory developed in disciplines that were established earlier. Most of the research done on distance education
could be ascribed to these, for example to general education,
pedagogics and andragogics, philosophy, psychology, sociology,
history, and economics.

It is only when such diverse studies concentrate on the concerns of distance education and emerge as consequences of a desire to attain expertise in distance education that it is possible to describe these united efforts as the beginnings of a new discipline. This is so when distance educators test the applicability of existing knowledge to their particular type of education and their target groups, and also discover new knowledge and 'new relationships within existing knowledge' (Jensen *et al.* 1964, on adult education).

The contents list of this book may be read as an articulated catalogue of research in the field, as the presentation of each chapter and section is based on research work. Other research areas, which have been given scant attention in this book, include economics and the history of distance education.

Sparkes' requirement that a discipline should lead to 'the publication of journals in the subject area' has been abundantly met. The following (with country of publication) should be mentioned:

The American Journal of Distance Education (USA)
Distance Education (Australia)
Epistolodidaktika (England)
Journal of Distance Education (Canada)
Open Learning (England)

To these should be added the newsletters and occasional publications of universities, schools, and professional bodies in the field such as:

Open Praxis. The Bulletin of the International Council for Distance Education
Open Campus (Australia: Deakin University)
Spotlight on Open Learning (of the British Training Agency)
Fernstudium aktuell (Deutsches Institut für Fernstudien an der Universität Tübingen)
Istruzione a Distanza (Universitá Degli Studi Di Roma La Sapienza)
Never Too Far (Unesco/Sukhothai Thanmathirat Open University)
Per Distans (Swedish National Organization for Distance Education).

Quite a few research departments have been established within and outside distance-teaching organizations. The British Open University has its Institute of Educational Technology (IET), which on the one hand contributes to R&D work related to the teaching of the University, to course development and evaluation, and on the other hand does independent distance-education research. The German FernUniversität has one service organization supporting the various faculties in their teaching, media development, evaluation etc. (Zentrum für Fernstudienentwicklung, ZFE), and also an autonomous research institute concentrating on problems of distance education independently of the immediate concerns of the FernUniversität (Zentrales Institut für Fernstudienforschung, ZIFF). The Open Learning Agency in Canada, Open Universiteit in the Netherlands, Deakin University and the University College of Southern Queensland in Australia as well as the Norwegian NKS and NKI schools are further examples of well-known distance-teaching organizations running their own departments for research on distance education. Research bodies wholly or partly unrelated to the actual teaching at a distance are, for example, the American Center for the Study of Distance Education at the Pennsylvania State University in the USA and Deutsches Institut für Fernstudienforschung at Tübingen University in Germany.

DISTANCE EDUCATION AS A UNIVERSITY TEACHING SUBJECT

Some universities regularly arrange courses and seminars on distance education. The University of Wisconsin at Madison should be mentioned as a pioneer. Credits towards degrees are sometimes awarded for this type of study.

Curricula have been developed for mainly postgraduate study of distance education and are offered, as seems logical, as distance-study courses by some universities. Among them are the FernUniversität (FeU) in Germany (Bååth 1984a; Holmberg 1982, 1983b), the South Australian College of Advanced Education (SACAE) (Mitchell 1982; Willmott and King 1984) and the University of Wisconsin with a programme leading to a 'Certificate of Professional Development in Distance Education'. The International Extension College in London offers a distance-education course preparing students for a University of London MA degree in distance education.

While there are considerable differences between the various courses of this type, as far as organization and media are concerned, their views of the subject, i.e. the discipline, largely coincide. Among other things they cover the following: the concept, theory, rationale, and philosophy of distance education, the distance students, study motivation, course planning and course development (instructional design), self-checking exercises, communication and support strategies, information technology, media, principles of adult education, organization and administration, systems and course evaluation. Issues of principles bearing on this teaching have been discussed by Willmott and King (1984) and the present author (Holmberg 1984). See also Kaufman (1984).

The consensus on the content of the discipline is strong also outside organized university teaching. This is apparent from various staff-training programmes for distance educators. An example from New Zealand has been presented by Nicoll (1986). The Association of European Correspondence Schools offers a comprehensive diploma course for distance educators taught by distance-education methods. This training is recognized by the British College of Preceptors, a body granted a Royal Charter as early as 1849 for the purpose of 'promoting sound learning and of advancing the interests of education'.

RECOGNITION

From what has been said it is evident that distance education meets the criteria mentioned and can, if these are accepted, be described as an academic discipline. There seems to be far-reaching unanimity about its content in research and university teaching.

There can be no doubt, however, that this claim is queried by many (as, for instance, the parallel claims of adult education have been rejected; see a discussion in the *Journal of Distance Education* I, 1 (1986) and IV, 1 Coldeway *et al.* (1989). Nevertheless, it seems reasonable to uphold it, although to many scholars it would evidently be more satisfactory to call distance education a field of study.

Sparkes asks in what ways an area of academic interest must develop to be 'acceptable to the academic community as a discipline' and answers that the following apply:

1 it must grow in degree of relevance to real and important problems . . .

2 it must grow in theoretical and conceptual depth;

3 it must develop its own 'conceptual structure'; that is, there must be a complex set of inter-relationships between its fundamental ideas.

(Sparkes 1983: 181)

This book should have shown that distance education is growing, and has been at least since the 1950s, in all of these respects. However, it must be conceded that on a further issue mentioned by Sparkes, the use made of distance-education theory and data by other disciplines, there is so far little to be adduced.

As further characteristics of a discipline Dressel and Mayhew (in discussing higher education as a field of study) mention the existence of 'a specialized vocabulary and a generally accepted basic literature' as well of 'some generally accepted body of theory and some generally understood techniques for theory testing and revision' (Dressel and Mayhew 1974: 3). The former evidently applies to distance education, whereas the latter – as shown in this book – is a concern of today's distance-education research.

What must in any case be admitted is that distance education is an area of research and academic teaching that constitutes a cohesive structure of theoretical and practical interest.

While this is decisive for its recognition as a discipline, the professionalization of distance educators beyond training programmes should also be considered. Contributions of relevance in this respect are Delling (1987a and 1992) on the scope of the profession; Coughlan (1980) on the mentor role (tutor styles and facilitation styles); Crick (1980) on the tasks of course developers (teams and their leaders); Meacham (1982) on change agents; Sewart (1980) on the role (and the support of) tutor-counsellors.

ON THE CHARACTER OF THE DISCIPLINE OF DISTANCE EDUCATION

As has been shown in the preceding chapters, distance-education research, and thus the discipline as a whole, has largely been concerned with problems of understanding and explaining its circumstances and conditions; the needs and requirements of its students; the measures taken to meet these needs and requirements; methodology; media use; organization and administration; evaluation of these measures and of complete distance-education systems from educational, social, and financial points of view. The search for understanding and explanation has in some cases resulted in attempts to find a kind of instrumental approach to improving distance education, i.e. facilitating distance students' learning. As shown in Chapter 9, these attempts have had some success in the spirit of Popper. The present author shares Popper's already quoted epistemological view, according to which the task of scholarship is both to bring about explanation and to provide for application and technology (see p. 180).

Some scholars are very pessimistic as to the practical technological part. It has been claimed that students' learning ability and readiness are determined by their learning experiences and habits, can only be partly improved and are above all largely irreversibly preconditioned by society. I do not share this belief in the dominance of social influence; I interpret the findings made and reported on about the impact of various kinds of course development and two-way communication as evidence of possibilities to apply cause–effect principles to the improvement both of distance education generally and of individual students' learning. The limitations of these possibilities have been discussed on pp. 180–1.

Most of the above exposition has concentrated on the internal problems of distance education, such as methods, without paying much attention to its milieu apart from its very prerequisites. There are scholars, however, who find it more important to investigate the role of distance education in society and how social conditions and distance education influence each other. In a paper published in 1991 Mick Campion and Patrick Guiton, both of Murdoch University in Western Australia:

> hope to begin to challenge the theoretical underpinning of policies which ignore, and hence deliberately or inadvertently, hide the fundamental importance of the economic, technological, demographic, cultural, political and social contexts within which a system of higher education operates. In essence we are arguing that... an emphasis on endogenous factors will no longer do.
>
> (Campion and Guiton 1991: 12)

Discussions among distance educators of what in comparison to industrial processes has been called Fordism and post-Fordism a related to power illustrate the trend towards research on exogenous factors. The social outcomes of distance education are thus coming to the fore. Anyone doing research on distance education must, independently of his or her own research orientation, be aware of these trends and take note of the fact that they are given priority in some research programmes (Evans 1991 and Edwards 1991).

In discussions of the kind mentioned a fear of alienation as a consequence of the industrial character of much distance education is often explicitly or implicitly in the foreground. This makes it important to demonstrate the fact that in distance education we actually have the only real one-to-one relationship between student and tutor that – but for Oxbridge tutorials – occurs in education. However 'industrial' the course development may be, mediated student–tutor interaction – in writing, on the telephone etc. – brings about personal contact between each student and his/her tutor. The importance of this one-to-one tutoring can hardly be exaggerated. It is also, as shown in Chapter 6 of this book, a most important and fertile research topic.

Endogenous and exogenous research of the kinds discussed undoubtedly characterize the discipline of distance education.

There are evidently good reasons to describe the discipline of distance education as both theoretical, in search of understanding and explanation, and practical or technological, applying principles that have been investigated with a view to facilitating learning and in other ways improving distance education.

REFERENCES

Abels, H., Heinze, Th., Horstkemper, M. and Klusemann, H. W. (1977) *Lebensweltanalyse von Fernstudenten. Qualitative Inhaltsanalyse – theoretische und methodologische Überlegungen. Werkstattbericht,* Hagen: Fern-Universität.

About Distance Education – a journal published by the International Extension College, London.

Ahlm, M. (1972) 'Telephone instruction in correspondence education. The functions of telephone instruction and an experimental study of its effects', *Epistolodidaktika* 1972, 2: 49–64.

Aitchison, J. and Aitchison, J. (1987) 'Text design in distance education: print and facilitating adult learning', *Papers* 7: 1–29, Pretoria: University of South Africa.

Allen, W. H. (1975) 'Intellectual abilities and instructional media design', *AV Communication Review* 23, 2: 39–170.

The American Journal of Distance Education, published by the Office for Distance Education of the College of Education at the Pennsylvania State University, University Park, PA: Pennsylvania State University.

Andrews, D. H. and Goodson, L. A. (1980) 'A comparative analysis of models of instructional design', *Journal of Instructional Development* 3, 4: 2–16.

Andrews, J. and Strain, J. (1985) 'Computer-assisted distance education: off-line and on-line American experiences', *Distance Education* 6, 2: 143–57.

Ansere, J. K. (1978) 'A profile of correspondence students in Ghana', *Epistolodidaktika* 2: 3–28.

—— (1982) 'The inevitability of distance education in Africa', in J. S. Daniel, M. A. Stroud and J. R. Thompson (eds) *Learning at a distance: A world perspective,* 53–61, Edmonton: Athabasca University/ICCE.

Ashhurst, J. (1985) *An evaluation of fleximode in the Victorian TAPE off-campus network in 1985,* Melbourne: Royal Melbourne Institute of Technology.

Atman, K. (1990) 'Psychological type elements and goal accomplishment style: Implications for distance education', in Moore, M.G. (ed.) *Con-*

temporary issues in American distance education, 136–50. Oxford: Pergamon.

Ausubel, D. P. (1968) *Educational psychology: a cognitive view*, New York: Holt, Rinehart & Winston.

Bååth, J. A. (1979a) *Correspondence education in the light of a number of contemporary teaching models*, Malmö: LiberHermods.

—— (1979b) *Postal two-way communication in correspondence education*, an EHSC workshop document, Malmö: LiberHermods.

—— (1980) *Postal two-way communication in correspondence education*, Lund: Gleerup.

—— (1981) 'On the nature of distance education', *Distance Education* 2, 2: 212–19.

—— (1987) 'A list of ideas for the construction of distance education courses', Appendix to B. Holmberg, *Distance Education: a short handbook* (3rd edn), Malmö: Hermods.

—— (1984a) 'Essentials of distance education', *Teaching at a Distance* 25: 120–2.

—— (1984b) 'Research on completion and discontinuation in distance education', *Epistolodidaktika* 1–2: 31–43.

—— (1986) 'Learning by written material: Psychological aspects with particular implications for correspondence education', *Epistolodidaktika* 2: 8–22.

—— (1989) 'Submission density, amount of submission questions, and quality of student–tutor dialogue – a comment on Holmberg & Schuemer', in Holmberg, B. (ed.) *Mediated communication as a component of distance education*, 81–8. Hagen: FernUniversität, ZIFF.

Bååth, J. A. and Månsson, N. O. (1977) *CADE – a system for computer-assisted distance education*, Malmö: LiberHermods.

Bajtelsmit, J. W. (1988) *Predicting distance learning dropouts: testing a conceptual model of attrition in distance study*, Bryn Mawr, PA: The American College.

—— (1990) 'Study methods in distance education: a summary of five research studies', in Moore, M. G. (ed.) *Contemporary issues in distance education*, 181–91. Oxford: Pergamon.

Balay, E. (1978) 'Factors associated with the completion and non-completion of correspondence courses', unpublished Master's thesis, University of Alberta.

Ballstaedt, S. P. and Mandl, H. (1982) 'Elaboration: Probleme der Erhebung und Auswertung', *DIFF-Forschungsberichte* 16, Tübingen: Deutsches Institut für Fernstudienforschung.

Ballstaedt, S. P., Molitor, S. and Mandl, H. (1987) 'Wissen aus Text und Bild', *Forschungsberichte* 40, Tübingen: Deutsches Institut für Fernstudien.

Barker, L. J., Taylor, J. C., White, V. J., Gillard, G., Khan, A. N., Kaufman, D. and Mezger, R. (1986) 'Student persistence in distance education: a cross-cultural multi-institutional perspective', *ICDE Bulletin* 12: 17–36.

Barrow, R. (1986) 'The concept of curriculum design', *Journal of Philosophy of Education* 20, 1: 73–80.

Bartels, J. (1982) *Absolventen*, Hagen: FernUniversität, ZFE.

—— (1983) *Studienabbrecher*, Hagen: FernUniversität.

Bartels, J. and Fritsch, H. (1976) 'Empirische Analyse des Studienabbruchs von Vollzeit- und Teilzeitstudenten nach dem ersten Studienhalbjahr an der FernUniversität', *ZIFF-Papiere* 11, Hagen: FernUniversität, ZIFF.

Bartels, J. and Wurster, J. (1975) *Erster Zwischenbericht über die studienbegleitende Erprobung der Studienmaterialien des Studienjahres 1975/76*, Hagen: FernUniversität.

—— (1979) *Evaluation, Konzepte und Erfahrungen an der FernUniversität*, Hagen: FernUniversität, ZFE.

Bartels, J., Helms, F. P., Rossié, U. and Schormann, J. (1984) *Studienverhalten von Fernstudenten. Eine vergleichende Untersuchung von Studienabbrechern und Studienfortsetzern*, Hagen: FernUniversität, ZFE.

Bates, A. W. (ed.) (1984) *The role of technology in distance education*, London/Sydney: Croom Helm.

Bates, A.W. (1990a) *Media and technology in European distance education*, Heerlen: European Association of Distance Teaching Universities.

—— (1990b) *A scan of the British Columbian Environment 1990–1993*, Vancouver: The Open Learning Agency.

—— (1993) 'Distance education in a changing world: the importance of policy research', in *Research in distance education*, Umeå: Distansrådet Umeå.

Battenberg, R. W. (1971) 'The Boston Gazette. March 20, 1728', *Epistolodidaktika* 1: 44–5.

Baynton, M. (1992) 'Dimensions of "control" in distance education, a factor analysis', *The American Journal of Distance Education* 6, 2: 17–31.

Beijer, E. (1972) 'A study of students' preferences with regard to different models for two-way communication,' *Epistolodidaktika* 2: 83–90.

Benkoe de Rotaeche, A. (1987) 'The influence of an instructional design upon learning of distance-education students in Venezuela', *ZIFF Papiere* 66, Hagen: FernUniversität.

Blom, D. (1986) 'Tutor-initiated telephone support for correspondence students at NKS', *Epistolodidaktika* 1: 51–62.

Bloom, B. S. *et al.* (1956 and 1964) *Taxonomy of educational objectives* I-II, New York: McKay.

Bock, M. (1983) 'Zur Repräsentation bildlicher und sprachlicher Informationen im Langzeitgedächtnis–Strukturen und Prozesse', in L. J. Issing and J. Hannemann (eds) *Lernen mit Bildern, AV-Forschung* 25: 61–94.

Boot, R. L. and Hodgson, V. E. (1987) 'Open learning: meaning and experience', in V. E. Hodgson, S. J. Mann and R. Snell (eds) *Beyond distance teaching – towards open learning*, 5–15, Milton Keynes: Open University Press.

Boucher, M. (1973) *Spes in arduis – a history of the University of South Africa*, Pretoria: University of South Africa.

Boud, D. (1988) 'Moving towards autonomy', in Boud, D. (ed.) *Developing student autonomy in learning*, London: Kogan Page.

—— (1990) 'Design for learning systems', in Eastcott, D., Farmer, B. and Lantz, B. (eds) *Aspects of Educational and Training Technology XXIII*,

Making learning systems work, 3–11, London: Kogan Page; New York: Nicholls.

Boud, D., Keogh, R. and Walker, D. (1985) 'What is reflection in learning?', in D. Boud, R. Keogh and D. Walker (eds) *Reflection: turning experiences into learning*, London: Kogan Page.

Bowles, J. C. (1987) 'Fleximode – a strategy for select groups or an option for all students?', *Programmed Learning and Educational Technology* 24, 3: 194–9.

Bradbury, Ph., Hinds, E., Humm, M. and Robbins, D. (1982) 'Innovations in independent study at North East London Polytechnic', in D. C. B. Teather (ed.) *Towards the community university. Case studies of innovation and community service*, 48–68, London: Kogan Page.

Brady, T. F. (1976) *Learner-instructor interaction in independent study programs*, Dissertation (unpublished), Madison, Wisc: University of Wisconsin.

Bratt, J. (1977) *Engelskundervisningens framväxt i Sverige. Tiden före 1850*, Stockholm: Föreningen för svensk undervisningshistoria.

Briggs, L. J. (1968) *Sequencing of instruction in relation to hierarchies of competence*, Pittsburgh: American Institute for Research.

Brockman, J. R. and Klobas, J. E. (1983) *Libraries and books in distance education*, Perth: Western Australian Institute of Technology.

Brown, B. and Fortosky, D. (1986) 'Use of television', in J. Mugridge and D. Kaufmann (eds) *Distance education in Canada*, 260–69, London: Croom Helm.

Bruner, J. S. (1971) *Towards a theory of instruction*. Cambridge: Harvard University Press.

Burt, G. (1977) 'How do readers comment on the structure of teaching materials?', *Teaching at a Distance* 10: 67–76.

Bynner, J. M. (1986) 'Masters teaching in education by distance methods', *Distance Education* 7, 1: 23–37.

Calvert, J. (1986) 'Research in Canadian distance education', in J. Mugridge and D. Kaufman (eds) *Distance education in Canada*, 94–110, London: Croom Helm.

Campion, M. and Guiton, P. (1991) 'Economic instrumentalism and integration in Australian external studies'. *Open Learning* 6, 2: 12–20.

Candy, P. (1987) 'Evolution, revolution or devolution: increasing learner control in the instructional setting', in Boud, D. and Griffin, V. (eds) *Appreciating adults' learning, from the learners' perspective*, London: Kogan Page.

Candy, P., Harri-Augstein, S. and Thomas, L. (1985) 'Reflection and the self-organized learner: a model of learning conversations', in D. Boud, R. Keogh and D. Walker (eds) *Reflection: turning experience into learning*, London: Kogan Page.

Casas Armengol, M. (1987) *Universidad sin clases: Educación a distancia en América Latina*, Caracas: OEA – UNA – Kapelusz.

Castro, A. S. (1987) *Teaching and learning as communication: the potentials and current applications of computer-mediated communication systems for higher distance education*, a Unesco conference document, Geelong: Deakin University.

Chafe, W. L. (1979) 'The flow of thought and the flow of language', in T. Givon (ed.) *Syntax and semantics 12, Discourse and syntax* 1: 59–181, New York: American Press.

—— (1980) 'The development of consciousness in the production of a narrative', in W. L. Chafe (ed.) *The pear stories: Cognitive, cultural, and linguistic aspects of narrative production*, 9–50, Norwood, N.J.: Ablex.

Chang, T. M., Crombag, H. F., van der Drift, K. D. J. M. and Moonen, J. M. (1983) *Distance learning: On the design of an Open University*, Boston: Kluwer-Nijhoff.

Chia, N. (1990) 'Measurement techniques in distance education: definition, classification, characteristics, selection and application'. *Epistolodidaktika* 1990: 51–93.

Childs, G. B. (1953) 'Supervised correspondence study', *4th ICCE-Proceedings*, 99–105, University Park, PA: ICCE.

—— (1965) 'Research in the correspondence instruction field', *7th ICCE Proceedings*, 79–84, Stockholm: ICCE.

—— (1971) 'Recent research developments in correspondence instruction', in O. MacKenzie and E. L. Christensen (eds) *The changing world of correspondence study*, 229–49, University Park, PA: Pennsylvania University Press.

Cirigliano, G. F. J. (1983) *La educación abierta*, Buenos Aires: El Ateneo.

Clark, R. E. (1975) 'Constructing a taxonomy of media attributes for research purposes', *AV Communication Review* 24, 2: 197–215.

Clyde, A., Crowther, H., Patching, W., Putt, I. and Store, R. (1983) 'How students use distance teaching materials: an institutional study', *Distance Education* 4, 1: 4–26.

Coldeway, D. O. (1986) 'Learner characteristics and success', in J. Mugridge and D. Kaufman (eds) *Distance education in Canada*, 81–93, London: Croom Helm.

Coldeway, D. O., Devlin, L.E. and Holmberg, B. (1989) 'Distance education as a discipline'. A debate, *Journal of Distance Education* IV, 1, 54–66.

Coldeway, D. O. and Spencer, R. E. (1982) 'Keller's personalized system of instruction: the search for a basic distance learning paradigm', *Distance Education*, 3, 1: 51–71.

Coleman, E. B. (1965) 'Learning of prose written in four grammatical transformations', *Journal of Applied Psychology* 49: 332–41.

Coltman, B. (1984) 'Environment and systems in distance counselling', *International workshop on counselling in distance education. Selected papers*, 45–57, Manchester: The Open University, ICDE.

Comenius, J. A. (1957) *Didactica magna*, photolithographic reprint of the Amsterdam edition of 1657 of *Opera didactica omnia*, Prague: Academia Scientiarum Bohemoslovenica.

Cookson, P. S. (1990) 'Persistence in distance education: a review', in Moore, M.G. (ed.) *Contemporary issues in American distance education*, 192–204, Oxford: Pergamon.

Cooper, A. and Lockwood, F. (1979) 'The need, provision and use of a computer-assisted interactive tutorial system', *Aspects of Educational*

Technology XIII (*Educational technology twenty years on*), 252–8, London: Kogan Page.

Coughlan, R. (1980) 'The mentor role in individualized education at Empire State college', *Distance Education* 1, 1: 1–12.

Crick, M. (1980) 'Course teams: myth and actuality', *Distance Education* 1, 2: 127–41.

Crocker, C. (ed.) (1982) *Library services in distance education: Proceedings of a national workshop*, Brisbane: Library Association of Australia.

Crombag, H. F. M. (1979) 'ATI: perhaps not such a great idea after all', *Tijdschrift voor Onderwijsresearch* 4, 4: 176–83.

Cross, K. P. (1976) *Accent on learning*, San Francisco and London: Jossey Bass.

Crothers, E. J. (1972) 'Memory structure and the recall of discourse', in J. B. Carroll and R. O. Freedle (eds) *Language comprehension and acquisition of knowledge*, New York: Wiley.

Cube, F. von (1968) *Kybernetische Grundlagen des Lernens und Lehrens*, Stuttgart: Klett.

Cunningham, J. (1987) 'Openness and learning to learn', in V. E. Hodgson, S. J. Mann and R. Snell (eds) *Beyond distance teaching – towards open learning*, 40–58, Milton Keynes: Open University Press.

Daniel, J. S. and Marquis, C. (1979) 'Interaction and independence: getting the mixture right', *Teaching at a Distance* 14: 29–44.

Davies, I. K. (1971) *The management of learning*, London: McGraw-Hill.

—— (1978) 'Objectives in curriculum design', in J. Hartley and I. K. Davies (eds) *Contributions to an educational technology*, 2: 135–51, London: Kogan Page.

Dawson, C. J. (1985) *A report on a hub class distance education project: Yr 11 and 12, Music Theory from Fremont High School to Jamestown High School, 1984–85*, Adelaide: University of Adelaide, Department of Education.

De Cecco, J. P. (1964) *Educational technology*, San Francisco: Holt, Rinehart & Winston.

Diehl, G. E. (1989) 'Some thoughts on delayed and immediate feedback – the effect of field scoring on time to completion in career development courses – comparison of two pre-test feedback modalities on end of course test performance', in Holmberg, B. (ed.) *Mediated communication as a component of distance education* 3–31. Hagen: FernUniversität, ZIFF.

Delling, R. M. (1966) 'Versuch der Grundlegung zu einer allgemeinen Fernunterrichtstheorie', *Epistolodidaktika* 4: 209–26.

—— (1987a) 'Professionalisierung und Fernstudium', *Fernstudium aktuell* 9, 1/2: 13.

—— (1987b) 'Towards a theory of distance education', *ICDE Bulletin* 13, January: 21–5.

—— (ed.) (1992) *Professionalisierung im Fernstudium*, Tübingen: Bund redlich Interessierter an der Erforschung der Fernunterrichtsprobleme.

Dewal, O. S. (1986) 'Open School, India: The preliminary years,

1979–1983. A case study', *Deakin Open Education Monographs* No. 3, Victoria: Deakin University, The Distance Education Unit.

Dewey, J. (1916) *How to think*, Boston: Heath.

Dieuzeide, H. (1985) 'Les enjeux politiques', in F. Henri and A. Kaye (eds) *Le savior à domicile. Pédagogique et problématique de la formation à distance*, Québec: Télé-Université.

Distance Education 1980– , the Journal of the Australian and South Pacific External Studies Association, Melbourne.

Dixon, T. (1992) 'Design principles for microcomputer-based learning software: a case study approach', *Epistolodidaktika* 1992: 1: 56–99.

Dochy, F. J. R. C. (1988) *The 'prior knowledge state' of students and its facilitating effect on learning: theories and research*, Heerlen: Open Universiteit, OTIC.

Doerfert, F. (1980) *Zur Wirksamkeit typografischer und grafischer Elemente in gedruckten Fernstudienmaterialien*, Hagen: FernUniversität, ZIFF.

Doerfert, F., Schuemer, R. and Tomaschewski, C. (1989) *Short descriptions of selected distance-education institutions*, Hagen: FernUniversität, ZIFF.

Doerfert, F. and See-Bögehold, C. (1991) *Abschlussbericht zum Arbeitsfeld Medien*, Hagen: FernUniversität, ZIFF.

Donehower, G. (1968) *Variables associated with correspondence study: A study to test twelve hypotheses* (unpublished MA thesis), Reno: Nevada University.

Donnachie, I. (1986) 'Distance teaching of history: a comparison of Open University and Deakin University approaches', *Open Campus* 12: 48–57.

Dressel, P. L. and Mayhew, L. B. (1974) *Higher education as a field of study*, San Francisco: Jossey-Bass.

Dubin, R. and Taveggia, T. (1968) *The teaching-learning paradox*, Eugene: University of Oregon, Center for the Advanced Study of Educational Administration.

Duchastel, Ph.C (1976) 'TAD 292 – Art and Environment and its challenge to educational technology', *Programmed Learning and Educational Technology* 13, 4: 61–6.

Dunnett, C. (1985) 'Communications' technology and resources of the school system', *Educational Media International* 4: 2–5.

Durbridge, N. (1982) *Audio cassettes in higher education*, Milton Keynes: The Open University (mimeo).

—— (1984) 'Audio-cassettes', in A. W. Bates (ed.) *The role of technology in distance education*, London: Croom Helm.

Education 21, 'The Open University system', May 1976: 1–7.

Edwards, R. (1991) 'The inevitable future? Post-Fordism and open learning', *Open Learning* 6, 2: 36–42.

Egan, K. (1976) *Structural communication*, Belmont, Calif.: Fearon.

Einstein, A. and Infeld, L. (1950) *Die Evolution der Physik*, Hamburg: Zsolnay.

El-Bushra, J. (1973) *Correspondence teaching at university*, Cambridge: International Extension College.

Elton, L. (1988) 'Conditions for learner autonomy at a distance', *Programmed Learning and Educational Technology* 25, 2: 216–24.

Elton, L., Oliver, E. and Wray, M. (1986) 'Academic staff training at a distance – a case study', *Programmed Learning and Educational Technology* 23, 1: 29–40.

Entwistle, N. J. (1978) 'Knowledge structures and styles of learning: a summary of Pask's recent research', *British Journal of Educational Psychology* 48: 255–65.

Epistolodidaktika, 1963–70, Hamburg: Walter Schultz Verlag.

Epistolodidaktika, 1971–72, Malmö: European Home Study Council (EHSC).

Epistolodidaktika, 1973–85, London: European Home Study Council (EHSC).

Epistolodidaktika, 1986- , London: Association of European Correspondence Schools (AECS).

Erdos, R. F. (1967) *Teaching by correspondence*, UNESCO source book (French version: *L'enseignement par correspondance*), London: Longman.

—— (1975a) *Establishing an institution teaching by correspondence*, Paris: UNESCO, International Bureau of Education.

—— (1975b) 'The system of distance education in terms of sub-systems and characteristic functions', in E. Ljoså (ed.) *The system of distance education*, 9–19, Malmö: LiberHermods.

—— (1992) *Teaching beyond the campus*, Glebe (Australia): Fast Books.

Ericsson, K. A. and Simon, H. A. (1980) 'Verbal reports as data', *Psychological Review* 87: 215–51.

Evans, T. (1984) 'Communicating with students at a distance', *Teaching at a Distance* 25: 108–10.

Evans, T. and King, B. (eds) (1991) *Beyond the text: contemporary writing on distance education*, Geelong: Deakin University Press.

Evans, T. and Nation, D. (1992) 'Theorising open and distance education', *Open Learning* 7, 2: 3–13.

Faust, G. W. and Anderson, R. C. (1967) 'Effects of incidental material in a programmed Russian vocabulary lesson', *Journal of Educational Technology*, 58: 3–10.

Faw, H. W. and Waller, T. G. (1976) 'Mathemagenic behaviours and efficiency in learning from prose materials: review, critique and recommendations', *Review of Educational Research* 46, 4: 691–720.

Fernstudium aktuell 1979- , Tübingen: Deutsches Institut für Fernstudien an der Universität Tübingen.

Fitzpatrick, J. (1982) 'The Australian schools of the air: the conundrum of who teaches', *Distance Education* 3, 2: 183–97.

Flinck, R. (1978) *Correspondence education combined with systematic telephone tutoring*, Kristianstad: Liber Hermods.

—— (1980) 'The research project on two-way communication in distance education: an overview', *Epistolodidaktika* 1–2: 3–10.

Foks, J. (1987) 'Towards open learning', in P. Smith and M. Kelly (eds) *Distance education and the mainstream*, 74–92, London: Croom Helm.

Forsythe, K. (1984) 'Satellite and cable', in A. W. Bates (ed.) *The role of technology in distance education*, 57–68, London: Croom Helm.

—— (1985) '*A web of diamonds: the learning system as a new paradigm for the information age*', Paper presented to the XXXII Annual World

Assembly of the International Council on Education for Teachers in Vancouver.

—— (1986) *Understanding the effectiveness of media in the learning process*, Paper presented at the World Congress of Education and Technology in Vancouver, May 1986, Victoria: Learning Systems Knowledge Network.

Fox, D. (1983) 'Personal theories of teaching', *Studies in Higher Education* 8, 2: 151–63.

Frase, L. T. and Silbiger, F. (1970) 'Some adaptive consequences of searching for information in a text', *American Educational Research Journal* 7: 553–60.

Fritsch, H. (1980) 'Nichtbewerber: Gründe von Interessenten, sich nicht an der Fernuniversität einzuschreiben', *ZIFF-Papiere* 32, Hagen: Fern-Universität, ZIFF.

—— (1989) 'PC Tutor', *ZIFF-Papiere* 75, Hagen: FernUniversität.

Fritsch, H. and Ströhlein, G. (1988) 'Mentor support and academic achievement', *Open Learning* 3, 2: 27–32.

Fritsch, H., Kueffner, H. and Schuch, A. (1979) *Entwicklung einer Studieneingangsberatung für Fernstudenten*, Hagen: FernUniversität, ZIFF.

Gaddén, G. (1973) *Hermods 1898–1973*, Malmö: Hermods.

Gage, N. L. (1963) *Handbook of research on teaching*, Chicago: Rand McNally.

Gage, N. L. (1978) *The scientific bases of the art of teaching*, New York: Teachers College Press.

Gagné, R. M. (1968) 'Learning hierarchies', *Educational Psychologist* 6: 1–9.

—— (1970) *The conditions of learning*, 2nd edn, New York: Holt, Rinehart & Winston.

—— (1977) *The conditions of learning*, 3rd edn, New York: Holt, Rinehart & Winston.

Ganor, M. (1988) 'Assignment construction and evaluation', in Sewart, D. and Daniel, J. (eds) *Developing distance education*, 207–10, Oslo: International Council for Distance Education.

—— (1990) 'On the structure of evaluation at a distance', in Croft, M., Mugridge, I., Daniel, J. and Hershfield, A. (eds) *Distance education: development and access* 167–72, Caracas: International Council for Distance Education.

—— (1991) 'Evaluation at a distance', in Schuemer, R. (ed.) *Evaluation concepts and practice in selected distance education institutions*, 80–8, Hagen: FernUniversität, ZIFF.

Garrison, D. R. (1990) 'An analysis and evaluation of audio teleconferencing to facilitate education at a distance', *The American Journal of Distance Education* 4, 3: 13–24.

Garrison, D. R. and Shale, D. (1990) 'A new framework and perspective'. In Garrison, D. R. and Shale, D. (eds) *Education at a distance: from issues to practice* 123–34, Malabar, Florida: Krieger.

Gaskel, A., Gibbons, S. and Simpson, O. (1990) ' "Taking off" and "bailing out" ' – correspondence counselling, *Open Learning* 5, 2: 49–54.

Gervais, R. (1987) 'Steps to your future', in A. Tait (ed.) *Second international workshop on counselling in distance education. Conference papers*, 37–46, Cambridge: Open University East Anglia, Cambridge.

Gibbons, A. S. (1977) 'A review of content and task analysis methodology', *Report Series* 2, San Diego: Courseware Inc.

Gibbs, G. and Durbridge, N. (1976) 'Characteristics of Open University tutors', *Teaching at a Distance* 6: 96–102 and 7: 7–22.

Gilliland, J. (1972) *Readability*, London: Hodder & Stoughton.

Glatter, R. (1968) 'The Manchester home study research project', *CEC Yearbook*, 34–52, Copenhagen: CEC.

Glatter, R. and Wedell, E. G. (1971) *Study by correspondence. An enquiry into correspondence study for examinations for degrees and other advanced qualifications*, London: Longman.

Göttert, R. (1983) 'Fernstudieninteressenten. Ihr Selbstbild und weiterer Studienverlauf', *ZIFF-Papiere* 47, Hagen: FernUniversität, ZIFF.

Graff, K. (1970) *Voraussetzungen erfolgreichen Fernstudiums. Dargestellt am Beispiel des schwedischen Fernstudiensystems*, Hamburg: Lüdke.

—— (1977) *Vorschläge für ein Projekt 'EDV-Buchhaltungsprogramm' im Rahmen des CMA-Projekts*, Zwischenbericht Projekt Standardisierte Testverfahren, Hagen: FernUniversität.

—— (1980) 'Die Jüdische Tradition und das Konzept des autonomen Lernens', *Studien und Dokumentationen zur vergleichenden Bildungsforschung*, Bd. 14, herausgegeben von Wolfgang Mitter, Weinheim und Basel: Beltz.

—— (1981) 'Management von Fernstudieneinrichtungen', in P. Clever, W. Hesshaus, M. Lücke and G. Mus (eds) *Ökonomische Theorie und wirtschaftliche Praxis*, Festschrift zum 65, Geburtstag von Rolf Hanschmann, Herne/Berlin: Verlag Neue Wirtschafts-Briefe.

Graff, K. and Holmberg, B. (eds) (1984) *Fernstudium im internationalen Vergleich–Erste Ergebnisse*, Zwischenbericht zum ZIFF-Forschungsprojekt Nr. 1–2.29, Hagen: FernUniversität, ZIFF.

—— (1988) *International study on distance education: a project report*, Hagen: FernUniversität, ZIFF.

Graff, K., Holmberg, B., Schuemer, R. and Wilmersdoerfer, H. (1977) *Zur Weiterentwicklung des Studiersystems der FernUniversität. Struktur und Ablauf*, Hagen: FernUniversität, ZIFF.

Granholm, G. (1971) 'Classroom teaching or home study – a summary of research on relative efficiency', *Epistolodidaktika* 1971, 2: 9–14 and 1973, 2: 6–10.

Groeben, N. (1972) *Die Verständlichkeit von Unterrichtstexten. Dimensionen und Kriterien rezeptiver Lernstadien*, Münster: Aschendorff.

Hall, W., Thorogood, G. and Carr, L. (1989) 'Using hypercard and interactive video in education: an application in cell biology', *Educational and Training Technology International* 26, 3: 207–14.

Halliwell, J. (1987) 'Is distance education by radio outdated? A consideration of the outcome of an experiment in continuing medical education with rural health care workers in Jamaica', *British Journal of Educational Technology* 18, 1: 5–15.

Handal, G. (1973) 'On the selection of relevant media/methods for defined educational purposes', in G. Granholm (ed.) *The selection of relevant media/methods for defined educational purposes within distance education*, 1–32, Oslo: NKI.

Hannum, W. H. and Briggs, L. J. (1982) 'How does instructional systems design differ from traditional instruction?', *Educational Technology*, Jan: 9–14.

Harary, F., Norman, R. Z. and Cartwright, D. (1965) *Structural models: An introduction to the theory of directed graphs*, New York: Wiley.

Harley, M. F. (1985) 'An alternative organizational model for early childhood distance education programs', *Distance Education* 6, 2: 158–68.

Hartley, J. (ed.) (1980) *The psychology of written communication*, London: Kogan Page.

Hartley, J. and Burnhill, P. (1977) 'Fifty guide-lines for improving instructional text', *Programmed Learning and Educational Technology* 14, 1: 65–73.

Hartley, J. and Trueman, M. (1979) 'Some observations on producing and measuring readable writing', *Aspects of Educational Technology* XIII (*Educational technology twenty years on*), 102–6, London: Kogan Page.

Hartmann-Anthes, P. and Ebbeke, K. (1991) 'COURSY. Correction, utility and research system', *ZIFF-Papiere* 85. Hagen: FernUniversität.

Haughey, M. (1991) 'Confronting the pedagogical issues', *Open Learning* 6, 3: 14–23.

Hawkridge, D. G. (1978) 'The University of Mid-America: an Open University analogue', *Teaching at a Distance* 13: 37–44.

Heidt, E. U. (1976) *Medien- und Lernprozesse*, Tübingen: Universitätsverlag.

—— (1978) *Instructional media and the individual learner*, London: Kogan Page.

Hellkvist, I. (1981, 1982) *Utvärdering av grundläggande vårdlärarutbildning som distansundervisning* I-II, Uppsala: Uppsala universitet, Avd. för pedagogisk utveckling och fortbildning.

Henderson, E. S. and Nathenson, M. B. (1976) 'Development testing: an empirical approach to course improvement', *Programmed Learning and Educational Technology 13*, 4: 31–42.

Henderson, E. S., Hodgson, B. and Nathenson, M. B. (1977) 'Developmental testing: the proof of the pudding', *Teaching at a Distance 10*: 77–92.

Henri, F. and Kaye, A. (1985) *Le savoir à domicile. Pédagogie et problématique de la formation à distance*, Québec: Presses de l'Université du Québec, Télé-université.

Herrmann, T. (1979) *Psychologie als Problem*, Stuttgart: Klett.

Hinds, E. (1987) 'The school for independent study and international links', *ZIFF-Papiere* 69, Hagen: Fern-Universität.

Hirst, P. H. (1970) 'The logical and psychological aspects of teaching a subject', in R. S. Peters (ed.) *The concept of education*, London: Routledge & Kegan Paul.

Hirst, P. H. and Peters, R. S. (1970) *The logic of education*, London: Routledge & Kegan Paul.

Holmberg, B. (1960) 'On the methods of teaching by correspondence', *Lunds universitets årsskrift*, N. F. Avd. 1 Bd. 54 Nr. 2, Lund: Gleerup.

—— (1969) 'Educational technology and correspondence education', *8th ICCE Proceedings*, 59–62, Paris: ICCE.

—— (1972) *Företagsplanering. Erfarenheter och synpunkter baserade på en arbetsmetod*, Malmö: Hermods.

—— (1973a) 'Supervised correspondence study – a Swedish case study based on experiences within the school system', *Epistolodidaktika* 2: 29–34.

—— (1973b) 'The Swedish Delta Project – a case study', in G. Granhom (ed.) *The selection of relevant media/methods for defined educational purposes within distance education*, Oslo: NKI, EHSC.

—— (1977a) *Distance education: a survey and bibliography*, London: Kogan Page.

—— (1977b) 'Das Leitprogramm im Fernstudium', *ZIFF Papiere* 17, Hagen: FernUniversität, ZIFF.

—— (1981a) 'Independent study for university degrees: distance study compared with the Keller Plan', *Distance Education* 2, 1: 39–53.

—— (1981b) 'Approaches to correspondence course evaluation', *Epistolodidaktika* 1981, 1: 3–29.

—— (1982) *Essentials of distance education* (a distance-study course based on a handbook and reader), German version: *Grundlagen des Fernstudiums*, Hagen: Fern-Universität, ZIFF.

—— (1983a) 'Guided didactic conversation in distance education', in D. Sewart, D. Keegan and B. Holmberg (eds) *Distance Education: International Perspectives*, 114–22, London: Croom Helm.

—— (1983b) 'Considerations concerning the content of a course in distance education', *EHSC Report of Proceedings*, Autumn workshop at Eastbourne, 44–53, London: Tuition House.

—— (1984) 'Professional development courses in distance education: a reply', *Distance Education* 5, 2: 237–38.

—— (1985a) *Status and trends of distance education* (second revised edition), Lund: Lector Publishing.

—— (1985b) 'Applications of distance education in Kenya', *Distance Education* 6, 2:242–47.

—— (1985c) 'The feasibility of a theory of teaching for distance education and a proposed theory', *ZIFF Papiere* 60, Hagen: FernUniversität, ZIFF.

—— (1986) *Growth and structure of distance education*, Beckenham: Croom Helm.

—— (1987) *Distance Education: a short handbook* (3rd edn), Malmö: Liber.

—— (1989a) 'The concepts and applications of distance education and open learning', *International Journal of Innovative Higher Education* 6, 1 and 2: 24–8.

—— (1989b) (ed.) *Mediated communication as a component of distance education*, Hagen: FernUniversität, ZIFF.

—— (1989c) 'Key issues in distance education: an academic viewpoint'. *European Journal of Education* 24, 1: 11–23.

—— (1992) 'An epistemological stand'. *Educational and Training Technology International* (ETTI) 29, 4: 269–78.

Holmberg, B. and Schuemer, R. (1989) *Tutoring frequency in distance education – an empirical study of the impact of various frequencies of assignment submission*, Hagen: FernUniversität, ZIFF (in preparation).

Holmberg, B., Schuemer, R. and Obermeier, A. (1982) *Zur Effizienz des gelenkten didaktischen Gespräches*, ZIFF-Projekt 2.6, Schlussbericht mit einer englischen Zusammenfassung (with an English summary), Hagen: FernUniversität, ZIFF.

Holmberg, R. G. and Bakshi, T. S. (1982) 'Laboratory work in distance education', *Distance Education* 3, 2: 198–206.

Horn, R. and Green, J. (1974) 'Information mapping', in A. Howe and A. J. Romiszowski (eds) *APLET Yearbook of Educational and Instructional Technology* 1974/75, 125–7, London: Kogan Page.

Hosford, P. L. (1973) *An instructional theory – a beginning*, Englewood Cliffs, N.J.: Prentice-Hall.

Huber, G. L., Krapp A. and Mandl, H. (eds) (1984) *Pädagogische Psychologie als Grundlage pädagogischen Handelns*, München: Urban & Schwarzenberg.

Hudgins, B. B. (1971) *The instructional process*, Chicago: Rand McNally.

Iley, J. (1983) 'Why a unit is not a book', *Teaching at a distance* 23: 76–7.

Isaacs, G. (1990) 'Course and tutorial CAL lesson design: helping students take control of their own learning', *Educational and Training Technology International* 27, 1: 85–91.

James, B. J. and Wedemeyer, C. A. (1959 and 1960), 'Completion of university correspondence courses by adults', *The Home Study Review* 1, 2: 13–20; also published in: *Journal of Higher Education* 30, 2: 87–93.

James, W. (1899) *The principles of psychology*, New York: Holt, Rinehart & Winston.

Jarvis, P. (1993) 'The learning process and late modernity', *Scandinavian Journal of Educational Research* 37, 3: 179–90.

Jenkins, J. and Perraton, (1980) 'The invisible college: NEC 1963–1979', *IEC Broadsheets on distance learning* no. 15, Cambridge: International Extension College.

Jensen, G., Liveright, A. A. and Hallenbeck, W. (1964) *Adult education. Outline of an emerging field of university study*. Place of origin not stated: Adult Education Association of USA.

Jevons, F. (1984) 'Distance education in mixed institutions: working towards parity', *Distance Education* 5, 1: 24–37.

Johnson, R. (1991) 'Recent developments in distance higher education in Australia', *ICDE Bulletin* 26: 11–22.

Jonassen, D. H. (ed.) (1984) *The technology of text: principles for structuring, designing, and displaying text* I-II, Englewood Cliffs, N.J.: Educational Technology Publications.

Jones, A. (1984) 'Computer assisted learning in distance education', in A. W. Bates (ed.) *The role of technology in distance education*, London: Croom Helm.

Journal of Distance Education (Revue de l'enseignment à distance) 1986-, Canada: Ottawa, Canadian Association for Distance Education.

Juler, P. (1990) 'Promoting interaction: maintaining independence: swallowing the mixture'. *Open Learning* 5, 2: 24–33.

Kammerer-Jöbges, B. (1992) *Betriebliche Nutzung.* Hamburg: Büro Kammerer-Jöbges.

Katzen, M. (1977) *The visual impact of scholarly journals,* Leicester: Leicester University, Primary Communication Research Centre.

Kaufman, D. (1982) *Course development: industrial or social process,* Paper presented at the American Educational Research Association, March 1982, New York.

—— (1984) 'Practice and theory of distance education: course blue print', *Distance Education* 5, 2: 239–51.

—— (1986) 'Computers in distance education', in J. Mugridge and D. Kaufmann (eds) *Distance education in Canada,* 296–309, London: Croom Helm.

Kaufman, D., Sketches, D. and Usukawa, S. (1982) *Visual design in distance education courses,* Richmond, B.C.: Open Learning Institute.

Kaye, A. and Rumble, G. (eds) (1981) *Distance teaching for higher and adult education,* London: Croom Helm/The Open University Press.

Kaye, T. (1985) *Computer-mediated communication systems for distance education. Report on a study visit to North America,* Milton Keynes: The Open University, IET.

Keegan, D. J. (1980a) 'On the nature of distance education', *ZIFF Papiere* 33, Hagen: FernUniversität, ZIFF.

—— (1980b) 'On defining distance education', *Distance Education* 1, 1: 13–36.

—— (1983) *Six distance education theorists,* Hagen: Fern Universität ZIFF.

—— (1986) *The foundations of distance education,* London: Croom Helm.

—— (1990) *Foundations of distance education,* London and New York: Routledge.

Kelly, P. (1982) *An overview of student use and appreciation of tuition,* Milton Keynes: The Open University, RTS Research Group.

Kelly, M. and Shapcott, M. (1987) 'Towards understanding adult distance learners', *Open Learning* 2, 2: 3–10.

Kember, D. (1982) 'External science courses: the practicals problem', *Distance Education* 3, 2: 207–25.

Kemmis, S. (1980) 'Program evaluation in distance education: against the technologization of reason', *Open Campus* 2: 19–48.

Kemmis, S. and Hughes, C. (1979) 'Curriculum evaluation in higher education: self-reflection in a critical community', *Open Campus* 3: 7–26.

Khoul, B. N. and Jenkins, J. (1990) *Distance education. A spectrum of case studies,* London: Kogan Page/International Extension College.

King, B. (1993) 'Open learning in Australia: government intervention and institutional response', *Open Learning* 8, 3: 13–25.

King, B., Sewart, D. and Gough, J. E. (1980) 'Support systems in distance education', *Open Campus* 3: 13–28.

Kirkwood, A. (1989) 'Enabling new students to examine their expectations of distance learning', *Educational and Training Technology International* 26, 1: 39–49.

Kjellman, M. (1985) *Utveckling av vårdlärarlinjens distansutbildning vid*

Uppsala universitet, Uppsala: Uppsala universitet, Institutionen för lärarutbildning.

Klafki, W. (1970) 'Die Inhalte des Lernens and Lehrens – das Problem der Didaktik im engeren Sinne', in W. Klafki *et al. Erziehungswissenschaft* 2: 55–88, Funk-Kolleg Erziehungswissenschaft, Frankfurt/Main: Fischer.

Klare, G. R. (1976) 'Judging readability', *Instructional Science* 5: 55–61.

Klare, G. R. and Smart, K. (1973) 'Analysis of the readability level of selected USAFI instructional materials', *Journal of Educational Research* 67: 176.

Knowles, M. (1975) *Self-directed learning. A guide for learners and teachers*, New York: Association Press.

Koeymen, U. S. (1983) *A model for organizing written instructional material in the context of a proposed model for an Open University in Turkey* (Unpublished Syracuse dissertation), Syracuse.

Küffner, H. (1979) 'LOTSE- Das computerunterstützte Korrektursystem für Einsendeaufgaben der FernUniversität', in M. J. Tauber *Der Computer als didaktisches und organisatorisches Hilfsmittel des Fernstudiums*, Hannover: Schroedel; Paderborn: Schoeningh.

Laaser, W. (1984) 'Didactic design of video instruction in distance education', *Epistolodidaktika* 1984: 1&2: 4–15.

—— (1986) 'Some didactic aspects of audio-cassettes in distance education', *Distance Education* 7, 1: 143–52.

Lambert, M. P. (1983) 'New course planning. The strategy and tactics of developing a home study course', *NHSC News*, Washington: National Home Study Council.

Lampikoski, K. and Mantere, P. (1976) *Didactic principles as tools in analyzing and developing a guidance system for distance education*, Distance education development project, Helsinki: The Institute of Marketing.

Landa, L. N. (1976) *Instructional regulation and control: cybernetics, algorithmization and heuristics in education*, Englewood Cliffs, N.J.: Educational Technology Publications.

Langer, J., Schulz von Thun, F. and Tasuch, R. (1974) *Verständlichkeit in Schule, Verwaltung, Politik und Wissenschaft*, München: Ernst Reinhardt Verlag.

Laurillard, D. (1978) 'The processes of student learning', *Higher Education* 8: 395–409.

Lebel, C. (1989a) 'En guise de réponse . . .', *Journal of Distance Education* IV, 1: 51–53.

—— (1989b) 'Le support à l'étudiant en enseignement à distance', *Journal of Distance Education* IV, 2: 7–24.

Lehmann, H. (1968) 'The systems approach to education', *Audiovisual*, Feb. 1968: 144–8.

Lehmann, T. (1975) *Educational outcomes from contract learning at Empire State College*. A paper presented to the American Association for Higher Education.

Lehmann, T. and Granger, D. (1991) 'Assessing at Empire State College – Strategies and methods used in evaluating distance education', in

Schuemer, R. (ed.) *Evaluation concepts and practice in selected distance education institutions*, Hagen: FernUniversität, ZIFF.

Lehmann, T. and Holtan, J.M. (1988) *Accounting for quality through assessment*, Albany: The Nelson A. Rockefeller Institute of Government/ Empire State College.

Lehner, H. (1978) *Die Steuerung von Lernprozessen auf der Grundlage einer kognitiven Lerntheorie*, Hagen: FernUniversität, ZIFF.

—— (1979) *Erkenntnis durch Irrtum als Lehrmethode*, Bochum: Kamp.

—— (1986) *Konstruktivismus und Fernstudium*, Hagen: FernUniversität, ZIFF.

Lehner, H. and Weingartz, M. (1985) 'Konfektionierung und Individualisierung im Fernstudium', *ZIFF-Papiere* 58, Hagen: FernUniversität.

Leslie, J. D. (1979) 'The university of Waterloo model for distance education', *Canadian Journal of University Continuing Education* VI, 1: 33–42.

—— (1986) 'Use of audiocassettes', in J. Mugridge and D. Kaufmann (eds) *Distance Education in Canada*, 234–46, London: Croom Helm.

Lewis, B. N. (1974) *New methods of assessment and stronger methods of curriculum design*, Milton Keynes: The Open University, IET.

—— (1975) 'Conversational man', *Teaching at a Distance* 2: 68–70.

Lewis, N. B. (1972) 'Course production at the Open University IV: the problem of assessment', *British Journal of Educational Technology* 2: 108–28.

Lewis, R. (1986) 'What is open learning?' *Open Learning* 1, 2: 5–10.

Lewis, R. and Spencer, D. (1986) *What is open learning?* London: Council for Educational Technology.

Lidman, S. (1979) 'Towards a more functional picture language', *Epistolodidaktika* 1: 21–41.

Lidman, S. and Lund, A. M. (1972) *Berätta med bilder*, Stockholm: Bonniers.

Likert, R. (1932) 'A technique for the measurement of attitudes', *Archives of Psychology* 140: 1–55.

Ljoså, E. (ed.) (1975) 'Why do we make commentary courses?', in E. Ljoså (ed.) *The system of distance education*, 112–18, Malmö: Hermods, ICCE.

—— (1977) 'Course design and media selection – some implications on co-operation between broadcasting, publishing and distance-education organizations', *Epistolodidaktika* 1979, 1: 75–84.

—— (1991) 'Distance education in the society of the future: from partial understanding to conceptional frameworks', in Holmberg, B. and Ortner, G.E. (eds) *Research into distance education*, Frankfurt am Main: Peter Lang.

—— (1992a) 'Distance education in a modern society', *Open Learning* 7, 2: 23–30.

—— (1992b) 'Experience with the electronic classroom', *Epistolodidaktika* 1992, 1: 44–9.

Ljoså, E. and Sandvold, K. E. (1983) 'The students' freedom of choice within the didactical structure of a correspondence course', in D. Sewart, D. Keegan and B. Holmberg (eds) *Distance education: Inter-*

national perspectives, 291–315 (also published in *Epistolodidaktika* 1983, 1: 34–62), London: Croom Helm.

Lockwood, F. and Cooper, A. (1980) 'CICERO: computer-assisted learning within an Open University course', *Teaching at a Distance* 17: 66–72.

Loser, F. and Terhart, E. (1977) *Theorien des Lehrens*, Stuttgart: Klett.

McConnell, D. (1982) 'CYCLOPS telewriting tutorials', *Teaching at a Distance* 22: 20–25.

Macdonald-Ross, M. (1973) 'Behavioural objectives – a critical review', *Instructional Science* 2: 1–52.

—— (1979) 'Language in texts: a review of research relevant to the design of materials of curricular materials', in L. S. Shulman (ed.) *Review of research in education* 6, Itasca, Ill.: Peacock.

Mace, E. (1976) ' "Rolling remake": an alternative approach to course design at the Open University', *Programmed Learning and Educational Technology* 13, 4: 25–30.

Mace, J. (1978) 'Mythology in the making: Is the Open University really cost-effective?', *Higher Education* 7: 295–309.

McGuire, A. (1973) 'Australia's school of the air', *ICCE Newsletter* 3, 3: 4–6.

McInnis-Rankin, E. and Brindley, J. (1986) 'Student support services', in J. Mugridge and D. Kaufmann (eds) *Distance education in Canada* 60–80, London: Croom Helm.

McIntosh, N., Calder, J. and Swift, B. (1976) *A degree of difference. A study of the first year's intake to the Open University of the United Kingdom*, Guildford: Society for Research in Higher Education.

McIntosh N., Woodley, A. and Morrison V. (1980) 'Student demand and progress at the Open University – the first eight years', *Distance Education* 1, 1: 37–60.

MacKenzie, K. (1974) 'Some thoughts on tutoring by written correspondence', *Teaching at a Distance* 1: 45–51.

Mager, R. F. (1962) *Preparing instructional objectives*, Palo Alto, California: Fearon.

Mager, R. F. and Beach, K. M. (1967) *Developing vocational instruction*, Palo Alto, California: Fearon.

Mandl, H. and Ballstaedt, S. P. (1982) 'Effects of elaboration on recall of texts', in A. Flammer and W. Kintsch (eds) *Discourse processing*, Amsterdam: North-Holland Publishing Company.

Mandl, H. (ed.) (1981) *Zur Psychologie der Textverarbeitung*, München: Schwarzenberg.

Mandl, H., Picard, E., Henninger, M. and Schnotz, W. (1991) 'Knowledge acquisition with texts by means of flexible computer-assisted information access', *Forschungsberichte* 54, Tübingen: Deutsches Institut für Fernstudien.

Markowitz, H. (1987) 'Financial decision making – calculating the costs of distance education', *Distance Education* 8, 2: 147–61.

Marland, P. (1989) 'An approach to research on distance learning', *British Journal of Educational Technology* 20, 3: 173–82

Marland, P., Patching, W., Putt, I. and Store, R. (1984) 'Learning from distance teaching materials: a study of students' mediating responses', *Distance Education* 5, 2: 215–36.

Marland, P. W. and Store, R. E. (1982) 'Some instructional strategies for improved learning from distance teaching materials', *Distance Education* 3, 1: 72–106.

Marshall, L. (ed.) (1984) *Independent study contracts*, a guide for students considering applying for independent study contracts and for staff who supervise them, Murdoch: Murdoch University.

Marton, F. and Säljö, R. (1976) 'On qualitative differences in learning', *British Journal of Educational Psychology* 46: 115–27.

Mason, R. (1989) *The use of computer networks for education and training*, London: Training Agency.

Mason, R. and Kaye, A. (eds) (1989) *Mindweave. Communication, computers and distance education*, Oxford: Pergamon.

Meacham, D. (1982) 'Distance teaching: innovation, individual concerns and staff development', *Distance Education* 3, 2: 244–54.

Mentoring 1. 'A newsletter', Leeds: Leeds Metropolitan University.

Merrill, M. D., Reigeluth, C. M. and Faust, G. W. (1979) 'The instructional quality profile: a curriculum evaluation and design tool', in H. F. O'Neil (ed.) *Procedures for instructional system development*, New York: Academic Press.

Merup, A. (1968) 'The computer in the administration of a correspondence school', *CEC Yearbook* 1868, 54–77, Copenhagen: CEC.

Milanesi, S. Buiges de (1978) 'ULSA trains its students "in-company" in 22 countries', in R. B. Wentworth (ed.) *Correspondence education: dynamic and diversified* I: 124–28, London: Tuition House.

Miller, G. A. (1951) *Language and communication*, New York: McGraw-Hill.

Minnis, J. R. (1990) 'Research project on "comparison of organizational climate of Thailand's distance teaching universities and the impact on collaboration" ', *Never Too Far* 15: 3–4, 6.

Mitchell, I. (1975) 'Carte blanche to organize the ideal distance education institute', in E. Ljosä (ed.) *The system of distance education* 1: 25–30, Malmö: Hermods, ICCE.

—— (1982) 'Learning to be a distance educator – by distance education', *Distance Education* 3, 2: 298–308.

—— (1992) 'Guided didactic conversation: the use of Holmberg's concept in higher education', in Ortner, G.E., Graff, K. and Wilmersdoerfer, H. (eds) *Distance education as two-way communication. Essays in honour of Börje Holmberg* 123–32, Frankfurt am Main: Peter Lang.

Mitchell, S. (1962) 'Supervised correspondence study for high schools and for adults taking high school courses', *The Home Study Review*, Spring 1962.

Möllers, P. (1981) *Computergestützte Lehre zum betrieblichen Rechnungswesen. Ein integriertes Modell*, Hagen: FernUniversität, ZIFF.

Moore, L. (1987) 'The Australian law of copyright and its application to distance education', *Distance Education* 8, 1: 18–37.

Moore, M. G. (1972) 'Learner autonomy: the second dimension of independent learning', *Convergence* 5, 2: 76–88.

—— (1975) 'Cognitive style and telematic (distance) teaching', *ICCE Newsletter* 5, 4: 3–10.

—— (1976) *Investigation of the interaction between the cognitive style of field independence and attitudes to independent study among adult learners who use correspondence independent study and self-directed independent study,* Unpublished doctoral dissertation, Madison: University of Wisconsin.

—— (1977) 'A model of independent study', *Epistolodidaktika* 1: 6–40.

—— (1981) 'Educational telephone networks', *Teaching at a Distance* 19: 24–31.

—— (1983) 'Self-directed learning and distance education', *ZIFF Papiere* 48, Hagen: FernUniversität, ZIFF.

—— (1986) 'Self-directed learning and distance education', *Journal of Distance Education* 1, 1: 7–24.

—— (1989) 'The theory of distance education: some research literature', in Tait, A. (ed.) *Interaction and independence* (conference papers) 150–66. Cambridge: Open University.

—— (ed.) (1990) *Contemporary issues in American distance education,* Oxford: Pergamon.

Moran, L. and Croker, S. W. (1981) *Take counsel with yourself: a self-directed counselling process,* Paper presented at regional symposium on distance teaching in Asia, Penang.

Morgan, A. (1984) 'A report on qualitative methodology in research in distance education', *Distance Education,* 5, 4: 252–67.

Morgan, A. (1985) 'What shall we do about independent learning?'. *Teaching at a Distance* 26: 38–45.

Morgan, A., Taylor, E. and Gibbs, G. (1982) 'Variations in students' approaches to studying', *British Journal of Educational Technology* 13, 2: 107–13.

Müller, K., Schneider, G. and Schulz, W. (1985) 'Teaching at a distance – reflections on the relationship between discipline-based and general teaching theory', *Distance Education* 6, 1: 91–101.

Nathenson, M. B. and Henderson, E. (1976) 'Developmental testing: a new beginning', *Teaching at a Distance* 7: 28–41.

—— (1980) *Using student feedback to improve learning materials,* London: Croom Helm.

Nation, D. and Elliott, C. (1985) *'I'm sorry to bother you at home but you said we could ring . . .',* Paper presented to the 13th ICDE world conference in Melbourne, on microfiche, Melbourne: ICDE.

Naughton, J. (Systems Group) (1986) *Artificial intelligence,* a research study by the Open University for the Training Technology Section of MSC, Sheffield: Manpower Services Commission.

Naylor, P., Cowie, H. and Stevenson, K. (1990) 'Using student and tutor perspectives in the development of open tutoring', *Open Learning* 5, 1: 9–18.

Neil, M. W. (1981) *Education of adults at a distance,* a report of the Open University's tenth anniversary international conference, London: Kogan Page.

Nicoll, D. (1986) 'Staff development in distance teaching', *Epistolodidaktika* 2: 104–13.

Nilsen, E. (1986) 'On the definition of correspondence education', *Epistolodidaktika* 1: 3–30.

Northcott, P. (1986) 'Distance education and open education: an exploration of the terms', *Open Campus* 12: 34–40.

Nuthall, G. and Snook, J. (1973) 'Contemporary models of teaching', in R. M. W. Travers (ed.) *Second handbook of research on teaching*, Chicago: Rand McNally.

Open Campus, occasional papers published by the Centre for Educational Services, Geelong: Deakin University.

Open Learning, 1986– , London: Longman.

Open Tech News, a periodical published in the mid–1980s. London: Manpower Services Commission.

Ortner, G. (1992) 'Does two-way communication require a new distance education technology?', in Ortner, G. E., Graff, K. and Wilmersdoerfer, H. (eds) *Distance education as two-way communication. Essays in honour of Börje Holmberg* 148–70. Frankfurt am Main: Peter Lang.

Osgood, C. (1952) 'The nature and measurement of meaning', *Psychological Bulletin* 49: 197–237.

Öster, L. (1965) 'Problems concerning the office organization of a large correspondence school', *CEC Yearbook 1965*, 70–88, Leiden: CEC.

Paine, N. (1984) 'Counselling: Defining the field', *International workshop on counselling in distance education: Selected Papers*, 16–20, Manchester: The Open University, ICDE.

Palola, E. G., Lehmann, T., Bradley, A. P. and Debus, R. (1977) *PERC handbook*, Saratoga Springs, N.Y.: Empire State College.

Parer, M. S. (1988) *Textual design and student learning*, Churchill, Victoria (Australia): Gippsland Institute of Advanced Education, The Centre for Distance Learning.

Parlett, M. and Hamilton, D. (1972) *Evaluation as illumination: a new approach to the study of innovatory programs*, Occasional paper 9, Edinburgh: University of Edinburgh, Centre for Research in Educational Sciences.

Pask, G. (1975a) *Conversation, cognition and learning*, Amsterdam: Elsevier.

—— (1975b) *The cybernetics of human learning and performance*, New York: Hutchinson.

—— (1976a) 'Conversational techniques in the study and practice of education', *British Journal of Educational Psychology* 46: 12–25.

—— (1976b) 'Styles and strategies of learning', *British Journal of Educational Psychology* 46: 126–48.

Pask, G. and Scott, B. C. E. (1972) 'Learning strategies and individual competence', *International Journal of Man-Machine Studies* 4, 3: 217–253.

Paul, R. (1990) *Open learning and open management. Leadership and integrity in distance education*, London: Kogan Page; New York: Nicholls.

Perraton, H. (1981) 'A theory for distance education', *Prospects* XI, 1: 13–24.

—— (1982) 'The cost of distance education', *IEC broadsheets on distance learning* 17, Cambridge International Extension College.

—— (1987) 'Theories, generalisation and practice in distance education', *Open Learning* 2, 3: 3–12.

Perry, Walter (1976) *Open University. A personal account by the first Vice-Chancellor*, Milton Keynes: The Open University.

—— (1984) *The state of distance-learning worldwide: the first report on the index of institutions involved in distance learning*, Milton Keynes: United Nations University, Centre for Distance Learning.

Perry, William (1970) *Forms of intellectual and ethical development in the college years*, New York: Holt, Rinehart & Winston.

Perspectives on distance education, An occasional paper to stimulate thought and discussion on the future of distance education in Alberta (1987), Edmonton: Alberta Education, Planning, Policy and Research Secretariat.

Peters, O. (1973) *Die didaktische Struktur des Fernunterrichts. Untersuchungen zu einer industrialisierten Form des Lehrens und Lernens.* Tübinger Beiträge zum Fernstudium 7, Weinheim: Beltz.

—— (1979) 'Some comments on the function of printed material in multi-media systems', *Epistolodidaktika* 1: 10–21.

—— (1983) 'Distance teaching and industrial production: a comparative interpretation in outline', in D. Sewart, D. Keegan and B. Holmberg (eds) *Distance education: International perspectives*, 95–113, London: Croom Helm.

—— (1989) 'The iceberg has not melted: further reflections on the concept of industrialisation and distance teaching', *Open Learning* 4, 3: 3–8.

—— (1990) 'Die chinesische Radio- und Fernsehuniversität', in Rehbom, H. and Tornow, J. (eds) *Jahrbuch 1990*, Hagen: Gesellschaft der Freunde der FernUniversität.

—— (1992) 'Some observations on dropping out in distance education', *Distance Education* 13, 2: 234–69.

Picard, E. (1992) 'Construction of knowledge structures in repeated reading'. *Forschungsberichte* 59, Tübingen: Deutsches Institut für Fernstudien.

Plessis, P. du (1987) 'Can the tables be turned? Likelihood that distance teaching at university can be more effective than attendance teaching', *Papers 1*, 9–18, Pretoria: University of South Africa.

Popham, W. J. (1987) 'Two-plus decades of educational objectives', *International Journal of Educational Research* 11: 31–41.

Popper, K. (1972) 'Naturgesetze und theoretische Systeme', in H. Albert (ed.) *Theorie und Realität*, Tübingen: Mohr.

—— (1980) *The logic of scientific discovery*, London: Hutchinson.

Posner, G. J. and Strike, K. A. (1976) 'A categorisation scheme for principles of sequencing content', *Review of Educational Research* 46: 685–90, London: Kogan Page.

—— (1978) 'Principles of sequencing content', in J. Hartley and I. K. Davies (eds) *Contributions to educational technology*, vol. 2, 165–9, London: Kogan Page.

Posz, A. C. (1963) 'Research results on personalization of instruction. Summarised in "from the editor's notebook" ', *The Home Study Review* 4, 3: 47–8.

Potvin, D. J. (1976) 'An analysis of the andragogical approach to the-didactics of distance education', in G. Granholm (ed.) *The system of distance education* 2: 27–30, Malmoe: Liber, ICCE.

Qvist-Eriksen, S. (1986) 'The organization of correspondence students at NKI', *Epistolodidaktika* 1: 81–5.

Rahmlow, H. F. (1971) 'Using student performance data for improving individualised instructional units', *Audio-visual Communication Review* 19, 2: 169–83.

Rayner, S. A. (1949) *Correspondence education in Australia and New Zealand*, Melbourne: Melbourne University Press.

Reigeluth, C. M., Merrill, M. D. and Bunderson, C. V. (1978) 'The structure of subject matter content and its instructional design implications', *Instructional Science* 7: 107–26.

Reiser, R. and Gagné, R. M. (1983) *Selecting media for instruction*, Englewood Cliffs: Educational Technology Publications.

Rekkedal, T. (1972a) 'Correspondence studies – recruitment, achievement and discontinuation', *Epistolodidaktika* 2: 3–38.

—— (1972b) *Systematisk elevoppfölging. En eksperimentell undersøkelse av virkningen av kontaktbrev til elever ved NKI-skolen* (with an English summary), Oslo: NKI.

—— (1983) 'The written assignments in correspondence education. Effects of reducing turn-around time' (a translation of 'Innsendingsoppgavene i brevundervisningen' of 1973), *Distance Education*, 4, 2: 231–52.

—— (1985) *Introducing the personal tutor/counsellor in the system of distance education*; Project report 2: Final report, Oslo: NKI.

—— (1989) *The telephone as a medium for instruction and guidance in distance education*, Oslo: NKI.

—— (1992) 'Computer mediated communication in distance education', in Ortner, G. E., Graff, K. and Wilmersdoerfer, H. (eds) *Distance education as two-way communication. Essays in honour of Börje Holmberg* 171–84. Frankfurt am Main: Peter Lang.

Rekkedal, T. and Ljoså, E. (1974) *Preproduserte laererkommentarer i brevundervisningen*, Oslo: Brevskoleraadet-Forsoeksraadet for skoleverket, NKI/NKS.

Rekkedal, T. and Vigander, K. (1990) *Forsøk med bruk av Telewriter i matematikundervisning*, Oslo: NKI.

Richey, R. (1968) *The theoretical and conceptual bases of instructional design*, London: Kogan Page.

Roberts, D. (1986) 'Student study patterns', *Open Learning* 1, 3: 34–7.

Robertson, B. (1987) 'Audio teleconferencing: low costs technology for external studies networking', *Distance Education*, 8, 1: 121–30.

Rogers, C. (1969) *Freedom to learn*, Columbus, Ohio: Merill.

Rogers, W. S. (1986) 'Changing attitudes through distance learning', *Open Learning* 1, 3: 12–17.

Romiszowski, A. J. (1981a) *Designing instructional systems*, London: Kogan Page.

—— (1981b) 'Strategies for the teaching of knowledge and skills', *Aspects of Educational Technology XV, Distance Learning and Evaluation*, 215–23, London: Kogan Page.

—— (1986) *Instructional development 2: Developing autoinstructional materials*, London: Kogan Page.

Rosberg, U. (1966) 'How should the most efficient correspondence course be designed?', *The Home Study Review* 7, 4: 17–19.

Ross, D. (1991) 'Project management in the development of instructional material for distance education: an Australian overview', *The American Journal of Distance Education* 5, 2: 24–30.

Ross, R. D. (1976) 'The institutionalization of academic innovations: two models', *Sociology of Education* 49.

Rothkopf, E. Z. (1970) 'The concept of mathemagenic activities', *Review of Educational Research*, 40: 325–36.

Rothkopf, E. Z. and Kaplan, B. (1972) 'Exploration of the effect of density and specificity of instructional objectives on learning from text', *Journal of Educational Psychology* 63: 295–302.

Rowntree, D. (1975) *Student exercises in correspondence texts*, Milton Keynes: The Open University Institute of Educational Technology.

—— (1974) *Educational technology in curriculum development*, London: Harper & Row.

—— (1986) *Teaching through self-instruction: A practical handbook for course developers*, London: Kogan Page.

Royce, J. R. (1978) 'How can we best advance the construction of theory in psychology?' *Canadian Psychological Review* 19, 4: 259–76.

Rumble, G. (1985) 'Distance education in Latin America: models for the 1980s', *Distance Education* 6, 2: 248–55.

—— (1986) *The planning and management of distance education*, Beckenham: Croom Helm.

—— (1992) *The management of distance learning systems*, Paris: Unesco.

Rumble, G. and Harry, K. (eds) (1982) *The distance teaching universities*, London: Croom Helm.

Saba, F. (1989) 'Integrated telecommunication systems and instructional transaction', in Moore, M. G. and Clarke, G. C. (eds) *Readings in principles of distance education* 29–37, University Park, PA: The American Center for the Study of Distance Education.

Salomon, G. (1972) 'Heuristic models for the generation of aptitude-treatment interaction hypotheses', *Review of Educational Research*, 42: 327–43.

Sanders, N. M. (1966) *Classroom questions. What kinds?*, New York: Harper & Row.

Sauvé, L., Gagné, P. and Lamy, T. (1989) 'La technologie éducative dans l'enseignement à distance, son role et sa place: une étude exploratoire', in Sweet, R. (ed.) *Post-secondary distance education in Canada. Policies, practices and priorities*, Athabasca: Athabasca University/Canadian Society for Studies in Education.

Saxe, A. F. (1965) 'The administration of a small correspondence school', *CEC Yearbook* 1965: 89–98, Leiden, CEC.

Saxe, B. (1965) 'The principles and methods of supervised correspondence study as applied in military educational programmes', *CEC Yearbook* 1965: 32–9, Leiden: CEC.

Schnotz, W. (1982) 'How do different readers learn with different text organizations?', in A. Flammer and W. Kintsch (eds) *Discourse processing: Advances in psychology* 8: 87–97, Amsterdam: North-Holland Publishing Co.

—— (1986) 'Kohärenzbildung beim Aufbau von Wissensstrukturen mit Hilfe von Lehrtexten, *Forschungsberichte 39*, Tübingen: DIFF.

Schnotz, W. (1990) *Aufbau von Wissensstrukturen: Untersuchungen zur mentalen Kohärenzbildung beim Wissenserwerb mit Texten*, Tübingen: Deutsches Institut für Fernstudien.

Schramm, W. (1977) *Big media, little media*, Beverly Hills: Sage Publications.

Schuemer, R. (1988) *Internationale Studie zum Fernstudium: Ergänzungsbericht – Versuch zur Klassifikation der Institutionen auf empirischer Basis*, Hagen: FernUniversität, ZIFF.

—— (ed.) (1991) *Evaluation concepts and practice in selected distance education institutions*, Hagen: FernUniversität, ZIFF.

—— (1993) *Some psychological aspects of distance education*, Hagen: FernUniversität, ZIFF.

Schuemer, R. and Ströhlein, G. (1991) 'Dropout-Forschung und Dropout-Prophylaxe: Zur Theorie und Methodologie', in Holmberg, B. and Ortner, G. E. (eds) *Research into distance education/Fernlehre und Fernlehrforschung*. 196–222. Frankfurt am Main: Peter Lang.

Schulz, T. (1989) 'Hypermedia. Eine neue Dimension in der Wissensverarbeitung', in Fischer, P. H. and Meynersen, K. (eds) *Interaktives Lernen mit neuen Medien. Möglichkeiten und Grenzen*, Tübingen: Deutsches Institut für Fernstudien.

Schwalbe, H. and Zander, E. (eds) (1984) *Fernkurse in der betrieblichen Weiterbildung*, Hardebek: Eulenhof.

Scriven, M. (1967) 'The methodology of evaluation', in R. W. Tyler, R. M. Gagné and M. Scriven (eds) *Perspectives of curriculum evaluation*, (AERA monograph series on curriculum evaluation 1) 39–83, Chicago: Rand McNally.

Seaborne, K. and Zuckernick, A. (1986) 'Course design and development', in I. Mugridge and D. Kaufmann (eds) *Distance education in Canada*, 37–49, London: Croom Helm.

Segal, C. (1990) 'Strategic planning: the Open Learning Agency experience', in Croft, M., Mugridge, I., Daniel., J. and Hershfield, A. (eds) *Distance education: development and access* 70–2. Caracas: International Council for Distance Education.

Serrander, O. (1979) *Utbildningskostnader i högskolan*, Stockholm: Universitets-och högskoleämbetet.

Sewart, D. (1980) 'Creating an information base for an individualized support system in distance education', *Distance Education 1*, 2: 171–87.

—— (1981) 'Distance teaching: a contradiction in terms?', *Teaching at a Distance* 19: 8–18.

—— (1983) 'Students and their progress', in D. Sewart, D. Keegan and B. Holmberg (eds) *Distance education: international persectives*, 165–8, London: Croom Helm.

—— (1984) 'Counselling in distance education – an overview, *Inter-*

national workshop on counselling in distance education: Selected papers, 7–11, ICDE, Manchester: The Open University.

Sewart, D., Keegan, D. and Holmberg, B. (eds) (1983) *Distance education: International perspectives*, Beckenham: Croom Helm. (Reprinted by Routledge, 1988.)

Shale, D. and Garrison, D.R. (1989) 'Evaluating a telewriting system to enhance audio-teleconferencing: a qualitative search for instructional design issues', in Bedard, R. (ed.) *Proceedings of the 8th annual conference of the Canadian Association for the Study of Adult Education*, Cornwall, Ontario: University of Ottawa.

Shavelson, R. J. (1974) 'Methods for examining representations of a science subject-matter structure in a student's memory', *Journal of Research in Science Teaching* 11: 231–49.

Shavelson, R. J. and Stasz, C. (1980) 'Some methods for representing structure of concepts in prose material', in J. Hartley (ed.) *The psychology of written communication*, 40–8, London: Kogan Page.

Sheath, H. C. (1972) 'Integrating correspondence study with resident study,' in H. A. Bern and F. Kulla (eds) *Ninth international conference on correspondence education: A collection of conference papers*, II: 286–9, Warrenton, Va.: ICCE.

Simpson, O. (1977) 'Post-foundation counselling', *Teaching at a Distance* 9: 60–7.

Sims, R. S. (1977) *An inquiry into correspondence education processes: Policies, principles and practices in correspondence education systems worldwide*, Unpublished ICCE-UNESCO report.

Singh, B. (1975) 'The role and organization of an ideal distance education institute', in E. Ljoså (ed.) *The system of distance education* 1: 31–8. Malmö Hermods, ICCE.

—— (1979) 'Distant education in developing countries – with special reference to India', in J. R. Hakemulder (ed.) *Distance education for development*, Bonn: German Foundation for International Development.

Skinner, B. F. (1968) *The technology of teaching*, New York: Appleton-Century-Crofts.

Smith, K. C. (1975) 'External studies at the University of New England: An exercise in integration', in E. Ljoså (ed.) *The system of distance education* 1: 161–9, Malmö: Hermods, ICCE.

—— (1979) *External studies at New England*, Armidale, NSW: The University of New England.

—— (1980) 'Course development procedures', *Distance Education*, 1, 1: 61–7.

Snellbecker, G. E. (1983) 'Is instructional theory alive and well?', in C. M. Reigeluth (ed.) *Instructional-design theories and models: an overview of their current status*, Hillsdale, N.J.: Lawrence Erlbaum.

Snowden, B. L. and Daniel, J. S. (1980) 'The economics and management of small post-secondary distance education systems', *Distance Education* 1, 1: 68–91.

Sparkes, J. J. (1982) 'On choosing teaching methods to match educational aims', *ZIFF Papiere* 39, Hagen: Fern-Universität, ZIFF.

—— (1983) 'The problem of creating a discipline of distance education', *Distance Education* 4, 2: 179–86.

Spencer, H. (1969) *The visible word*, London: Lund Humphries.

Spotlight on Open Learning, a journal published by the Manpower Services Commission, Sheffield: Manpower Services Commission.

Staaf, P. (1973) *Utveckling av en utbildningsmodell: Analys, planering, konstruktion, uppföljning*, Stockholm: Landstingsförbundet.

Stake, R. (1977) 'Formative and summative evaluation', in D. Hamilton, D. Jenkins, C. King, B. MacDonald and M. Parlett (eds) *Beyond the numbers game: A reader in educational evaluation*, London: Macmillan.

Stein, L. S. (1960) 'Design of a correspondence course', *Adult Education* 10: 161–6.

Strike, K. A. and Posner, G. J. (1976) 'Epistemological perspectives on conceptions of curriculum organization and learning', in L. S. Shulman (ed.) *Review of research in education*, Itasca, III: Peacock.

Svensson, L. (1973) 'Val av utbildningsmetod. Mål – och medieanalys med pedagogiska, tekniska och ekonomiska synpunkter', *Dokumentation Hermods vårkonferense 1973*, Malmö: Hermods.

Swanepoel, E. (1987) 'Student support in distance learning', *Papers* 5: 183–99, Pretoria: University of South Africa.

Tate, O. (1986) 'Monitoring and evaluating the performance of a distance education institution', *Epistolodidaktika* 2: 77–103.

Taylor, F. J. (1977) 'Acquiring knowledge from prose and continuous discourse', in M. J. A. Howe (ed.) *Adult learning: Psychological research and application*, 107–23, London: Wiley.

Taylor, P. and Tomlinson, D. (1985) 'Primary distance education: Population, problems and prospects', *Research Series* No. 2, Nedlands, W.A.: The University of Western Australia, National Centre for Research on Rural Education.

Taylor, R. (1991) 'The Blooming of education', *Epistolodidaktika* 2: 33–8.

Teaching at a Distance 1974–85 (new title from 1986– : *Open Learning*), Milton Keynes: The Open University.

Tergan, S.-O. (1979) 'Der Einfluss von Textverständlichkeit und Orientierungshinweisen auf den Lernerfolg von Funkkollegiaten', *DIFF Forschungsberichte* 2, Tübingen: Deutsches Institut für Fernstudien.

—— (1983) *Textversïndlichkeit und Lernerfolg im angeleiteten Selbststudium*, Wienheim: Beltz.

Thomas, L. F. and Harri-Augstein, E. S. (1977) 'Learning to learn: The personal construction and exchange of meaning', in M. J. A. Howe (ed.) *Adult learning: Psychological research and applications*, London: Wiley.

Thornton, R. and Mitchell, J. (1978) *Counselling the distance learner: A survey of trends and literature*, Adelaide: Adelaide College of Advanced Education.

Thorpe, M. (1979a) 'The student special support scheme: a report', *Teaching at a Distance* 15: 1–14.

—— (1979b) 'When is a course not a course?', *Teaching at a Distance* 16: 13–18.

—— (1986) 'How to develop good exercises, assignments and tests' *Epistolodidaktika* 2: 27–50.

—— (1987) 'Conference report: Association of European Correspondence Schools (AECS) autumn congress 1986 in Munich', *Open Learning* 2, 2: 56.

—— (1988) *Evaluating open and distance learning*, Harlow: Longman.

Thorpe, M. and Grugeon, D. (eds) (1987) *Open learning for adults*, Harlow/Essex: Longman.

Tight, M. (1987) 'London University external developments', *Open Learning*, 2, 2: 49–51.

Tinker, M. A. (1969) *Legibility of print*, Ames, Iowa: Iowa State University Press.

Tinto, V. (1975) 'Dropout from higher education: a theoretical synthesis of recent research. *Review of Educational Research* 45, 1: 89–125.

Tomlinson, D., Coulter, F. and Peacock, J. (1985) 'Teaching and learning at home: Distance education and the isolated child', *Research Series*, No. 4, Nedlands: The University of Western Australia, National Centre for Research on Rural Education.

Tuckey, C. J. (1993) 'Computer conferencing and the Electronic White Board in the United Kingdom: a comparative analysis', *The American Journal of Distance Education* 7, 2: 58–72.

Valcke, M. M. A., Martens, R. L., Poelmans, P. H. A. G. and Daal, M. M. (1993) 'The actual use of embedded support devices in self-study materials by students in a distance education setting. *Distance Education* 14, 1: 55–84.

Valkyser, H. (1981) *Fernstudiensystemkonforme Beratung und Betreuung als didaktische Elemente einer Zweiweg-Kommunikation im Fernstudium – unter besonderer Berücksichtigung bisheriger Erfahrungen an der FernUniversität* (Dissertation), Hagen: FernUniversität.

Verduin, J. R. and Clark, T. A. (1991) *Distance education. The foundation of effective practice*, San Francisco and Oxford: Jossey Bass.

Villarroel, A. (ed.) (1987) *Aspectos operativos en universidades a distancia*, Caracas: Universidad Nacional Abierta.

Vivian, V. (1986) 'Electronic mail in a children's distance course: trial and evaluation', *Distance Education*, 7, 2: 237–60.

Wångdahl, A. (1979) *Correspondence education combined with face-to-face meetings*, EHSC workshop papers, Malmö: LiberHermods.

—— (1980) 'Who are the correspondence students and what about their handicap of isolation?', *Pedagogical Reports* 130, Lund: Lund University, Department of Education.

Wagenschein, M. (1975) *Verstehen lernen*, Weinheim: Beltz.

Wagner, L. (1972) 'The economics of the Open University', *Higher Education* 1, 2: 159–83.

—— (1977) 'The economics of the Open University revisited', *Higher Education* 6, 3: 359–81.

Waller, R. (1977a) *Three functions of text presentation*, Notes on Transforming 2, Milton Keynes: The Open University, IET.

—— (1977b) *Typographic access structures for educational texts*, Milton Keynes: The Open University, IET.

REFERENCES

—— (1979) 'Four aspects of graphic communication', *Instructional Science* 8, 3: 213–22.

Ward, R. N. (1954) *A study of college correspondence study completions*, Lincoln: University of Nebraska (a master's thesis).

Wedemeyer, C. A. (1971) 'Independent study', in L. Deighton (ed.) *The Encyclopedia of Education*, 4: 548–57, New York: Macmillan and Free Press.

—— (1981) *Learning at the back door. Reflections on non-traditional learning in the lifespan*, Madison: University of Wisconsin.

Weingartz, M. (1980) *Didaktische Merkmale selbstinstruierender Studientexte*, Hagen: FernUniversitäet, ZIFF.

—— (1981) *Lernen mit Texten*, Bochum: Kamp.

—— (1990) *Selbständigkeit im Fernstudium*, Hagen: FernUniversität, ZIFF.

—— (1991) 'Der Lernvertrag. Ein effektiver Beitrag zur Förderung autonomen Lernens', in Holmberg, B. and Ortner, G. E. (eds) *Research into distance education/Fernlehre und Fernlehrforschung*, 180–91, Frankfurt am Main: Peter Lang.

Weinstein, C. E., Underwood, V. L., Wicker, F. W. and Cubberly, W. E. (1979) 'Cognitive learning strategies: verbal and imaginal elaboration', in H. F. O'Neil and C. Spielberger (eds) *Cognitive and affective learning strategies*, 45–75, New York: Academic Press.

Weissbrot, E. (1969) 'Specific aspects of supervised correspondence study with school children, *8th ICCE Proceedings*, 163–77, Paris: ICCE.

Weltner, K. (1977) 'Die Unterstützung autonomen Lernens im Fernstudium durch integrierende Leitprogramme', *ZIFF-Papiere* 17: 2–42, Hagen: FernUniversität, ZIFF.

White, M. A. (1982) 'Distance education in Australian higher education – a history', *Distance Education* 3, 2: 255–78.

Willén, B. (1981) *Distance education at Swedish universities*, Uppsala: Almqvist & Wiksell.

Williams, I. and Gillard, G. (1986) 'Improving satellite tutorials at the University of the South Pacific', *Distance Education* 7, 2: 261–74.

Williams, M. and Williams, J. (1987) 'A student-operated support network for distance learners', *ICDE Bulletin* 13: 51–64.

Willmott, G. and King, B. (1984) 'Professional development courses in distance education', *Distance Education*, 5, 1: 116–30.

Willows, D. M. and Houghton, H. A. (eds) (1987) *The psychology of illustration*, New York: Springer.

Wilmersdoerfer, H. (ed.) (1978) *CMA-Schlussbericht–Projekt Standardisierte Testverfahren. Teil. A: LOTSE*, Hagen: FernUniversität, ZIFF.

Winders, R. (1984) 'The Plymouth audio-conferencing network', *Teaching at a Distance*, 25: 51–7.

Winter, A. and Cameron, M. (1983) *External students and their libraries*, Geelong: Deakin University.

Woodley, A. (1983) 'Why they declined the offer', *Teaching at a distance* 23: 2–7.

—— (1986a) 'Correspondence schoolchildren in Alaska', *Open Learning*, 1, 3: 47–9.

—— (1986b) 'Distance students in the United Kingdom', *Open Learning*, 1, 2: 11–13.

Worth, V. (1982) 'Empire State College/State University of New York Center for Distance Learning', *DERG Papers* 7, Milton Keynes: The Open University.

von Wright, G. H. (1987) *Vetenskapen och förnuftet*, Borgå: Bonniers.

Wright, T. (1987) 'Putting independent learning in its place', *Open Learning*, 2, 1: 3–7.

Wyant, T. G. (1974) 'Network analysis', in A. Howe and A. J. Romiszowski (eds) *APLET Yearbook of Educational and Instructional Technology* 1974/75: 129–31, London: Kogan Page.

Young, M., Perraton, H., Jenkins, J. and Dodds, T. (1980) *Distance teaching for the third world*, London: Routledge & Kegan Paul.

Zhao, Y. (1988) 'China: its distance higher education system', *Prospects* 18, 2: 218–28.

INDEX